Advance Praise

The literary artistry of the Gospel of Luke makes it an ideal text for careful literary analysis. Andrew Arterbury's new book, *Reading Luke: A Literary and Theological Commentary*, offers precisely that—a perceptive and sensitive reading of Luke's narrative, informed by strategic probes of the cultural environment in which Luke wrote. Arterbury provides a reliable guide to this Gospel and to the theological vision that comes to expression in Luke's artful narrative.
—*John Carroll*
Harriet Robertson Fitts Memorial Professor of New Testament
Union Presbyterian Seminary

Andrew Arterbury carefully yet succinctly walks us through Luke's Gospel. Along the way he rightly keeps in mind the larger context of this Gospel and its intertextual relation to Israel's earlier Scriptures.
—*Craig S. Keener*
F. M. and Ada Thompson Professor of Biblical Studies
Asbury Theological Seminary

READING LUKE

Smyth & Helwys Publishing, Inc.
6316 Peake Road
Macon, Georgia 31210-3960
1-800-747-3016
© 2019 by Andrew E. Arterbury
All rights reserved.

Library of Congress Cataloging-in-Publication Data

Names: Arterbury, Andrew E., author.
Title: Reading Luke : a literary and theological commentary / by Andrew E.
   Arterbury.
Description: Macon : Smyth & Helwys, 2019. | Includes bibliographical
   references.
Identifiers: LCCN 2018061570 | ISBN 9781641731164 (pbk. : alk. paper)
Subjects: LCSH: Bible. Luke--Commentaries.
Classification: LCC BS2595.53 .A78 2019 | DDC 226.4/07--dc23
LC record available at https://lccn.loc.gov/2018061570

Disclaimer of Liability: With respect to statements of opinion or fact available in this work of nonfiction, Smyth & Helwys Publishing Inc. nor any of its employees, makes any warranty, express or implied, or assumes any legal liability or responsibility for the accuracy or completeness of any information disclosed, or represents that its use would not infringe privately-owned rights.

Reading Luke

A Literary and Theological Commentary

Andrew E. Arterbury

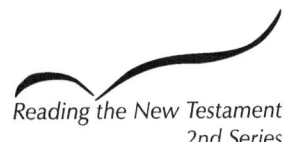

Also by Andrew E. Arterbury

Engaging the Christian Scriptures: An Introduction to the Bible
(co-authored with W. H. Bellinger, Jr., and Derek S. Dodson)

*Entertaining Angels:
Early Christian Hospitality in Its Mediterranean Setting*

To my students—
past, present, and future—
who challenge me to
read Luke's Gospel more faithfully

Contents

Acknowledgments xiii
Editor's Foreword xv

Introduction to the Gospel of Luke 1
Literary Sources 1
Date and Authorship 2
Relationship to the Book of Acts 4
Intended Audience 5
Genre 6
Methodology 6

A Proper Beginning, Luke 1:1–4:13 9
Introduction 9
The Prologue to Luke's Gospel (1:1-4) 10
Announcing the Births of John and Jesus (1:5-56) 11
    John's Birth Foretold (1:5-25) 11
    Jesus' Birth Foretold (1:26-38) 14
    Mary Visits Elizabeth and Praises God (1:39-56) 15
The Birth, Naming, and Growth of John (1:57-80) 17
The Birth, Naming, and Growth of Jesus (2:1-52) 19
The Ministry of John the Baptist (3:1-20) 23
Preparation for the Ministry of Jesus (3:21–4:13) 26
    Jesus' Baptism (3:21-22) 26
    Jesus' Genealogy (3:23-38) 28
    The Temptation of Jesus (4:1-13) 29

Jesus' Galilean Ministry, Luke 4:14–9:50 33
Introduction 33
Jesus' Inaugural Sermon (4:14-30) 33

Jesus' Power and Authority (4:31–6:49)..37
   An Overview of Jesus' Authority (4:31–5:11)...............................37
   Authority to Cleanse and Transform (5:12–6:11)........................40
   Authority to Call Disciples (6:12-16)...46
   Authority to Teach Disciples (the Sermon on the Plain) (6:17-49)...48
Jesus' Prophetic Ministry in Capernaum and Nain (7:1-50)..................53
Jesus and His Followers (8:1-21)...63
Jesus' Power over Nature, Demons, Disease, and Death (8:22-56).........67
Commissioning the Twelve (9:1-9)..74
Feeding the Five Thousand (9:10-17)...77
Peter's Confession and Jesus' Transfiguration (9:18-36).........................78
The Disciples' Inadequacies (9:37-50)..82

Jesus' Journey to Jerusalem, Luke 9:51–19:44..................................85
Introduction..85
Rejected by Samaritans (9:51-62)..86
Commissioning the Seventy-two (10:1-24)..89
Loving Neighbor and Loving God (10:25-42).......................................93
Teaching about Prayer (11:1-13)...96
Dialoguing with Disciples and Adversaries (11:14–13:9).......................98
Healing and Parables (13:10–17:10)...106
   Healing a Crippled Woman (13:10-17).......................................106
   The Kingdom of God (13:18-35)...108
   Conversing with Pharisees (14:1-35)..110
   More Parables and Teaching (15:1–17:10)..................................116
      Parables about "Lost" Things (15:1-32)................................116
      Parables about Wealth (16:1-31)...120
      Exhorting his Disciples (17:1-10)..130
More Healing and Teaching (17:11–18:8)..132
   Cleansing Ten Lepers (17:11-19)..132
   Teaching about the Kingdom of God (17:20–18:8)......................134
On Approaching God with Humility, Not Arrogance (18:9–19:27).....137
   Parable of a Pharisee and Tax Collector (18:9-14).........................137
   Receiving Children (18:15-17)...141
   The Rich Ruler (18:18-30)..141
   Foretelling his Death (18:31-34)..148
   "Seeing" Jesus Properly (18:35–19:10)..148
   The Parable of the Pounds (19:11-27)..156
Entry into Jerusalem (19:28-44)..159

Contents

Jesus in Jerusalem, Luke 19:45–24:53 165
Introduction 165
Jesus' Ministry in Jerusalem (19:45–21:38) 165
    Disrupting the Temple (19:45-48) 166
    Challenges to Jesus' Authority (20:1-44) 167
    The Temple's Fate (20:45–21:38) 178
The Death of the Messiah (22:1–23:56a) 185
    Conspiring against Jesus (22:1-6) 185
    The Last Supper (22:7-38) 187
    The Mount of Olives (22:39-53) 196
    Jesus' Trials and Innocence (22:54–23:25) 200
    Jesus' Crucifixion and Burial (23:26-56a) 206
The Resurrection of the Messiah (23:56b–24:53) 213
    The Empty Tomb (23:56b–24:12) 214
    On the Road to Emmaus (24:13-35) 215
    Appearing to the Disciples (24:36-43) 218
    Commissioning the Disciples (24:44-49) 219
    Jesus' Ascension (24:50-53) 220

Works Cited 223

Acknowledgments

I need and want to acknowledge Baylor University and its administration—President Linda Livingstone and the Office of the Provost—for their ongoing support of my academic research. The university generously provided me with release time to work on this project. In addition, this study was supported in part by funds from the Arts & Humanities Faculty Research Program and the Vice Provost for Research at Baylor University. I also wish to thank the deans (Drs. Todd Still, Terry York, and Dennis Tucker) and faculty of Baylor University's Truett Seminary who supported, encouraged, and assisted me in numerous ways as I wrote this book.

I am incredibly grateful to Dr. Rebecca Poe Hays, who read the entire manuscript of *Reading Luke* and provided highly valuable suggestions for ways to improve both its content and its grammar. Likewise, I want to thank Val Fisk, who served admirably as my graduate assistant while I wrote this commentary.

I would also like to thank Smyth & Helwys Publishing and in particular Leslie Andres, whose editorial oversight and suggestions were most appreciated. Further, I would like to thank the series editor, Dr. Todd Still, for inviting me to contribute to this distinguished series. I am honored to be linked with the fine scholars who have written volumes for the Reading the Old Testament and Reading the New Testament collections.

As always, I am forever indebted to and thankful for my amazing wife, Kristin, and our wonderful sons, Timothy and Daniel. I could not ask for a more supportive or loving family. I am proud just to be associated with them.

Finally, while I plan to investigate the Gospels and Acts for many more years to come, this project has forced me to think broadly about the significant streams of influence that shaped and formed my understanding of Luke's Gospel. As a result, I would like to express immense gratitude for the following people:

- For my mother, Earlene Brown, who first taught me to read the Scriptures, and my father, Elvis Arterbury, who encouraged me throughout this project.
- For faithful pastors who have exegeted Luke's Gospel for the congregations of which I was a part: Rodney Reeves, David Bush, Steve Hollaway, Scott Walker, Julie Pennington-Russell, Jim Coston, Mary Alice Birdwhistell, and Matt Snowden.
- For dear friends and fellow ministers with whom I have had rich conversations about Luke's Gospel: Dan Baumgartner, Steve Beard, Kimlyn Bender, Derek Dodson, Eric Holleyman, Mike Stroope, Dennis Tucker, and Doug Weaver.
- For those who first taught me about the Gospels and Acts: A. K. M. Adam, Brian Blount, Sharyn Dowd, Beverly Gaventa, Donald Juel, Naymond Keathley, and Ulrich Mauser.
- Finally, for those who guided my doctoral studies on Luke's writings—Charles Talbert and my dissertation supervisor, Mikeal Parsons.

These people and many more have influenced my understanding of Luke in wonderfully positive ways. The errors, oversights, and oversimplifications present in this commentary are exclusively my own.

Editor's Foreword

Like its predecessor (Reading the New Testament) and its companion series (Reading the Old Testament), Reading the New Testament: Second Series seeks to help readers—whether students or scholars, ministers or laypeople—gain a greater understanding of and appreciation for biblical texts in their original contexts. To this good end, commentaries in this series attend not only to lexical, historical, and critical concerns but are also attuned to and interested in, as the subtitle of each volume signals, literary matters and theological meaning.

Whereas some commentaries are committed to the necessary and salutary task of commenting on every jot and tittle (see Matthew 5:18), works in this series seek to trace the thought and observe the craft of biblical authors in a less atomistic manner. While attending to various trees, they are also intent on not missing the forest. Relatedly, while technically undergirded and academically informed, the commentaries within this series are intended for and are meant to be accessible and valuable to a broad readership. The seventeen volumes that will make up Reading the New Testament: Second Series, then, are written by scholars but are not exclusively, or even primarily, for scholars.

Contributors to this commentary series are accomplished academics, experienced teachers, capable communicators, and professing Christians who are committed to explicating Scripture thoughtfully, clearly, and sympathetically. To the extent that this series results in people reading the twenty-seven New Testament documents with greater skill, care, insight, devotion, and joy, the contributors and editor of Reading the New Testament: Second Series will be grateful and gratified.

Todd D. Still
Baylor University
George W. Truett Theological Seminary
Waco, TX

Introduction to the Gospel of Luke

By means of this introduction, I am primarily seeking to introduce the readers of this commentary to my own assumptions about the Gospel according to Luke. In most, if not all, instances, I espouse opinions that are commonplace among scholars who have studied Luke's Gospel over the last century. Nevertheless, it is important for me to identify the assumptions on which my reading of this narrative about the life of Jesus is built.

Literary Sources

Along with the vast majority of Lukan scholars, I am convinced that Luke knew of and had access to other written accounts of Jesus' life. Luke makes that exact point when he says, "many have undertaken to set down an orderly account of the events that have been fulfilled among us, just as they were handed on to us by those who from the beginning were eyewitnesses" (1:1-2, NRSV). (Unless otherwise noted, all translations in this commentary will come from the New Revised Standard Version of the Bible.) In addition, it appears that Luke relied on some of those source documents as he wrote his Gospel (1:1-3).

For instance, along with many others, I am convinced that the author of Luke (and the author of Matthew) had access to a manuscript of Mark's Gospel. Slightly more than a third of the material in Luke's Gospel appears to be drawn directly from Mark. Given that at times we can see verbatim or near-verbatim agreement between the two, it is far more likely that Luke had access to a hard copy of Mark as opposed to an oral tradition that was simply linked to Mark's Gospel.

In addition, Luke and Matthew share in common a significant amount of Jesus' teachings. These shared teachings make up about 20 percent of Luke's Gospel (Garland, *Luke*, 24–25). Because this teaching material, which appears exclusively in Luke and Matthew, also exhibits verbatim or near-verbatim similarities, most think a literary link, as opposed to a shared oral tradition, likewise existed between Luke and Matthew. Currently, the scholarly community relies largely on one of two prominent theories to explain the origins of this overlapping teaching material in Luke and Matthew.

The first is known as the Two-Source Hypothesis. Those who advocate for this hypothesis argue that both Luke and Matthew independently relied on Mark's Gospel and another unnamed (and now lost) source document that exclusively preserved Jesus' teachings. Scholars refer to this unnamed source document, which has never been found, as "Q"—an abbreviation for the German word *quelle*, which means "source." Reliance on Mark's Gospel explains the shared elements that are found in all three of the Synoptic Gospels (Matthew, Mark, and Luke). Reliance on "Q" explains the overlapping teaching materials that are only found in Matthew and Luke.

The second theory is known as the Farrer theory, which British New Testament scholar Austin Farrer first articulated in 1955. Scholars who support this theory argue that Matthew relied on Mark's Gospel while writing his own account of Jesus' life. Later, Luke then relied on both Mark's Gospel and Matthew's Gospel as he wrote his own. Both the triple tradition (material shared by Matthew, Mark, and Luke) and the double tradition (material shared by Matthew and Luke) can be explained if Luke had access to both Mark and Matthew.

In this introduction, I will not weigh the strengths and weakness of the Two-Source Hypothesis versus the Farrer theory. Both theories are plausible, and both face challenges. As a result, in this commentary, I will simply assume that Luke had access to multiple literary sources, one of which was Mark's Gospel. In other words, within this commentary, I will assume that Luke drew from Mark's Gospel and either Matthew's Gospel or another source document that Matthew also used when relaying Jesus' teachings.

Finally, Luke included a good bit of material about Jesus' words and deeds in his Gospel that are unique to Luke—approximately 40 percent of Luke's Gospel (C. F. Evans, *Saint Luke*, 26–27). For instance, the parable of the good Samaritan (10:29-37) and Jesus' encounter with Zacchaeus (19:1-10) are only found in Luke's Gospel. Consequently, Luke had access to and relied on additional oral traditions (or written sources) about Jesus—frequently referred to by scholars as "L material"—when he added the material that is unique to his Gospel.

Date and Authorship

Because I assume that Luke relied on Mark while writing his Gospel and because I believe that Mark wrote around the time of the fall of the temple in Jerusalem (70 CE), I date Luke late in the first century CE. Like many others, I assume that Mark wrote somewhere between 65 and 75 CE given his literary emphases on suffering and on Jesus' prediction of the fall of the temple in Mark 13 (e.g., Hooker, *Saint Mark*, 8). In addition, following the lead of many others, I surmise that Luke likely wrote his Gospel between 80 and 100 CE (e.g., Talbert, *Reading Luke*, 1). A date within that range affords time for Mark's Gospel to have been copied and distributed widely, provides Luke with enough time to investigate "everything carefully from the very first" (1:3), and still predates the references to Luke's Gospel that we begin to see late in the second century CE (e.g., Irenaeus, *Haer.*, 3.1.1).

The author of the Gospel of Luke never identifies himself, though "the masculine participle in 1:3 makes it impossible for the author to be a woman" (Bovon, *Luke*, 1:8). Instead, the only other biographical detail related to the author emerges when the author refers to the stories of Jesus that have been "handed on to us by those who from the beginning were eyewitnesses" (1:2). Consequently, the author of Luke appears to be a second-generation Christian rather than an eyewitness to Jesus' ministry. As a result, it is best to acknowledge that this narrative about Jesus' life was composed by an anonymous, second-generation Christian about whom we know little.

In the latter half of the second century CE, once all four of the canonical Gospels started to circulate as a collection, we begin to see evidence that Christian tradition linked this Gospel with Luke, the Gentile traveling companion of Paul and a physician (e.g., Irenaeus, *Haer.*, 3.1.1; Eusebius, *Hist. eccl.*, 3.4; see Fitzmyer, *Luke*, 1:38). We have clear evidence that a physician named Luke ministered and worked alongside Paul. For example, in Phlm 24, Paul refers to Luke as his "fellow worker." In 2 Tim 4:11, the author (Paul or another person writing in Paul's name) indicates that Luke is with him. Finally, in Col 4:14, Paul refers to Luke as "the beloved physician." Our struggle, however, is that we have no ability to verify that Christians in the late second century CE were correct in their assessment of who wrote this Gospel one hundred to one hundred and twenty-five years earlier (Parsons, *Luke*, 5).

As a result, I will frequently refer to the author of this Gospel as Luke for convenience's sake. I am not, however, assuming that the anonymous author is the physician who traveled with Paul (see e.g., Cadbury, *Making of Luke-Acts*, 50) nor am I ruling that idea out. Rather, based on the sophisticated prologue with which the author begins and the literary artistry and rhetorical skill that are present throughout the text, I believe that this author was a well-educated, second-generation Christian who relied on Greek as his native language and who was well versed in what came to be known as the Old Testament (OT) (Bovon, *Luke*, 1:8).

Relationship to the Book of Acts

Scholars frequently debate the relationship between the Gospel of Luke and the Acts of the Apostles. Notice, for example, that both books are dedicated to Theophilus (Luke 1:4: Acts 1:1), both books share similar vocabulary and literary structure, and both books share similar literary and theological motifs. In addition, at the beginning of Acts, the author refers to his "first book," which implies that Acts is the second of a two-book series (Acts 1:1). Whereas the Gospel narrates the life of Jesus (Acts 1:1-5), the Acts of the Apostles describes the birth, growth, and ministry of the Christian movement in the wake of Jesus' death, resurrection, and ascension. Moreover, whereas the Gospel ends with Jesus' final instructions and ascension (Luke 24:50-53), Acts begins with those two elements (Acts 1:6-11).

Given these similarities, I agree with most scholars and assume that the same person wrote both Luke and Acts. At that point, scholarly opinion about the relationship between Luke and Acts diverges into two main viewpoints:

1. From the beginning the author set out to write one unified narrative about Jesus and his followers that was contained on two scrolls. Many scholars in this camp refer to the pair of books as "Luke-Acts" (e.g., Cadbury, *Making of Luke-Acts*, and Verheyden, *The Unity of Luke-Acts*).

2. The author wrote Acts later as a sequel to Luke rather than as one continuous narrative (e.g., Parsons and Pervo, *Rethinking the Unity of Luke and Acts*; Parsons, *Luke: Storyteller*, 40–50).

In this commentary, I agree with Parsons and Pervo that it is better to speak of Luke and Acts rather than Luke-Acts—largely because the early canon lists (or lists of authoritative biblical books) never place the two books side by side (Parsons, *Luke*, 10–11) and because their manuscripts appear to have circulated separately (i.e., their reception histories vary from one another) (Gregory, *Reception of Luke and Acts*, 300–301). In other words, I opt not to use the title "Luke-Acts" because there is no evidence that Christians in the first several centuries treated the books of Luke and Acts as one continuous story.

Nevertheless, I remain convinced that Luke not only anticipated his later work on the Acts of the Apostles even as he wrote his Gospel but also that he made editorial decisions about Luke's Gospel based on what he planned to do in Acts. Consequently, while I think Luke easily stands on its own as a complete literary work, I also believe it is best to keep one eye on Acts while reading Luke's Gospel. The words and deeds of Jesus' disciples in Acts often

Introduction to the Gospel of Luke

help to illustrate and interpret Jesus' own words and deeds in the Gospel. Furthermore, when Luke refers to "the events that have been fulfilled among us" (1:1), he may have envisioned not only events from Luke's Gospel but also events from the book of Acts, like the inclusion of Gentiles among the people of God beginning in Acts 10 (C. F. Evans, *Saint Luke*, 4; Garland, *Luke*, 27–30). As a result, I will frequently cite the Acts of the Apostles throughout this commentary as a sequel to Luke's Gospel.

Intended Audience

Luke dedicates his Gospel to "most excellent Theophilus" so that he "may know the truth concerning the things about which" he has "been instructed" (1:3-4). Even though Luke dedicates his Gospel to an individual, it is clear that he expected many other people to read it as well. Regardless, while referring to Theophilus as the book's addressee, Luke indicates that he likewise envisions Theophilus to be one of the book's beneficiaries. By means of this Gospel, Luke hopes to strengthen the confidence of Theophilus (and Luke's other readers) in regard to the things about which he has already been instructed about Jesus. Consequently, Theophilus provides an important clue about the audience that Luke first envisioned for his Gospel.

In light of the prologue (1:1-4) and at the most obvious level, Luke envisions an audience within the Greek-speaking Roman Empire that already possesses some knowledge of the life and teachings of Jesus. Along these lines, Richard Bauckham argues that Luke wrote for a general Christian audience living in the Mediterranean basin in the late first century (1998, 46). Similarly, François Bovon claims that Luke envisioned "three target groups: educated Gentiles, Hellenistic Jews, and Christians unsettled by rumors (Luke 1:4; Acts 22:30)" (*Luke*, 1:9). Rather than writing to Christians in one specific community (e.g., Ephesus), Luke likely cast a wide net while targeting Christians throughout the Roman Empire. If so, Luke hoped to narrate the story of Jesus in a manner that would embolden his Christian readers to remain faithful and confident followers of Jesus in their various Mediterranean contexts.

Moreover, when considering his audience, Luke likely envisioned readers (and listeners) from diverse socioeconomic backgrounds. On the one hand, Luke places great emphasis on Jesus' reactions to the people at the margins of society throughout his Gospel (e.g., the poor, the sick, widows, etc.). On the other hand, it is equally important to note that Luke gives significant attention to matters of wealth and status in his Gospel. For example, Luke addresses Theophilus with the Greek term *kratistos*, or "most excellent"—a term that generally refers to a person of significant status and wealth in

Roman antiquity (cf. Acts 23:26; 24:3; 26:25) (Garland, *Luke*, 55–56). In addition, Luke highlights tax collectors (e.g., Zacchaeus in 19:1-10) and Roman centurions in his writings (Luke 7:1-10; 23:47; Acts 10). Luke therefore likely anticipated that some first-century Christians who possessed significant social status and/or wealth would read or hear this narrative about Jesus as well as the poor and oppressed. If so, Luke's inclusion of Jesus' teachings about avoiding greed (e.g., 12:15) and aiding those in need (e.g., 12:32-34) may well have been tailored for people like Theophilus (1:3) and those disciples whom Jesus instructs to live as servants rather than as people with the power and demeanor of Gentile kings and benefactors (22:24-26). In essence, in addition to a message of good news for the downtrodden, Luke may have also hoped Gentile "opinion formers" of his day (Stanton, *Gospels*, 80) would hear a word of redirection in this biography of Jesus. Luke frequently lifts up Christian virtues as a distinct alternative to the honor/shame culture of Greek and Roman society. In short, Luke appears to write for a Christian audience that mirrors the wide array of people who respond favorably to Jesus or the good news about Jesus within the narratives of Luke and Acts—Jewish and Gentile Christians, male and female Christians, rich and poor Christians.

Genre

Debates about the genre of the four Gospels have been extensive. Some argue that the Gospels constitute their own unique genre (Bultmann, *History of the Synoptic Tradition*, 371). Others argue that Luke and Acts together constitute historiography (Sterling, *Historiography and Self-Definition*). Still others argue that the Gospel writers composed ancient biographies of the life of Jesus (see, e.g., Talbert, *What is a Gospel?*; Burridge, *What Are the Gospels?*). In this commentary, I align myself with those who argue that Luke and the other Gospel writers composed ancient biographies of Jesus. If so, Luke's primary literary objective would be to reveal Jesus' character to his readers while using Jesus' words and deeds to highlight his public accomplishments (Parsons, *Luke*, 14–15).

Methodology

In this commentary, I am seeking to read the final form of the text from both a literary and theological angle of vision in keeping with the intent of the Reading the New Testament series. To aid me in both endeavors, I will give preference to Luke's first readers. In other words, I will ask how the first readers (or listeners) likely made sense of both the literary form of the text and the theological convictions embodied within the text. To ask about the readers that Luke first envisioned when he wrote this Gospel is to ask about late-first-century Jewish and Gentile Christians who were products of and enmeshed within the cultures of the Mediterranean basin.

Finally, when citing the biblical text, I will rely on the New Revised Standard Version. Also, when helpful, I will also supply Greek vocabulary in a transliterated format based upon the Nestle-Aland 28th/United Bible Society 4th edition of the Greek New Testament.

A Proper Beginning

Luke 1:1–4:13

Introduction

Luke presents a carefully crafted introduction to his biography about Jesus of Nazareth in the first four and a half chapters of his book. First, Luke introduces his Gospel by writing a sophisticated prologue that resembles those found in ancient Greek histories, biographies, and scientific treatises. In doing so, Luke proves himself to be an accomplished writer who is comfortable with the Greek language. Furthermore, Luke's authorial audience, the readers whom Luke first envisioned as he wrote this Gospel, likely consisted of Gentile Christians who could appreciate such a prologue.

Thereafter, Luke begins with the angelic announcements about the impending births of both John the Baptist and Jesus. In the process, Luke establishes a pattern, which he utilizes throughout the first four chapters, whereby he compares John the Baptist and Jesus extensively. In particular, by means of this close comparison, or *synkrisis*, Luke clearly demonstrates that while similar to John, Jesus is far greater. In the process, Luke also makes it clear that no animosity exists between John and Jesus. Instead, Luke informs us that John and Jesus are relatives (1:36).

In the third chapter, Luke then provides a vivid depiction of John the Baptist's prophetic ministry along with noteworthy responses from the crowd, tax collectors, and soldiers. Yet when John is shut up in prison (3:20), the narrative shifts to focus entirely on Jesus' prophetic ministry, which resembles John's ministry but far surpasses it. In particular, Luke introduces the motif of Jesus as the "Son of God," which appears in three consecutive passages: Jesus' baptism, genealogy, and temptation. All three passages highlight Jesus' faithfulness as the Son of God over against the children of God in the past who have not proven faithful.

The Prologue to Luke's Gospel (1:1-4)

Unlike the other canonical Gospels, Luke begins with a sophisticated prologue to his Gospel that resembles those found in ancient histories such as those written by Dionysius of Halicarnassus, ancient biographies such as Philo's *Life of Moses*, and a variety of Hellenistic treatises—especially scientific treatises (Fitzmyer, *Luke*, 1:288; Talbert, *Reading Luke*, 7–11; Alexander, *The Preface*, 167). This four-verse sentence, which is written in a polished Greek style, tells us a good bit about the author of this book and perhaps some about his audience. While Luke will utilize a variety of writing styles throughout the rest of Luke and Acts, from the outset his readers should be keenly aware of his refined rhetorical and literary skills. At the outset, Luke demonstrates that he is capable of great erudition as he constructs an orderly account (1:3) that will enable his readers to be confident concerning the truth about Jesus (1:4).

Second, Luke dedicates his Gospel to "most excellent Theophilus" (1:3). The term translated as "most excellent" or most noble (Gk. *kratistos*) was an honorific title that was frequently, though not exclusively, applied to persons of elevated status or official position (cf. Acts 23:26; 24:3; 26:25) (Culy, Parsons, and Stigall, *Luke*, 5; see also Alexander, *The Preface*, 188–90, and Cadbury, *Making of Luke-Acts*, 314–15). The name "Theophilus" has engendered debate beginning as early as the early church fathers (e.g., Ephiphanius, *Pan.* 51.429; Origen, *Hom. Luc.* 1). When translated literally, it means "friend of God." As a result, for centuries exegetes have asked whether the name "Theophilus" refers symbolically to all those who are friends of God.

Far more likely, however, *kratistos* ("most excellent") in 1:3 refers to an actual person of noble status. Consequently, Theophilus may have been the wealthy patron who sponsored Luke and took responsibility for distributing the book after its completion (Garland, *Luke*, 56). Another possibility relates to whether the name Theophilus functions as a pseudonym for a high-ranking Roman official who sponsored Luke but who desired to remain anonymous due either to political caution or selfless humility (Streeter, *The Four Gospels*, 559). The best evidence lies with either of these last two options. Most likely, Theophilus was Luke's wealthy patron.

Regardless, the common Greek name "Theophilus" likely tells us something about Luke's intended audience as well (see the introduction above). In the most straightforward reading of Luke 1:3, Luke addresses his Gospel to a Christian of elevated status within the context of the Roman Empire. As a result, Richard Hays concludes, "Part of Luke's literary achievement is to

A Proper Beginning

make the foreboding story of Jesus seem reasonable and inviting to a more cultured readership in the Hellenistic world" (*Moral Vision*, 113).

Finally, Luke's characterization of his entire Gospel (and possibly of the Acts of the Apostles as well; see Bovon, *Luke*, 1:17-18) in Luke 1:1 is noteworthy. Luke perceives Jesus' entire life span as "events that have been fulfilled among us." Whereas Matthew aims to demonstrate how specific events in Jesus' life fulfill specific Old Testament (OT) prophecies, Luke draws upon the OT in a wholly different manner. Most often, Luke portrays Jesus' life and ministry as evidence that God has fulfilled God's promises to Israel: "Scripture is read not as a book of oracular predictions about future events but as a book of promises to God's chosen people, promises that have been made good in the dramatic events of Jesus' ministry, death, and resurrection as well as in the subsequent experience of the church" (Hays, *Moral Vision*, 113–14).

Announcing the Births of John and Jesus (1:5-56)

To introduce the story of Jesus, Luke utilizes an ancient Greek rhetorical technique called *synkrisis* or comparison. In his first three chapters, Luke repeatedly begins with John the Baptist, whom he portrays in an exceedingly positive light. Luke depicts John the Baptist as a great prophet much like those found in the OT. Luke then shows how Jesus is similar to John and yet far greater than John in every respect. For example, Luke narrates the conception, birth, naming, and growth of John and Jesus in a parallel fashion throughout Luke 1–2. By comparing Jesus to a great prophet like John the Baptist in a side-by-side format, Luke is able to accentuate the profound significance of Jesus, who has no equal.

John's Birth Foretold (1:5-25)

Luke begins his biography of Jesus by narrating the miraculous conception of John the Baptist. As he does so, Luke utilizes a literary style that resembles the Septuagint (LXX), the Greek translation of the Hebrew Bible—a style that Luke will mimic throughout the first two chapters of his Gospel. In the process, Luke alludes to a variety of OT images and concepts. For example, in Luke 1:5-7 Luke refers to a king, a priest, the priestly order of Abijah (cf. 1 Chr 24:10), Aaron, the commandments of the Lord, and a barren woman—all within the first three verses of Luke's narrative about Jesus. This editorial decision suggests that Luke knew that many of his first readers were keenly aware of the OT. More important, it implies that God's redemptive work did not begin in Luke 1 with the conceptions of John and Jesus. Unlike Mark (1:1) and Matthew (1:1), Luke will not even mention Jesus' name until

1:31. Rather, Luke uses these OT allusions, echoes, parallels, and stylistic features to indicate that the story of God's redemptive work in the world (or "salvation history") began long ago. It simply reaches its climactic turning point during the life, death, and resurrection of Jesus.

Luke also sets the scene for a dramatic miracle when he introduces John's parents. He tells us that both Zechariah and Elizabeth are "righteous before God, living blamelessly according to all the commandments and regulations of the Lord" (1:6). Yet despite their devotion to God, Elizabeth is barren. For those familiar with the OT stories of Sarah (Gen 18:9-15), Rebekah (Gen 25:21), Rachel (Gen 30:22-24), and Hannah (1 Sam 1:1-20), the combination of Elizabeth's devotion and barrenness suggests that God may once again intervene and miraculously open Elizabeth's womb just as God did on rare occasions in the OT. Luke therefore elevates his readers' hopes and expectations as he introduces Zechariah and Elizabeth.

As the priestly order of Abijah performs their semiannual duties at the temple in Jerusalem, Zechariah is chosen for what will likely be a once-in-a-lifetime privilege of offering incense inside the sanctuary of the temple complex. As he does so, the people outside of the sanctuary are praying (1:8-10). This seemingly offhanded comment helps set up a much larger conversation about prayer in Luke's Gospel. Repeatedly, Luke highlights the importance of prayer in his biography about Jesus—far more than the authors of the other Gospels. In particular, Luke sets up a correlation between prayer and revelation or divine enlightenment (Crump, *Jesus the Intercessor*, 21). Notice, for instance, that the people are praying in 1:10, and an angel of the Lord, who delivers the Lord's message, arrives in 1:11; in 1:13, Luke also tells us that Zechariah had previously prayed for a descendant. We will see this same combination of prayer and revelation at numerous other points in Luke's writings (e.g., Luke 3:21-22; 9:28-36; 22:41-44; Acts 12:6-17).

The interaction between Zechariah and the angel of the Lord unfolds in a manner that is reminiscent of OT call stories (e.g., Exod 3:2-12, Judg 6:11-24) (Tannehill, *Luke*, 42–44). Similar to the encounters between an angel of the Lord and Moses (Exod 3) and an angel of the Lord and Gideon (Judg 6), Luke narrates Zechariah's experience in a similar pattern:

(a) An angel of the Lord appears (1:11).

(b) Zechariah is frightened (1:12).

(c) The angel delivers an unexpected call or message from the Lord (1:13-17).

(d) Zechariah objects to the angel's charge with reasons why the calling is nonsensical (1:18).

(e) Finally, the angel provides a sign that authenticates the angel's instructions (1:19-20). Unfortunately for Zechariah, his own inability to speak will serve as the sign that substantiates God's calling in Luke 1. Zechariah will be mute until the birth of John.

That Luke narrates Gabriel's instructions to Zechariah in the same literary style and sequence that writers used when describing OT call stories in the past is highly significant. In particular, Luke likely hoped his readers would recognize that the same God who intervened on behalf of God's people in the past is once again intervening to rescue his people in Luke's day. Notice, for example, that Gabriel predicts blessings that will extend far beyond the barren couple. Rather, the child to be born to Zechariah and Elizabeth will be a great prophet like Elijah and will "turn many of the people of Israel to the Lord their God" (1:16-17). This new event, which Luke narrates like a familiar OT call story, bridges God's work in the past with God's new work in the present. As distinct from the calls of Moses and Gideon, however, Gabriel now reports far more about what God will do and considerably less about what Zechariah will do (1:13-17). Regardless, Luke's use of a familiar literary form builds expectations for his readers from the outset of this Gospel. Moreover, Luke will use the same literary form again when Gabriel announces Jesus' birth to Mary (1:26-38) and to a group of shepherds (2:8-20).

Elizabeth reacts to her pregnancy and the birth of her son much like Hannah reacts in 1 Sam 1:18-28. In antiquity, barrenness brought great distress to couples and in particular to married women. Descendants not only carried on the family name and property but, in Hebraic thought, they also provided a type of life beyond death for deceased family members. For Elizabeth, however, the Lord's miraculous intervention does even more. It removes the sense of disgrace that she feels when she interacts with other people (1:25). Often in the ancient world, it was assumed that God willed barrenness upon a woman or a couple as a consequence of God's displeasure (e.g., Gen 16:2; 30:22-24). Luke has already informed his readers that both Elizabeth and Zechariah are "righteous before God" (1:6); their barrenness is not a consequence of sin. Nevertheless, Elizabeth experiences God's rescue and vindication in Luke 1:24-25. God removes the disgrace or reproach that Elizabeth endured when she was with other people. As a result, here at the beginning of Luke's Gospel Elizabeth functions as a foretaste of God's salvific work in the time of Jesus. Triumphantly and confidently, Elizabeth now proclaims that the Lord has "looked favorably on me" (1:25). By the end of Luke and Acts, many others burdened by numerous forms of oppression will be capable of making similar, triumphant declarations.

Jesus' Birth Foretold (1:26-38)

Next, Luke narrates the angel Gabriel's announcement of Jesus' conception to Mary. Immediately, we learn that the virgin Mary is betrothed to Joseph, who is a descendant of David (1:27). Thereafter, Luke once again relies heavily upon the style and form of an OT call story to narrate this event (e.g., Exod 3:2-12; Judg 6:11-24).

(a) An angel of the Lord appears to Mary. This time, however, Luke includes Gabriel's greeting to Mary in which he refers to her as "favored one" (1:28).

(b) The angel seeks to calm Mary's fears by again declaring that Mary has found "favor" or grace (Gk. *charis*) with God (1:30).

(c) The angel proclaims the call or message from God. Here Gabriel declares that Mary, a virgin, will conceive a child. In addition, Mary, as opposed to the baby's father (cf. 1:13) is directed to name the baby "Jesus" (1:31). As we saw with Gabriel's appearance to Zechariah (1:13-17), Luke again accentuates what God will do far more than what the human is called to do, as is common in OT call stories.

(d) Mary objects to the angel's proclamation, though her question seems to spring from an actual desire for understanding rather than the desire to avoid God's call as we routinely see in OT call stories (1:34; cf. Exod 3:11; Judg 6:15).

(e) The angel provides a sign that will validate his words. In this case, the surprising news that Mary's much older relative, Elizabeth, is pregnant (1:36) will function as the corroborating sign.

(f) Finally, Luke adds an additional step to the familiar OT call story format, one not even seen in Zechariah's encounter with Gabriel in Luke 1:8-20. The youthful Mary believes Gabriel (1:45) and boldly vows obedience to God (1:38). Like a devout disciple, Mary simply wants the Lord's will to be done. Just as Elizabeth provides a foretaste of all those who will experience the Lord's favor in Luke's writings (1:24-25), here Mary provides a foretaste of what true discipleship and obedience will look like throughout Luke and Acts. She merely says, "Here am I, the servant of the Lord; let it be with me according to your word" (1:38). She desires to cooperate fully with the redemptive plan of God as it unfolds in the world.

Beyond the stylistic and generic observations about Luke's narration of 1:26-38, it is important to take note of the theological claims that Luke establishes in this unit. First, he sets forth important christological claims about Jesus from the outset of his Gospel by means of Gabriel's words. Jesus is the great Son of God who will inherit the Davidic throne, reign over Israel forever, and establish an unconquerable, everlasting kingdom (1:32-33, 35). These convictions about Jesus guide both Luke and Acts. Second, Luke sets forth important pneumatological claims through Gabriel's words. He identifies the Holy Spirit as "the power of the Most High" (1:35). The same power of God that hovered over the waters and spoke creation into being is now at work once again, causing a virgin to give life to a child (Brown, *Birth of the Messiah*, 314). Hereafter, this same Holy Spirit will continue to be the unseen power that propels God's salvific intervention in the world and enables God's purposes to be accomplished throughout both Luke and Acts.

Finally, Gabriel's restatement in 1:37 of what was first proclaimed in Gen 18:14 LXX affirms the Scriptures as an authentic and authoritative revelation of God (Bovon, *Luke*, 1:53). In Gen 18 when the Lord sent three angelic visitors to inform Abraham and Sarah that she would give birth to a son despite their old age, Sarah laughed in disbelief. An angel then informed her that nothing is impossible for God. Now in Luke 1:37, Gabriel is once again using those same words in a near-verbatim fashion to assure Mary that she, too, will give birth to a son. What God said in the past to Sarah remains true in the present for Mary.

Connecting Sarah and Mary, however, creates a slight disjuncture. One might have thought that Gabriel would have alluded to Gen 18:14 LXX when speaking with Zechariah and Elizabeth (1:8-20) rather than Mary (1:26-38). Zechariah and Elizabeth's barrenness in their old age more closely resembles the circumstances of Abraham and Sarah in Gen 18. By restating those same words in a slightly different context, however, Gabriel's declaration about God takes on an even greater force. John's conception to Zechariah and Elizabeth ought to remind Luke's readers of God's miraculous and redemptive works in the past. Occasionally, God has intervened and opened the womb of a barren woman as part of God's broader work on behalf of God's chosen people. The conception of an important child between a barren couple almost serves as a hallmark of God's divine power in the OT. The OT Scriptures, however, never speak about a virgin birth. God, through Mary, is now doing something unthinkable and dramatically new. It is precisely because God is doing something novel in the conception of Jesus that Gabriel needs to remind Mary (1:37)—and Luke needs to remind his readers—of the word of the Lord that was first spoken to Sarah in Gen 18:14 LXX.

Mary Visits Elizabeth and Praises God (1:39-56)

During her unconventional pregnancy, Mary seeks out and relies on the hospitality of her kinfolks in the Judean hill country for approximately three months (1:39-40, 56). When Elizabeth and Mary initially greet one another, it leads to two speeches—a brief one from Elizabeth (1:42-45) and a longer one from Mary (1:46-55). Both speeches reveal a great deal about Jesus.

(1) Luke 1:42-45. The leaping of John the Baptist in her womb prompts Elizabeth's speech. Notably, at that point the Holy Spirit fills Elizabeth. Readers should now realize that the Holy Spirit is the driving force behind the unfolding plan of God, which Luke is describing in Luke and Acts (cf. Acts 2). First, the Holy Spirit enabled Mary to conceive in 1:35, and now the Holy Spirit enables Elizabeth's boisterous celebration of Mary's pregnancy in 1:41-45. Remarkably, when Elizabeth, who is simultaneously pregnant with her own son, encounters the unborn Jesus in Mary's womb, she refers to Jesus as "my Lord" (1:43). Elizabeth's comments participate in the much larger Lukan conversation about John and Jesus. John's birth and his ministry are vitally important, but even John's mother can recognize the supremacy of the unborn Jesus.

(2) Luke 1:46-55. Mary's speech, often called the "Magnificat" due to the first word of the Latin text, functions like a hymn of praise and has a strong correlation with Hannah's song in the wake of Samuel's birth (1 Sam 2:1-10). As we have already seen, Luke greatly honors Mary. While Zechariah hears about the miraculous conception of his son (1:8-20) before Mary hears about the conception of Jesus (1:26-38), Mary holds the honored position of praising God first due to Zechariah's muteness (1:46-55; cf. 1:67-79). In addition, Luke allots far more space to Mary's words of praise (1:46-55) than Elizabeth's words of praise (1:42-45).

Mary's "Magnificat," which features two strophes or stanzas, sets forth major themes for Luke's Gospel. The first stanza runs from 1:46-50. Mary begins by depicting her own experiences as an individual servant or slave (Gk. *doulos*) of the Lord (1:48). In particular, she designates God as her "Savior" (1:47), though hereafter Luke will include references to Jesus as "Savior" (Luke 2:11; Acts 5:31; 13:23). With one exception in John 4:42, Luke is the only Gospel writer who employs the term "savior" (Gk. *sōtēr*) when referring to God or Jesus. The term is far more common in Greek and Roman literature. Roman writers, for instance, routinely referred to Roman emperors, military leaders, and gods as "saviors." In particular, Caesar Augustus was praised as a "savior" because his militaristic rise to power in 27 BCE ended the Roman civil wars, thereby saving the Roman people and bringing peace to the empire (e.g., the Priene calendar inscription). Mary, however, boldly identifies the Lord as her "Savior." In particular, she claims that God has extended mercy (Gk. *eleos*) to her. Unlike the militaristic Roman "saviors," the strength of Mary's God is located in God's mercy (Carroll, *Luke*, 49).

Furthermore, Mary's pregnancy portends an even fuller expression of God's mercy—namely "God's saving action for the downtrodden nation" of Israel (Hays, *Echoes of Scripture*, 196).

The second stanza runs from 1:51-55 and mirrors the first stanza. Rather than describing how God has shown mercy to her as an individual servant, however, Mary's praise now begins to spread outward. She praises God for the communal mercy (Gk. *eleos*) shown to God's servant or child (Gk. *pais*) Israel (1:54). Mary recalls the ways in which God has rescued and aided Israel in past generations. Her reference to the powerful arm of God that scatters the proud and brings down the powerful from their thrones echoes numerous OT texts that describe God's deliverance of the Hebrew people from Egypt (e.g., Exod 6:1, 6; 15:16; Deut 3:24). Similarly, OT texts from the postexilic period routinely depict Israel or the Israelites as the poor and oppressed whom God aids while opposing their enemies (e.g., Isa 61:1; 66:2; Ps 40:17; 70:5; 86:1; 109:22) (Brown, *Birth of the Messiah*, 242; Levin, "Poor in the Old Testament," 253–73). Most important for both Luke and Acts, Mary declares that God's faithful care for Israel over many generations is a fulfillment of the promises God made to Abraham (1:55; Gen 12:1-3; 15:18). Luke repeatedly depicts Jesus' arrival as a fulfillment of the Abrahamic covenant (e.g., Luke 1:73; Acts 3:25) (Dahl, "Story of Abraham," 150–56).

In the midst of these two powerful stanzas about how God has already functioned as a "Savior" for Mary and Israel, Mary's song also provides a foreshadowing function. God has not only reversed the fortunes of Israel in the past and Mary in the present but will also, as Mary's hymn notes, initiate a great, future reversal through the birth of Jesus. In the past, God has reversed the fortunes of the proud and powerful and the lowly (1:51-52). The implication is that God will soon do so again. "In remembrance of his mercy" and "according to the promise he made" to Abraham, God is again intervening in the present and future through Jesus (e.g., Acts 4:12; 16:31). In short, Mary's reflective testimony also functions for Luke's readers as a prophecy that will find its fulfillment over the course of Luke and Acts. This prophecy carries hope for the servants of God, but it likewise carries a warning for those with proud hearts and powerful thrones (1:51-52).

The Birth, Naming, and Growth of John (1:57-80)

In Luke 1:57-80, the author chronicles the birth (1:57-58), naming (1:59-79), and growth of John the Baptist (1:80). Thereafter, Luke will narrate Jesus' birth (2:1-20), naming (2:21-38), and growth (2:39-52) in a parallel fashion. As we saw with the annunciations of John (1:8-20) and Jesus (1:26-38), Luke again utilizes the ancient Greek rhetorical technique of *synkrisis* or comparison to highlight the grandeur of Jesus. Throughout the first three chapters, Luke portrays John as an exemplary prophet of God (1:15-17). The angel Gabriel even compares John to Elijah (1:17). Yet Luke repeatedly demonstrates in these same chapters the supremacy of Jesus by showing how Jesus far exceeds even the best attributes of a faithful servant like John.

(1) Luke 1:57-58. John's birth is an important event within the hill country of Judea. Both relatives and neighbors rejoice. In particular, all involved are mindful of the great mercy that God has shown to the barren Elizabeth. God has removed the source of her shame and opened her womb.

(2) Luke 1:59-66. The naming of John the Baptist is also an important event within his home region. As a devout Jewish family, Zechariah and Elizabeth circumcise and name John on the eighth day of his life (1:59-60; cf. Lev 12:2-3). Confusion reigns due to Zechariah's muteness and the couple's desire to be obedient to the Lord's instructions (1:13). Previously, Zechariah's doubtful questioning led Gabriel to punish Zechariah with muteness in 1:18-20. Now, however, Zechariah's obedience immediately leads to the return of his speech (1:63-64).

(3) Luke 1:67-79. As soon as he is able to speak, Zechariah begins to praise God (1:64). His praise of God is captured in the form of a hymn. Zechariah's "Benedictus" takes its name from the first word of the Latin translation of the text. Much like Mary's song (1:46-55), Zechariah's song falls into two stanzas (1:67-75 and 76-79). In addition, as in the "Magnificat," Luke introduces and reinforces major theological themes in his Gospel by means of Zechariah's hymn.

First, notice again that the Holy Spirit is guiding the most important events at the beginning of Luke (1:35, 41, 67). Second, much like John's mother acknowledged the superiority of Jesus (1:43), here also John's father uses his first words after nine months of muteness to prophesy about Jesus (1:68-75) even before he turns his attention to his son, John (1:76-79). Moreover, Zechariah offers exceedingly high praise for the unborn Jesus. He characterizes the upcoming birth of Jesus as the means by which "the Lord God of Israel . . . has looked favorably on his people and redeemed them" (1:68). He depicts Jesus as a great king when he literally says that Jesus will be a mighty horn of salvation: "In scripture a 'horn,' as of a wild buffalo or a bull, is a symbol of strength" (e.g., Ps 18:3; 75:5-6; 148:14) (Tannehill, *Luke,* 59). Third, like Mary (1:54-55), Zechariah depicts the arrival of Jesus as a manifestation of God's faithfulness to his promises. God has remembered the Abrahamic covenant (1:72-75; cf. Gen 12:1-3). In other words, God is once again showing mercy (Gk. *eleos*) to or blessing his people (1:72; cf. 1:50, 54).

In the second stanza (1:76-79), Zechariah now prophesies about the importance of his son, John. In particular, John will serve as a great prophet who will go before Jesus (1:76). Like Elijah (1:16-17), John will call God's people to repentance, which in turn will lead to forgiveness of their sins (1:76-77). Most important, John represents the firstfruits of God's mercy (Gk. *eleos*), which is dawning like a new day (1:78). Notice also that Luke again stresses God's mercy, which appears twice in Mary's song (1:50, 54) and twice in Zechariah's song (1:72, 78).

(4) Luke 1:80. Finally, Luke ends his section on John's birth and infancy by briefly commenting on John's growth (1:80). In particular, Luke informs his readers that John grows both physically and in spirit. John's maturation and formation, however, does not take place within Jerusalem. He does not live in the city, participate in typical religious activities, or fraternize with other religious leaders. Rather, John is the ultimate outsider who remains in the wilderness from his boyhood until it is time for his prophetic ministry as an adult.

The Birth, Naming, and Growth of Jesus (2:1-52)

As previously noted, Luke places the conception, birth, naming, and growth of Jesus in a parallel format with John's development. In each instance, however, Luke demonstrates the clear superiority of Jesus over John. That dynamic is most obvious in the birth of Jesus. For instance, whereas Luke describes John's birth in two verses (1:57-58), he dedicates twenty verses to the birth of Jesus (2:1-20). In addition, whereas John was born in his home region, Mary gives birth in Judea after Jesus' parents leave their hometown of Nazareth in the northern territory of Galilee in order to travel to the city of Bethlehem (2:1-7). This change of context then allows far more people to celebrate the birth of Jesus as compared with John.

(1) Luke 2:1-7. Two themes are immediately apparent in the first half of Luke's narration of Jesus' birth. First, Luke discloses that Jesus' birth is a worldwide event. On the one hand, his birth is significant for Luke's readers who are steeped in the OT. Importantly, Joseph, Jesus' father, is a descendant of David (2:4), which means that Jesus is likewise in the line of Israel's greatest king. This revelation reinforces Gabriel's pronouncement that "the Lord God will give to him the throne of his ancestor David" (1:32). In essence, Luke shows his readers that Jesus is the anointed descendant of David through whom God will fulfill his covenant to establish an everlasting kingship (1:33, 2:11; cf. 2 Sam 7:13-16).

On the other hand, Jesus' birth is also highly significant for Luke's readers who are steeped in Roman culture and history. Caesar Augustus, the greatest ruler of the Roman people, is an unwitting accomplice in the birth of Jesus. Octavius (or Octavian), whom his adopted father Julius Caesar renamed "Augustus," became the first ruler of the Roman Empire. He reigned from 27 BCE until 14 CE and was renowned for the "peace" that he brought to the Roman people as he extinguished the Roman civil wars through military force. Here, however, we see that even Caesar Augustus serves the greater interests of the God of Abraham, Isaac, and Jacob. Due to Augustus's decree, Joseph and Mary travel to David's hometown, thereby enabling a proper context for the birth of the new Davidic king (Parsons, *Luke*, 50). Furthermore, by 2:11, the angels of God are attributing to Jesus titles that were frequently associated with both David and Augustus—Messiah and Savior, respectively. The angels declare that God has now brought true "peace" to earth through Jesus, as opposed to Caesar Augustus (2:14).

Second, Luke lays the groundwork for a metaphorical association between Jesus and food or nourishment, which appears throughout his Gospel (Parsons, *Luke*, 52). For instance, Bethlehem, the birthplace of Jesus, literally means "the house of bread" (2:4). In addition, when Jesus was born, Mary placed him in an animal's feeding trough (2:7). Because numerous descendants of David likely all arrived in Bethlehem at the same time for the registration (2:1-2), the guest room (2:7; Gk. *kataluma*; cf. Luke 22:11) of Joseph's kinfolks was already in use (Culy, Parsons, and Stigall, *Luke*, 69; Malina and Rohrbaugh, *Social-Scientific Commentary*, 297). As a result, when Jesus is born, Mary lays her baby in the best accommodations that her relatives can provide—a manger. That Jesus is born in a town named for bread and sleeps in a location that supplies food to animals sets the stage for later Lukan passages that more explicitly associate Jesus with human food (e.g., 22:19). From the outset, Luke lays the groundwork for a depiction of Jesus as nourishment for the world.

(2) Luke 2:8-20. The second half of Jesus' birth story in Luke's Gospel comes in 2:8-20. Again, the comparison between the birth of John (1:57-58) and the birth of Jesus (2:1-20) is instructive. In the wake of John's birth, neighbors and relatives rejoice with Elizabeth because they perceive that God has shown mercy to Elizabeth (1:58). The immediate response to Jesus' birth, however, is far grander (2:8-20). For instance, beyond family members, a multitude of angels and strangers rejoice over Jesus' birth (2:13-14, 20). Rather than rejoicing within John's home region (1:58), Jesus' birth has a cosmic impact—both in the heavens and on earth. Moreover, rather than praising God for showing mercy to Elizabeth (1:58), the angel of the Lord announces "good news of great joy for *all the people*" (emphasis added; 2:10).

In addition, Luke narrates the angel's encounter with the shepherds in the pattern of an OT call story. As a result, the angel's interaction with the shepherds represents the third such call story within the first two chapters of Luke. As previously noted, Luke narrates Gabriel's annunciation of John's birth to Zechariah (1:8-20) and Gabriel's annunciation of Jesus' birth to Mary (1:26-38) in an OT call story format (e.g., Exod 3:2-12, Judg 6:11-24). Notice that Luke presents the same type of material in the same sequence when he tells his readers about the shepherds in Luke 2:8-20.

(a) An angel, representing the very presence of God, appears (2:9).

(b) The angel reassures the shepherds and tells them not to be afraid (2:10).

(c) The angel speaks the word of the Lord, which provides an explanation of what God is doing (2:11).

(d) Finally, the angel provides a sign intended to reassure the shepherds about the veracity of the angel's proclamation. In this instance, when the shepherds find a baby lying in an animal's feeding trough—a truly unexpected sight—they will know for sure that the Lord has spoken to them (2:12).

While narrating the angel's encounter with the shepherds, however, Luke drastically alters the generic elements of the call narrative pattern. The Lord's call of the shepherds even differs from the first two call stories in Luke's Gospel. As was the case with Moses, Gideon, Zechariah, and Mary, when God calls someone to action, that person typically objects or asks clarifying questions. In contrast, Luke characterizes the shepherds in an exceedingly positive light. The angel never calls them to action; he simply declares what God has done. The shepherds then commission one another to action (2:15). Moreover, unlike other call stories, the shepherds never raise objections to the angel's pronouncement. Whereas Moses provides excuses about why he cannot speak to Pharaoh in Exod 3, the shepherds immediately rush off to find the Christ child. In the first century, shepherds were often thought of as unrefined social misfits for whom others had little regard (see, e.g., Culpepper, "Luke," 9:65). Here, however, Luke portrays these socially suspect shepherds as spiritually sensitive and eagerly obedient servants of God. They take the initiative, act with obedience, and do so with haste (2:15-20). Furthermore, God gives these people of low social status the honored position of speaking the same words and rejoicing in the same manner as the angels of heaven.

Notably, in the OT God only occasionally intervenes and calls someone like Moses to action. In Luke's Gospel, however, God has now intervened on three occasions in a short span of time. The implication is that God is active at this historical juncture. God is breaking in and initiating the redemption of God's people. A Messiah and Savior has been born (2:11; cf. comments on 1:46-55). In addition, God is now working through unusual means. God is working through people whom Luke's readers likely would not have anticipated: God has worked through an elderly barren couple, a young betrothed virgin, and overlooked shepherds all in the first two chapters of this Gospel. God is decisively intervening in history, but God is doing so through unexpected people and in unexpected ways.

(3) Luke 2:21-39. Luke narrates the naming and circumcision of Jesus in two parts. We read about Mary and Joseph's actions in 2:21-24, 39, and we hear Simeon and Anna's prophesies about Jesus in 2:25-38. While discussing Mary and Joseph, Luke again depicts them as faithful and obedient followers of God. They circumcise Jesus on the eighth day as the Law prescribes (e.g., Lev 12:2-3), and they name him Jesus as Gabriel directed (1:31). In addition, they follow the postpartum purification instructions found in the Mosaic Law when they offer a poor family's sacrifice of two turtledoves and two pigeons in the temple (2:22-24; cf. Lev 12:6-8). Luke stresses the degree to which Mary and Joseph faithfully follow the Law of Moses by noting their obedience to it on five occasions within this unit (2:22, 23, 24, 27, 39).

As we have seen throughout Luke 1–2, Luke constructs a *synkrisis* or comparison between John and Jesus at this point. Once again, he depicts events from the life of Jesus—in this instance, his naming and circumcision—as far more grandiose than the corresponding events in John's life (1:59-79; 2:21-39). For example, John's own father, Zechariah, prophesies about John's future ministry (1:76-79). Yet two total strangers in the temple, Simeon and Anna, prophesy about the importance of Jesus' birth and future ministry (2:25-38). Most important, whereas Zechariah says that John "will go before the Lord to prepare his ways" (1:76), the Holy Spirit guides Simeon to declare that Jesus is both God's Messiah (2:25-27) and God's salvation (2:30). Whereas John's ministry will impact the Jewish people, Jesus will be "a light for revelation to the Gentiles" as well (2:30; cf. Luke 3:6). Here Simeon quotes from Isa 49:6. In the book of Isaiah, the phrase likely means that God will demonstrate his strength to the nations (or Gentiles) as he rescues exiled Israelites who have been scattered abroad (Kaminsky and Stewart, "God of All the World," 139). Luke, however, appears to reframe the phrase. It now appears to foreshadow the day when Gentiles will also experience the salvation of God (e.g., Acts 10:34-48). If so, then Simeon's prophecy sets the tone for the remaining portions of Luke and Acts.

(4) Luke 2:40-52. Luke again compares John and Jesus when describing their maturation process and the transition from their infancy to their public ministry. Yet whereas Luke accomplished his purposes with John in one verse (1:80), he provides two growth statements about Jesus (2:40, 52) and an example story that highlights Jesus' God-endowed wisdom (2:41-51). While Luke portrays John in a positive light, he shows his readers that Jesus is exponentially greater.

Luke mentions Jesus' wisdom in both summaries about his growth (2:40, 52). Luke uses a passive participle to indicate that Jesus was filled (presumably by God) with wisdom in 2:40, but then Luke also uses an imperfect tense in 2:52 to portray Jesus as continuously growing in wisdom. As a result, Jesus both receives God-given wisdom from the beginning and actively grows in that wisdom as he similarly grows in size and in favor with God and humans.

Luke alone among the Gospel writers then includes a story about Jesus at the age of twelve. In particular, the story demonstrates Jesus' wisdom, even as a child (2:48; Gk. *teknon*). As we already saw with Simeon and Anna, the temple is identified as the "Father's house" (v. 49) and offers a hospitable context for Jesus at this point in his life. (Obviously, later in 19:45-46, Luke will place the temple in a highly negative light after religious interlopers take over the house.) The emphasis of this unit, however, falls upon Jesus' understanding and his answers (2:47). Everyone, including his parents and the teachers, are amazed at him. Thus, Luke demonstrates for his readers that Jesus does not acquire his wisdom and understanding from his parents, the teachers, John the Baptist, or anyone else. Instead, from the beginning Luke indicates that Jesus' wisdom and understanding come from God.

The Ministry of John the Baptist (3:1-20)

The final *synkrisis* or comparison between John and Jesus that Luke sketches for his readers revolves around their public ministries. For example, Luke indicates that both men spend time in the wilderness before embarking on their ministries (3:2-4; 4:1-13) (Parsons, *Luke*, 62). Notably, though, Luke will narrate the ministry of John in twenty verses (3:1-20), but he will take the rest of the book to describe the far grander ministry of Jesus. Furthermore, in this unit (3:1-20), John's ministry of faithful proclamation and baptism serve in part to set the stage for the even more momentous event of Jesus' baptism (3:21-22).

As we saw in 2:1-7, Luke aims to locate the events surrounding John's ministry, and, more important, Jesus' life in their proper historical setting. Unlike the heroes of the legendary Greek and Roman epics like Odysseus and Aeneas, Luke's biography of Jesus takes place at a specific time in human history (3:1-2). By means of these historical details, Luke seeks to establish further for Theophilus and his readers the veracity of his account of Jesus' life (1:4). In the process, Luke again reinforces the concept that God's intervention in the world through Jesus has "universal implications" given that he cites both Roman and Jewish rulers (3:1-2) (Parsons, *Luke*, 64).

From the beginning Luke decisively depicts John the Baptist as a prophet (1:76-77; 7:26). Unlike Mark who simply says that John appears preaching and baptizing (Mark 1:4-8), Luke first establishes John's prophetic calling. Before anything else, the word of God prompts John while he is still in the wilderness (1:80; 3:2). Thereafter, his ministry consists of calling his fellow Jews to repent from their sins and to mark that repentance with baptism (3:3; cf. 1:76-77). Notably, Luke's readers can observe from the beginning of this Gospel that "forgiveness is available outside the temple system" (Carroll, *Luke*, 91). Luke then explains the importance of the prophet John by citing "the words of the prophet Isaiah" (3:4). As Luke does so, he expands Mark's reference to Isa 40:3 (Mark 1:3). Luke quotes Isa 40:3-5, which ends by declaring the worldwide mission of God: "all flesh shall see the salvation of God" (3:6). Much like Simeon's prophecy in 2:32, here again from the outset Luke foreshadows the spread of the gospel that will take place throughout the rest of Luke and Acts.

Luke also greatly expands Mark's account of the content of and the response to John's preaching in 3:7-20. Rather than speaking exclusively to the Pharisees and Sadducees as Matthew has it (Matt 3:7), Luke says that John addresses "the crowds" (3:7). Like an eighth-century Hebrew prophet, John confronts the people's hypocrisy. In particular, John seems to suggest that their actions do not match their oral pledges to God (3:8a). John stresses to his fellow Jews that they cannot claim Abrahamic heritage without also seeking to live like Abraham, whom Philo describes as embodying the "living law" of God (Philo, *Abr.* 5). As a result, judgment awaits the crowds if they fail to repent. The present-tense verbs in 3:9 "suggest that judgment is already underway in John's preaching" (Carroll, *Luke*, 92).

The reaction to John's preaching is both encouraging and informative. The crowds respond favorably to John's compelling preaching. They desire to repent and avoid judgment. Yet the identity of those expressing contrition is surprising. Luke does not show the Pharisees, Sadducees, religious leaders, or rulers pledging repentance (7:30). Rather, the crowds (3:10), tax collectors (3:12), and soldiers (3:14) ask John how they can bear fruits worthy of repentance (3:8). John replies and centers his comments on the responsible stewardship of possessions and generous care for others. If the crowd has adequate resources, he encourages them to share. He prohibits tax collectors from fleecing taxpayers, and he directs soldiers to be content with their wages while avoiding the misuse of their power. Here John's ministry and teaching foreshadow Jesus' ministry and teaching both in Luke and in Acts, even though the impact of Jesus' prophetic ministry will dwarf that of John's. For example, similar types of people will respond to Jesus as respond to John—crowds, tax collectors, and centurions (e.g., 9:10-11; 19:1-10; 23:47-48; Acts 10:1-48). Furthermore, Jesus will repeatedly teach people to be generous stewards of their resources while avoiding the misuse of their power (e.g., 12:13-15; 22:24-27).

As a result, it is not surprising that all of the crowds contemplate whether John is the Messiah (3:15), even though Luke has informed his readers that John merely prepares the way for the Messiah (1:76; 3:4). In response, John draws an important distinction between his baptism and the Messiah's baptism. John employs a water baptism when the repentant people of God desire forgiveness of sins. The Messiah, however, whom John himself characterizes as greater and more powerful, will employ a baptism of the Holy Spirit and fire (3:16). John's prophecy ultimately finds its fulfillment in Acts 2 when the Holy Spirit arrives at Pentecost (Acts 2:1-42). At the beginning of Acts, Jesus likewise refers to Pentecost as a baptism of the Holy Spirit, while also contrasting John's water baptism with the impending Spirit baptism (Acts 1:5).

The contrast between John's water baptism and the Messiah's "Holy Spirit and fire" baptism appears to revolve around differing durations of impact. Water baptism evokes images of washing and cleansing, but the duration is temporary. Conversely, fire is associated with purification (e.g., with metals; cf. Num 31:21-23; Zech 13:9; Mal 3:2-3), and its impact is considered permanent. Fire burns the dross away. Similarly, Luke will narrate the permanent endowment of God's Spirit upon the Jesus followers in the book of Acts. In essence, a baptism of "the Holy Spirit and fire" connotes permanent changes rather than temporary ones.

In addition, this contrast between John's baptism and the baptism of the Messiah—whom Luke has already identified as Jesus for his readers (2:11)—helps to sum up the *synkrisis* or comparison between John and Jesus that Luke has artfully constructed since Luke 1:5. John and his parents embody the best traits of God's people under the previous covenant(s). Zechariah the priest and his wife Elizabeth resemble Abraham and Sarah in Genesis. Moreover, Luke tells us they were "righteous before God" and "living blameless according to all the commandments" (1:6). The birth of their son, John, reminds us of Samuel's birth (1:13-15; 1 Sam 1:1-27). John is "great in the sight of the Lord," and he is "the prophet of the Most High" (1:76; 7:28-29).

Even John, however, proclaims that one far "more powerful" and worthy is coming after him (3:16-17). In 3:16-17, John does not depict Jesus as one who will continue John's prophetic ministry; instead, Jesus is one who will usher in an altogether different type of ministry. In short, in 3:15-17, Luke depicts Jesus as doing something new. What Jesus does will be greater than what has come before him—a work of God that is neither temporary nor short-lived, but permanent.

Finally, in 3:18-20, Luke concludes his narration of John's ministry before narrating Jesus' ministry. Herod Antipater, the tetrarch—or Rome's client ruler—of Galilee and Perea, shuts up John in prison (cf. 7:18-35; 9:7–9). Unlike Mark who communicates extensively about how the dysfunctional family dynamics of Herod, his wife, and his daughter result in John's death (Mark 6:17-29), Luke greatly abbreviates this event. In doing so, Luke accentuates a simple but clear contrast between the faithful prophet and the corrupt ruler—much like we encounter in the OT (e.g., Elijah and King Ahab in 1 Kgs 18–21; Garland, *Luke*, 160). When Herod Antipater (or Antipas) divorces his wife in order to marry his half-brother's ex-wife, John rebukes the ruler. John's bold actions then lead to his imprisonment and eventual demise (9:7-9); John's tragic ending also ominously foreshadows the outcome of Jesus' prophetic ministry in Luke 22–23.

Preparation for the Ministry of Jesus (3:21–4:13)

Jesus' Baptism (3:21-22)
Unlike Matthew (3:13-17) and Mark (1:9-11), who speak of John baptizing Jesus, Luke puts the spotlight solely on Jesus. Having mentioned John's imprisonment (3:20), Luke does not even refer to John at Jesus' baptism (3:21-22). Instead, Luke's narration of John's ministry is complete. Now, it is time to focus on Jesus and his ministry. Similar to the way that Luke alternated between John and Jesus when narrating their annunciations (1:8-20 and 1:26-38) and births (1:57-80 and 2:1-52), Luke now moves the discussion from John's ministry (3:1-20) to Jesus' ministry (3:21–24:53).

Despite its brevity, this passage about Jesus' baptism is theologically rich. First, Luke compares Jesus to "all the people" (3:21). Jesus is not separate from the crowd; rather he is one of them. He simply joins the masses in the act of baptism (Craddock, *Luke*, 50). He does not demand individual attention or pomp and circumstance. Rather, "he submits to the same obedience and conditions required by Israel" (Garland, *Luke*, 168). Luke has already depicted Jesus at his birth as a Jewish king who is born into a spiritually devout family of humble means (1:32-33; 2:11, 21-24). Now, he shows a worthy yet humble Jesus being baptized among the masses of repentant sinners (3:16, 21).

Second, Luke depicts Jesus' baptism as an anointing and empowerment by the Holy Spirit as well as an affirmation by God (Tannehill, *Luke*, 83–86). Previously Luke informed his readers that Jesus' conception was due to the miraculous intervention of the Holy Spirit (1:35). Now that same Spirit anoints and imbues him with divine power to carry out and fulfill God's redemptive purposes (e.g., 4:1, 14, 18-19; Acts 10:38). In other words, Luke's focus is not exclusively or even primarily on the baptism. Rather, Luke places the emphasis on God's divine empowerment of Jesus by means of the Holy Spirit. Luke wants his readers to understand that God's Spirit will be the illuminating force that guides and enables Jesus' words and actions.

In addition, among the Gospel writers, Luke alone adds another important detail. After the baptism is complete (aorist participle), Jesus is in the ongoing process of praying (present participle) when the heavens open and the Holy Spirit descends upon him (3:21). Throughout his Gospel, Luke greatly accentuates the link between prayer and the presence of the Holy Spirit for his readers. Both here at Jesus' baptism and later at Pentecost (Acts 1:12-14, 24; 2:1-13), prayer precedes the arrival of the Holy Spirit. Furthermore, Luke creates a strong correlation between prayer and divine revelation (e.g., 6:12-16; 9:28-31; 23:34, 46). For example, clarity about the Lord's will frequently arrives amid prayer in Luke's Gospel. In this instance, Jesus' faithful act of praying "provides the appropriate state of receptivity" for the Holy Spirit's empowerment and God's declaration from heaven (Tannehill, *Luke*, 84).

Finally, God's declaration about Jesus' identity is as important as the promise of the Holy Spirit's enablement. God speaks directly to Jesus saying, "You are my Son, the beloved; with you I am well pleased" (3:22). The Lord's words echo two OT texts, Ps 2:7 and Isa 42:1. "You are my Son" corresponds with Ps 2, which celebrates the coronation of Israel's king. "The Beloved; with you I am well pleased" corresponds with Isa 42, a servant song that celebrates God's chosen servant in a postexilic context. Here at Jesus' baptism, however, the two ideas are merged together: "In combination, they present the divine perspective that Jesus is the Servant-Messiah" (Garland, *Luke*, 169). Here, God articulates both his approval of and his purposes for Jesus. Even though Jesus is amid repentant sinners, he is clearly not one of them. Yet God also assures Jesus of his matchless identity. Gabriel had already informed Mary of Jesus' identity as the Son of God (1:32, 35). Now the Father relays the same message directly to Jesus. Hereafter, Luke will repeatedly build on this title, Son of God, to clarify further Jesus' role (e.g., Luke 4:3, 41; 22:70; Acts

9:20). The only other occasion in which Luke directly quotes the voice of God will be at the transfiguration (9:35).

Jesus' Genealogy (3:23-38)

Matthew opens his Gospel with Jesus' genealogy, thus placing Jesus' ancestry even before the miraculous conception of Jesus (Matt 1:1-18). Luke, however, delays discussing Jesus' genealogy until after Jesus is a full-grown adult who is about to embark on his public ministry (3:23). Surprisingly, Luke does not include Jesus' genealogy when he narrates Jesus' conception, birth, naming, or boyhood appearance in the temple—all of which could have provided a proper context for Jesus' genealogy. Rather, Luke elects to discuss Jesus' human ancestry, and in particular his legal status as Joseph's son (3:23), after Luke has first anchored Jesus' identity in the Father-Son relationship between God and Jesus as verbalized in the baptismal scene (1:32, 35; 2:49; 3:22): "Luke inserts the genealogy at this point because this is where Jesus' role as Son of God empowered by the Spirit begins" (Nolland, *Luke*, 1:173). Because God's declaration at Jesus' baptism most effectively sets the stage for Jesus' genealogy, Luke moves directly from one to the other.

Other notable differences exist between Jesus' genealogy in Luke and the one in Matthew. Of these differences, two greatly illumine Luke's theological arguments about Jesus. First, whereas Matthew's genealogy moves forward through time like familiar OT genealogies, Luke's genealogy moves backward. Matthew begins with Abraham and moves forward in time while noting who begets whom. As a result, the emphases in Matthew fall on Israel's history and each father's role in begetting his descendant. Luke, however, is focused not on fatherhood but on sonship, as we already saw at Jesus' baptism (3:21-22). Luke begins with Jesus and moves backward in time noting who is "the son of" whom. By focusing on sonship rather than fatherhood, Luke expands the broader theme of Jesus as the Holy Spirit-empowered, beloved *Son of God* as we heard in 3:22. Furthermore, Luke depicts Jesus as the fulcrum of world history by means of his genealogy. In the genealogy, Luke works backward from Jesus to the beginning of humanity. Hereafter, Luke will work forward in time toward Jesus' passion, the church, and the age to come. As a result, Jesus clearly functions as the pivot point in God's grand salvation history (Conzelmann, *Theology of St. Luke*, 185–86).

Second, Luke traces Jesus' lineage along a different trajectory and over a longer duration than Matthew does. For instance, Matthew traces Jesus' ancestry from Abraham (Matt 1:2), through David and Solomon (Matt 1:6-7), and to Jesus (Matt 1:16). Luke, however, moves backward in time from Jesus (3:23), through David's son Nathan (3:31), past Abraham (3:34), and to Adam, whom Luke also identifies as a "son of God" (3:38). In doing so, Luke demonstrates far more interest in the entirety of the human race as opposed to Israel alone. Abraham, for instance, was seen as the original ancestor of the Israelites, but Luke links Jesus all the way back to Adam, the original ancestor of all humanity. Because Luke has already mentioned the worldwide scope of God's redemptive work through Jesus (2:32; 3:6), he appears to connect Jesus to the whole world by means of his ancestry. In addition, unlike Matthew, Luke does not trace Jesus' lineage through Solomon, whose descendants committed many missteps as the kings of Judah. Rather, he traces Jesus' lineage through David's son, Nathan, as the book of Zechariah does. As a result, Nolland claims that unlike Matthew, "Luke focuses on the failures of the history of Israel (Acts 7:7-53) and sees the end of the Solomonic line in Jer 22:24-30. The Davidic promise must be carried forward through another of David's sons, and of these only the house of Nathan has any ongoing place in Scripture (Zech 12:12)" (*Luke*, 1:174). Finally, Luke sets up a vivid contrast between Jesus as the Holy Spirit-empowered, beloved Son of God (3:22) and Adam as the son of God who failed to obey God's commands (3:38). God is "well pleased" with Jesus, but God banished Adam from the garden (Gen 3:22-24).

The Temptation of Jesus (4:1-13)
It is no accident then that Luke moves directly from God's declaration of Jesus as the beloved Son of God at the baptism (3:22) to Jesus' genealogy that refers to Adam as a son or descendant of God (3:38) and finally to Jesus' temptation in which the devil tempts Jesus to act more like the disobedient Adam than the Son in whom God is well pleased (Tannehill, *Luke*, 85–87). For instance, the devil quotes God's own words to Jesus in the wilderness just as the serpent twists God's words in the garden of Eden (Gen 3:1-7). Notice that the devil begins the first and third temptation by saying, "If you are the Son of God" (4:3, 9), thereby questioning the validity of God's declaration at the baptism. In addition, after Jesus quotes Scripture to refute the devil's first two temptations in 4:4 and 4:8, the devil himself quotes Ps 91:11-12 out of context in an attempt to mislead Jesus (4:10-11). Many ancient and modern scholars have believed that Ps 91 expresses trust in God's protection against demonic forces. Psalm 91 was part of a four-psalm Dead Sea Scrolls (DSS) collection that was read during exorcisms in the first century (Craig Evans, "Jesus and Evil Spirits," 43–58). As a result, the devil, who is deemed to be synonymous with "the serpent," "the dragon," "the enemy," and Satan in first-century Jewish and Christian texts, misuses a passage of Scripture that chronicles God's protection against evil forces. Instead of citing Ps 91 to

fend off the demonic realm, the devil astonishingly quotes it while hoping to persuade Jesus to pledge allegiance to him.

Even more than the contrast between Adam and Jesus, Luke primarily contrasts the experiences of the Hebrew people with those of Jesus. Here, Luke first accentuates the way in which Jesus' time in the wilderness resembles the experiences of the Hebrew people as they journeyed through the Sinai wilderness. For instance, in Matthew's Gospel, Jesus first endures forty days in the wilderness without food. Jesus' temptation then takes place at the conclusion of that time period, perhaps over the course of one day (Matt 4:1-11). Luke, however, paints a vastly different picture. The devil tempts Jesus over the entirety of the forty days in the wilderness (4:1-2). In addition, these wilderness temptations of Jesus are akin to the wilderness temptations the Hebrews faced (Deut 8:2). The Hebrews sinned when they grumbled about the lack of food (Exod 16:1-12), worshipped idols (Exod 32:1-35), and tested God (Deut 6:16). Similarly, the devil tempts Jesus with hunger (4:3), false worship (4:7), and testing God (4:13). Even more clearly, when Jesus quotes Scripture, he quotes passages from Deuteronomy that portray Moses as entreating the Hebrew people to avoid temptation once they arrive in Canaan. Jesus quotes Deut 8:3, 6:13, and 6:16 in response to the devil's three temptations (4:4, 8, 12).

The comparison between the Hebraic people and Jesus primarily aims to create a sharp distinction between the two. Whereas the Hebrews submitted to temptations in the wilderness, Jesus resists them. Whereas the Israelites were unable to remain faithful to God, Jesus' allegiance to God never wavers. Luke signals this victorious outcome from the outset when he refers to the presence of the Holy Spirit (4:1-2).

Luke has already highlighted the role of the Holy Spirit in Jesus' life from the beginning of his Gospel. Jesus was conceived of by the Spirit (1:35). Those who prophesied about Jesus were filled with the Holy Spirit (1:67; 2:25, 27). John claims that Jesus will one day "baptize you with the Holy Spirit," and at Jesus' baptism the Holy Spirit descends upon Jesus as an act of anointing and empowerment (3:22; Acts 10:38). So it is not surprising that Luke accentuates the role of the Holy Spirit again in the temptation narrative in 4:1 and 4:14. Luke informs his readers that Jesus is full of and led by the Holy Spirit before he even ventures into the wilderness (4:1). Furthermore, Luke again mentions that Jesus is "filled with the power of the Spirit" as Jesus leaves the wilderness and returns to Galilee (4:14).

By emphasizing the presence of the Spirit at the beginning and end of the temptation narrative, Luke thereby implies that Jesus remained full of and empowered by the Holy Spirit throughout the entirety of the forty-day ordeal. As a result, Jesus' temptation in the wilderness unfolds in a manner different from the experience of the Hebrews in the Sinai wilderness. Where Israel failed, Jesus succeeds due to the presence and power of the Spirit. The devil desires to shape Jesus' fundamental identity and use of power, yet Jesus refuses to yield to the devil's direction. Instead, the Spirit of God defines Jesus' role and directs his actions.

Matthew concludes Jesus' temptation by saying in part, "Then the devil left him" (Matt 4:11). Luke likewise says that the devil left him, but then Luke adds a temporal qualifier: "until an opportune time" (4:13). Rather than the devil's finale, Luke indicates that the devil has only departed temporarily. In the process, Luke portrays the devil as even more determined, cunning, and perhaps powerful than Mark or Matthew do. Luke's qualification about the devil's departure prepares his readers for what comes next. They must be on the lookout, waiting for the devil to resurface.

While Jesus relays his futuristic vision of Satan falling from heaven in 10:17-20, Luke does not speak of Satan's active intervention again until Luke 22:3 when Satan enters Judas. Shortly thereafter, Jesus tells his disciples at the Last Supper that Satan has demanded to sift them all like wheat (22:31-34). As a result, although Jesus' refusal to yield to the devil in 4:1-13 provides a final, definitive answer about Jesus' loyalties, a larger cosmic battle still exists in Luke's writings. In particular, Jesus' disciples will remain vulnerable to Satan's attacks throughout this Gospel. Whereas Jesus is full of the Spirit (3:22; 4:1), Judas opts in the end to be filled with Satan (22:3). In Luke's anthropology, a person must choose which power will enliven him or her. Jesus has already made his decision, but others have not.

Jesus' Galilean Ministry

Luke 4:14–9:50

Introduction

Beginning in Luke 4:14, Luke introduces the prophetic ministry of the adult Jesus. In particular, in this second major unit in Luke's Gospel, Luke establishes the fullness of Jesus' identity, character, message, and power as a prophet of God. Jesus' public ministry begins when Jesus enters the synagogue at Nazareth, reads from the sacred scrolls of Isaiah, claims a prophetic anointing, and declares that God's promises to Israel as chronicled in Scripture are now fulfilled in his arrival and ministry. Those in the synagogue, however, attempt to kill Jesus when he declares that the Gentiles will also be recipients of God's merciful favor.

Thereafter, conflict between Jesus and the Jewish religious authorities continues to grow as Jesus teaches the people, recruits disciples, heals the sick, exorcizes demons, and ushers in the kingdom of God. Through each of these deeds, the author demonstrates how Jesus functions as a prophet of the Lord. Like the great prophets—Moses, Elijah, Elisha—Jesus, too, proclaims the Lord's word (e.g., 6:17-49; cf. Deut 5), heals people (5:12-16; cf. 2 Kgs 5), raises the dead (7:11-17; cf. 1 Kgs 17:17–24), and exerts his power over nature (8:22-25; cf. 1 Kgs 17:1–16). As God has worked through the prophets in the past, so God is again working in the present through Jesus, but in an even greater way.

Jesus' Inaugural Sermon (4:14-30)

To understand the importance of Luke 4:14-30 within Luke's Gospel, it is helpful to consider the same story within Mark's Gospel. Mark, whose Gospel almost certainly serves as one of Luke's primary source documents, narrates Jesus' visit to the synagogue at Nazareth toward the end of Jesus' Galilean ministry in Mark 6:1-6. Luke, however, fronts this story. Whereas Luke typically follows the same chronological sequence as Mark, this passage represents one of the few instances in which Luke intentionally alters Mark's chronology. Luke transports Jesus' hometown visit from the end of the Galilean ministry (as in Mark) to the beginning of Jesus' public ministry.

By converting this brief story from the latter half of Jesus' Galilean ministry in Mark into the inaugural event of Jesus' public ministry in his Gospel, Luke has greatly increased the literary and theological importance of this event. Other clues that point to this conclusion include the fact that Luke greatly expands the amount of space dedicated to this event—seventeen verses rather than Mark's six verses. In particular, Mark never refers to the content of Jesus' teaching but indicates that the unbelieving crowd in Nazareth discounts Jesus due to Jesus' status as a hometown boy. Luke, however, supplies his readers with the content of Jesus' teaching in the synagogue at Nazareth. His teaching in Nazareth then outlines his role as God's prophet—a theme that runs throughout Luke's Gospel. Furthermore, only Luke indicates that those in attendance morph into an angry mob not because of Jesus' hometown affiliation with Nazareth but because of the content of Jesus' teaching. In short, by placing this story at the outset of Jesus' public ministry and by emphasizing the content of his teaching, Luke suggests that Jesus' visit to the synagogue in Nazareth provides an overarching introduction to his prophetic ministry.

For example, Luke relies on Jesus' inaugural sermon in the Nazareth synagogue to set the stage for a variety of conversations to which he will return throughout the course of Luke and Acts. First, Luke continues to focus heavily on the role of the Holy Spirit in Jesus' life and ministry. Luke has already shown his readers that the Holy Spirit was present and active at Jesus' birth (1:35), baptism (3:22), and temptation (4:1). Similarly, Luke now informs his readers that Jesus is full of the Holy Spirit—God's own empowering force—as he begins his public ministry (4:14; Acts 10:38). As a result, Luke demonstrates for his readers that Jesus will do nothing outside the will of God. God not only approves of Jesus, as was clear at the baptism, but will also constantly and continuously animate Jesus' actions throughout his public ministry by means of the Holy Spirit.

In addition, Jesus' comments in Nazareth provide the first occasion in which he openly announces to those in his day that God's Spirit has anointed and empowered him. While teaching in the synagogue, Jesus quotes Isa 61:1-2a (4:18-19). The quote begins by saying, "the Spirit of the Lord is upon me." Shortly thereafter Jesus claims, "Today this scripture has been fulfilled in your hearing." As a result, Jesus announces to those present that the Holy Spirit is sanctioning, guiding, and empowering him to carry out his teaching and healing ministry (cf. Acts 10:38).

Second, while Luke has already depicted Jesus as Savior, Messiah, and Son of God in this Gospel (e.g., 2:11; 3:22), Luke especially portrays Jesus as a prophet of God in this particular thematic segment, or pericope. Whereas Mark only uses the word "prophet" once in Mark 6:1-6, Luke uses the word "prophet" four times (4:17, 24, 27), refers to three prophets by name (4:17, 25, 27), and quotes from the prophetic book of Isaiah (4:18-19). Moreover, the text Jesus quotes is itself noteworthy. Isaiah 61:1-2a describes the call and work of God's prophet (Croatto, "Jesus, Prophet like Elijah," 455). The prophet explains that the Lord has anointed him to speak on God's behalf while also advocating for the poor and the oppressed (terms that were at times literally and metaphorically synonymous with Israel or the Israelites) (Levin, "Poor in the Old Testament," 260–65). This description easily fits the work of various OT prophets like Isaiah, Amos, and Micah. Here, however, Jesus claims that the same call applies to him (4:21).

Throughout this second major unit in Luke's Gospel that runs from 4:14 to 9:50, the author will continue to demonstrate how Jesus functions as a prophet of the Lord. Jesus will proclaim the Lord's word through his teachings (e.g., 6:17-49). In addition, he will heal people (5:12-16), raise them from the dead (7:11-17), and demonstrate his power over nature (8:22-25). The people through whom God worked in the OT to perform similar miraculous deeds were the great prophets like Moses, Elijah, and Elisha. Now God will do even greater things through Jesus. Notably, however, Luke will go on in his Gospel to stress that Jerusalem always kills God's prophets (13:33-34). Therefore, when those in the synagogue attempt to kill Jesus in 4:28-29, it both reinforces Jesus' identity as a prophet and foreshadows the suffering that Jesus will surely endure as a prophet of the Lord.

Third, within his prophetic role, Jesus distinctively focuses his message on the grace and mercy of God rather than on God's judgment. In addition to bringing good news to the poor, captives, blind, and oppressed, Jesus also proclaims that "the year of the Lord's favor" has arrived (4:19, 21). The "favorable year" alludes to the year of Jubilee when all captives were to be released and the land was supposed to revert to its original tribe (Lev 25). As far as we know, no king ever enacted the year of Jubilee, but Jesus, as a herald of the kingdom of God, now announces this dramatic reversal of fortunes. Jesus proclaims that the long-awaited year of Jubilee has finally arrived.

This focus on God's mercy is even more obvious when Jesus elects to stop short in his reading of Isa 61:2. He only proclaims "the year of the Lord's favor" and not "the day of vengeance of our God" as Isaiah did (Isa 61:2b), even though Jesus clearly knows about and refers to "the days of vengeance" much later in Luke's Gospel (21:22). As a result, due to Jesus' gracious emphasis on the Lord's favor rather than the Lord's vengeance, the people praise him and his message. For instance, the people in the Nazareth synagogue initially respond well to Jesus' remarks while specifically commenting on "the gracious (Gk. *charis*) words that came from his mouth" (4:22). They recognize that Jesus' message consists of very good news.

By the end of the passage, those in the synagogue have switched from speaking well of Jesus and being amazed at his gracious words (4:22) to raging against him and seeking to kill him (4:28). Even then, the mercy and grace of God constitute the bedrock of Jesus' words and actions. When those in the synagogue hear Jesus' declaration about God's gracious intervention into world affairs, they likely understand it as a reference to God's mercy toward the Jewish people, as it was in Isaiah's day. As noted above, especially in a postexilic context, Israel or the Israelites were frequently referred to as the poor and oppressed whom God aids while opposing their pagan overlords (e.g., Isa 61:1; 66:2; Ps 40:17; 70:5; 86:1; 109:22) (Levin, "Poor in the Old Testament," 260–65).

Jesus, however, does not stop there. Instead, he continues to speak. In particular, he provides two examples that illustrate the gracious message he is proclaiming. The first recalls when God mercifully sent Elijah to help the widow at Zarephath (4:25-26; 1 Kgs 17:8-16). The second recalls when God mercifully sent Elisha to help Naaman the Syrian (4:27; 2 Kgs 5:1-14). The offensive element in both examples revolves around the fact that God showed mercy to a Gentile at the same time that many Jewish people were likewise in need. In essence, Jesus highlights God's occasional mercy for the Gentiles in the OT. For the Jews of Jesus' day who were continually oppressed by the Romans, this message no longer sounded like good news. Both Jesus' examples of God's grace toward the Gentiles as well as the angry reaction of those in the Jewish synagogue foreshadow events that will take place in the book of Acts. God will extend mercy to the first Gentile convert in Acts 10, and God's prophets (Christian prophets) will be rejected in a variety of synagogues throughout Acts (e.g., Acts 13:44-46). Consequently, Luke 4:14-30, at the outset of Jesus' prophetic ministry, already foreshadows these events and establishes patterns that we will see in Acts.

Finally, Jesus balances power and grace in his response to the mob that seeks to kill him (4:28-30). In Mark's narration of this event, the unbelief of those in the synagogue moderately restricts Jesus' power (Mark 6:5-6). Luke, however, does not adopt Mark's ending. Instead, Luke demonstrates that Jesus' power and authority remain undiminished in the face of rejection. When facing an angry mob that seeks to kill him, Jesus simply passes through their midst. Jesus' power has not been compromised. At the same time, Jesus does not use his power and authority to enact vengeance on the mob. The fact that he simply departs further emphasizes the theme of God's grace that we see throughout this pericope, and it sets the tone for how Jesus and his disciples will respond to rejection throughout Luke and Acts.

Jesus' Power and Authority (4:31–6:49)

After firmly establishing Jesus' identity in Luke 1:5–4:30, Luke now sketches the contours of Jesus' power and authority in 4:31–6:49. While Luke will continue to round out and build on both of these conversations throughout his Gospel, by Luke 6:49 his readers should know that Jesus, as Son of God, possesses the power of God in every realm. In particular, in this literary unit, Luke shows that Jesus has authority over diseases, demons, and disciples alike.

An Overview of Jesus' Authority (4:31–5:11)

In Luke 4:31–5:11, the author builds on what we have already learned about Jesus at the baptism (3:21-22), the temptation (4:1-13), and his inaugural sermon at Nazareth (4:14-30)—namely that he is the Messiah and Son of God empowered by the Holy Spirit who announces God's good news to the poor and oppressed (4:34, 41). In particular, by means of 4:31–5:11, Luke begins to supply his readers with evidence to substantiate these claims. Luke will continue to chronicle and verify Jesus' authority and power throughout this second major division in Luke's Gospel, which runs from 4:14 to 9:50.

(1) Luke 4:31-44. This brief unit (4:31-44) has four parts: 4:31-37; 4:38-39; 4:40–41; and 4:42-44. Marking its beginning and ending are references to Jesus' ongoing practice of teaching in Jewish synagogues "throughout the Roman province of Judea" even though, at this point, Jesus remains in the northern territory of Galilee (4:31-33, 44; cf. Acts 10:37) (Culy, Parsons, and Stigall, *Luke*, 153; see also Marshall, *Luke*, 198–99). The four parts of this unit highlight Jesus' authoritative actions even though the various contexts at first appear to be dissimilar. For example, Luke shows his readers that Jesus, as the Son of God (4:34, 41), has the authority to teach, exorcise demons, and heal diseases (4:32, 36, 43). In the process, Luke utilizes a chiastic pattern to narrate these events, and in each case he first narrates a specific event before moving to multiple manifestations of the same type of event. For instance, the unit can be outlined this way:

(a) 4:31-32, Jesus teaches in a synagogue
    (b) 4:33-35, Jesus exorcises a demon
        (c) 4:38-39, Jesus heals Simon's mother-in-law
        (c') 4:40, Jesus heals many with diseases

(b') 4:41, Jesus exorcises multiple demons
(a') 4:44, Jesus teaches in multiple synagogues

In each context, Jesus, as the Son of God, has the authority to proclaim good news and relieve oppression just as he announced in his inaugural sermon in Nazareth (4:18-19, 43). In other words, Jesus' deeds of liberation and restoration in this passage (4:31-44) now confirm the veracity of his words from the previous unit. While in the synagogue at Nazareth, Jesus announced release for captives and recovery of sight for the blind (4:18-21). Jesus' deeds now enact his words (Green, *Luke*, 221).

Furthermore, it is important in this unit to notice how Luke merges the various conversations about teaching, exorcising demons, and healing. For instance, Jesus rebukes (Gk. *epitimaō*) demons and sicknesses alike because both are examples of the oppression that he seeks to alleviate. Both demons and sicknesses prevent life as God intended it (4:35, 39, 41; cf. Acts 10:38). Likewise, Jesus' power to teach and to exorcise demons springs forth from the same authority to speak on God's behalf in 4:31-37.

Even those who reject Jesus and his authority, either human (4:28-29) or demonic (4:33-34), are ultimately connected through their opposition to Jesus as the Son of God. Notice, for example, that this passage begins with Jesus teaching in the Capernaum synagogue in 4:31-32, just as Jesus previously taught in the Nazareth synagogue in 4:16. And, as we saw in 4:14-40, resistance to Jesus soon arises from amid the people gathered in the synagogue (4:33-34). Startlingly, in this instance, a man who has an unclean, demonic spirit is in the synagogue. Whereas Jesus is full of the Holy Spirit, this man is full of an unholy spirit (4:14, 33) (Parsons, *Luke*, 84–85). This detail not only paints an increasingly negative picture for Luke's readers of the first-century Galilean synagogues that reject Jesus' authority and power but also links the responses of the angry mob in Nazareth (4:28-29) with the demon-possessed man in Capernaum (4:33-34). Their rejection of Jesus unites them.

After Jesus rebukes and exorcises the demon from the man at Capernaum, however, the people marvel at Jesus' "utterance" or his word (Gk. *logos*). In this instance, it is the word(s) of Jesus that demonstrates his authority and power (4:36). Like God at the creation of the world (Genesis 1), Jesus, as the Son of God, merely has to speak a word to dispel the demons. He likewise teaches with words and heals with words (4:39). In essence, Jesus declares "good news" whenever he teaches, exorcises demons, and/or heals the sick (4:43), just as he announced at the synagogue in Nazareth (4:18-22). All three actions illustrate the nature of God's coming kingdom (4:43). All three actions reinforce Jesus' identity as the Son of God who possesses the authority and power of God.

(2) Luke 5:1-11. When Matthew (4:18-22) and Mark (1:16-20) first introduce Peter, James, and John as disciples in their respective Gospels, they do not indicate that the fishermen had any prior experiences with Jesus. Jesus simply walks up, commands them to follow, and they obey. Luke, however, provides a clear rationale for the decisions of Peter, James, and John. First, Luke has already chronicled Jesus' teaching and miracles beginning in 4:14. Jesus taught and ministered in Nazareth (4:16), Capernaum (4:31), a deserted place (4:42), and a variety of Jewish synagogues (4:44). In addition, Jesus proclaims the word of God beside the lake where the fishermen are working and even from within their own fishing boats (5:1, 3). Furthermore, after speaking to the crowds, Jesus instructs the weary fishermen to let their nets down into the water after failing to catch anything throughout the night. When they do as Jesus instructs, they catch a remarkably large number of fish (5:4-7). In essence, before Peter, James, and John follow Jesus in 4:11, Luke establishes a clear rationale as to why the fishermen are willing to leave everything behind and follow him. These fishermen hear Jesus' teaching (5:1, 3), personally interact with him (5:4-10), and observe Jesus performing a great miracle (5:4-7; cf. 4:38-39) before Jesus ever calls them as his disciples (5:11).

Unlike the demons who correctly identify Jesus as the Son of God and Messiah in 4:34 and 41, Peter, James, and John do not yet associate those titles with Jesus (cf. 9:20). After hearing Jesus teach and watching him perform this miraculous deed, however, they likely deem Jesus to be a great prophet of God since prophets like Moses, Elijah, and Elisha both spoke the word of the Lord and performed miraculous actions that only God could enable (e.g., 1 Kgs 17:8-24). Notice, for example, that Jesus' instruction to throw the nets into the water despite a failed night of fishing sets up a prophecy-fulfillment pattern. Like a prophet, Jesus knows what will happen before the event occurs. The outcome about which Jesus hints comes to fruition when they lower their nets into the water. Luke has already gone to great lengths to portray Jesus as a great prophet of God in 4:14-30, a designation that Jesus affirms in 4:18-19, 21, and 24. In addition, unlike Matthew and Mark, Luke reveals a great deal to his readers about Jesus when Jesus takes the time to sit down in the boat, teach the crowds, and interact directly with Peter. In doing so, Luke demonstrates that Jesus has great care for the crowds and his disciples. He is not the aloof stranger who simply passes through town barking out commands.

When Peter, James, and John leave everything and follow Jesus, they become Jesus' first disciples (5:11). Luke clearly illustrates that Jesus has the authority to call disciples to follow him. Unlike Matthew and Mark, however, Luke not only provides a clearer picture of Jesus' initial interactions with Peter, James, and John but also provides a clearer picture of Peter's response to Jesus (5:8-10). Through the great catch of fish, Peter senses that God is at work in and through Jesus in an intimate and real way. Peter responds much like Isaiah when Isaiah encounters the Lord's presence in the temple (Isa 6:5). Peter refers to Jesus as Lord (Gk. *kurios*), falls at Jesus' knees, and confesses his sin (5:8). Perhaps Luke hoped that his readers might see similarities between Peter's response and Saul's first encounter with Jesus in Acts 9:4-5, when Saul also falls to the ground and addresses Jesus as Lord (Gk. *kurios*). In short, while Peter does not fully understand Jesus' identity at this point, he already seems to be aware that the God of Abraham, Isaac, and Jacob is at work in and through Jesus in a unique way. By narrating Peter's response, Luke has likewise provided a more complete picture for his readers of a disciple's proper response to Jesus.

Authority to Cleanse and Transform (5:12–6:11)
Luke continues to demonstrate to his readers in a systematic fashion what it means for Jesus to be the Holy Spirit-empowered Son of God (3:21-22). Luke has already illustrated that Jesus has the authority and power to teach, expel demons, and call disciples. In Luke 5:12–6:11, Luke now demonstrates that Jesus also has the authority and power to cleanse, forgive, transform, and save. He also possesses the authority to interpret the Scriptures. In the process, Luke will introduce the Pharisees and the scribes to his readers for the first time, and he includes the Pharisees in four consecutive controversy stories in Luke 5:17-26; 5:27-39; 6:1-5; and 6:6-11.

(1) Luke 5:12-16. Astonishingly, Jesus heals a leper in Luke 5:12-16, a dramatic miracle that he will repeat again in 17:11-19. In a contemporary setting, leprosy refers to a bacterial infection known as Hansen's Disease. Those who suffer with Hansen's Disease frequently lose the ability to feel pain in their extremities, which then increases their risk of losing limbs due to undetected injuries and infections. In antiquity, however, the term "leprosy" (Gk. *lepra*) was much broader and referred to a variety of skin maladies. Furthermore, it was commonly assumed that skin maladies were God's punishment upon the leper due to sin (Lev 14:18-20). As a result, no human cure to this disease existed. It was believed that only God could heal this sickness. Leprosy therefore resulted in the declaration of the victim as ceremonially unclean, which meant the leper could not participate with his or her

fellow Israelites in their ceremonial worship practices (Lev 13:2-3). In addition, the leper was quarantined from other humans for fear that others might catch the ailment. If, however, the leper experienced healing due to the mercy of God, then the leper showed himself or herself to a priest. Only priests, as witnesses to the work of God, could declare the person well. Afterward, the priest would instruct the former leper to make the proper sacrifices to God that would eventually result in the former leper being declared "clean" and therefore approved for participation in communal worship (Lev 14:2-32).

In 5:12-16 neither the leper nor Jesus follow the typical protocols. The leper possesses an astounding confidence in Jesus' authority and power to heal him when he addresses Jesus as Lord (Gk. *kurios*) and says, "if you choose, you can make me clean" (5:12). When Jesus agrees to help the man, he first touches the man and shows no concern whatsoever that the contagion might spread to him or render him unclean (5:13). Instead, Jesus simultaneously heals the man's leprosy and declares the man to be clean (5:13). Here, Jesus enacts divine healing, demonstrates that his power is greater than the power of leprosy, and declares the man to be clean without any reliance on priests or the sacrificial system. By means of this story, Luke reveals to his readers that Jesus has the power and authority to cleanse and to restore. When Jesus finally instructs the man to show himself to the priest and to make sacrifices, those actions are not effectual actions. Instead, they simply provide a testimony about what God has already done through Jesus (5:14).

(2) Luke 5:17-26. Luke continues to reveal to his readers the extent of Jesus' power and authority as the Son of God in 5:17-26. Luke has now demonstrated that Jesus has the power to speak on God's behalf, expel demons, heal diseases, and cleanse an "unclean" leper. Now, for the first time in this Gospel, Luke informs us that Jesus has the authority and power to forgive sins. In addition, for the first time, Luke introduces the Pharisees and the teachers of the law as opponents of Jesus.

Notably, the Pharisees and teachers of the law initially appear interested in Jesus and his teaching ministry. Luke indicates that these laypeople, who held strictly to the Mosaic Law, have come from "every village of Galilee and Judea and from Jerusalem" in order to listen to Jesus' teaching (5:17). Their receptivity, though, quickly gives way to skepticism and accusations (5:21-22). Here, Luke depicts the Pharisees not so much as outright enemies of Jesus or of the kingdom of God that Jesus proclaims (4:43) but rather as skeptics who cannot believe what Jesus is declaring.

At the same time, these skeptical Pharisees also function as an obstruction to those who desire to see Jesus. Because the Pharisees are sitting around Jesus, they physically block the pathway of the paralytic and his friends. To get "in front of Jesus," the friends must first remove tiles from the roof and then lower the paralytic down (5:18-19). Finally, after the Pharisees and lawyers see the previously paralyzed man walk, they are amazed, glorify God, and are filled with awe (5:26). Yet their criticism of Jesus will only fester throughout the remainder of Luke's Gospel. Luke does, however, provide a glimmer of hope that even these skeptical Pharisees, who block others on the pathway to Jesus, may one day recognize Jesus' power and believe in him. For instance, "some believers who belonged to the sect of the Pharisees" are present in Acts 15:5 for the Jerusalem Council.

More important, Jesus' healing of the paralytic in 5:17-26 demonstrates that Jesus has many types of power—including the power to forgive sin. For example, in 5:17 Luke says that "the power of the Lord was with him to heal." Here, Luke continues to highlight the intimate relationship between God and Jesus. As Luke first illustrated at the baptism (3:21-22), the Holy Spirit both anoints and empowers Jesus to fulfill his God-ordained role as the Son of God. Jesus and his prophetic ministry fall within and indeed provide the climax for the overarching history of God's redemptive work in the world. Jesus' power is not separate from the Lord's power. When Jesus declares that the paralytic's sins are forgiven, however, it creates no small disturbance among the crowd gathered around him (5:20-21). In particular, the Pharisees charge Jesus with blasphemy due to their belief that "God alone" can forgive sins. Jesus responds that he could have simply healed the man and told him to walk. Instead, by declaring the man's sins forgiven, the Pharisees now know that God has also given Jesus the authority to forgive sins (5:24). In essence, Luke clarifies for his readers that as the Son of God, Jesus even possesses the power and authority to forgive sins, which belongs to God alone.

Ultimately, in this passage Luke demonstrates to his readers that Jesus has a relationship with God that is unlike any that has been seen before. The power and work of Yahweh are manifest in Jesus. The God of Abraham, Isaac, and Jacob continues to work in the world to rescue his people, but now God is accomplishing that work through Jesus. In addition, the redeeming work of God realized through Jesus is not compartmentalized. The Pharisees are wrong to think that God has granted God's words to Jesus without also granting to Jesus God's power to heal and forgive sins. In turn, Jesus informs the Pharisees that it does not matter whether he informs the man that he is healed or forgiven (5:23-24). Both phrases point toward the fullness of God's power and both point toward a comprehensive redemption. "The Spirit of the Lord . . . has anointed" Jesus to bring wholeness to the poor, captives, blind, and oppressed no matter the form that their afflictions take (4:18-19).

Jesus brings about a multifaceted transformation in the paralytic's life, not just partial improvement. The man walks home glorifying God after Jesus restores wholeness to his life, which encompasses both his body and his soul.

Finally, it should be noted that Jesus uses the title "Son of Man" for the first time in 5:24. Luke likely inherits this title from his Markan source (Mark 2:10), but the meaning of the title was already ambiguous in Mark's Gospel. As a result, the meaning of the title in Luke's Gospel is equally difficult to pin down. In the OT, the title "Son of Man" often functions as a self-referential phrase whereby someone identifies himself as one human among other humans (e.g., Ps 8:4; Ezek 2:1). Similarly, when Matthew narrates Jesus' healing of the paralytic, he does not include the title "Son of Man" at all. Rather Matthew concludes with the idea that God has granted a human (Jesus) authority to heal disabilities (Matt 9:8b). Luke makes that same point in 5:17. Alternatively, by the first century, it is equally true that for Luke and his readers, the title "Son of Man" would have at times evoked images of the apocalyptic figure from Dan 7:13-14. The apocalyptic figure from Daniel was frequently associated with the coming Messiah who will judge and rule the world (see e.g., Fitzmyer, *Luke*, 1:584–85). In 5:24, Luke highlights Jesus' authority to forgive sins, which is an extension of his authority to judge (Acts 10:42). Consequently, when Luke's first readers encountered this pericope, they may have heard the "Son of Man" title as a reference either to Jesus' humanity or to his role as the apocalyptic judge. Jesus may have adopted the "Son of Man" title in order to be "deliberately mysterious and ambiguous" (Caird, *Saint Luke*, 94). Regardless, it is best to evaluate Luke's usage of this title on a case-by-case basis.

(3) Luke 5:27-39. The call of Levi constitutes the second of four consecutive controversy stories in which the Pharisees raise questions about Jesus and his unorthodox ministry in Luke 5:17–6:11. Since at least the third century CE, some Christian exegetes have asked whether the Levi referred to in 5:27-32 is the same person as Matthew, the apostle (6:15) (Bock, *Luke*, 1:493). Neither Mark nor Luke, however, connect these two names. Rather, the assertion derives from comparing Matt 9:9-13 with Mark 2:13-17 and Luke 5:27-32. The author of Matthew narrates a story about the apostle Matthew that is similar to the story that Mark and Luke tell about Levi. In the end, however, we do not have enough evidence to know whether Matthew also went by the name Levi or whether they are separate people. Regardless, this debate does not obfuscate Luke's reasons for including this pericope.

Jesus seeks out and calls Levi to follow him in 5:27-28. Given that Luke has already narrated the call of Peter, James, and John in 5:1-11, it is not surprising that Jesus is now gathering more disciples. The surprising detail pertains to Levi's work as a tax collector. He collects taxes from those traveling from city to city (Bock, *Luke*, 1:493). As a tax collector, Levi would have been viewed by his fellow Jews as one who opted to serve Rome with more devotion than he showed to God (Bovon, *Luke*, 1:189). As a result, many would have considered Levi to be a "sinner."

Luke, however, lifts up Levi as an ideal disciple. After Jesus singles him out and calls him to follow, Levi repents and obeys. Only Luke indicates that Levi leaves everything (e.g., his tax booth) and follows Jesus (5:28). Moreover, Levi hosts a great banquet in his home in honor of Jesus and invites other tax collectors to attend (5:29). Quite simply, Levi illustrates ideal discipleship in Luke because he repents fully. His greatest loyalty now belongs to Jesus rather than his money-making endeavors in his tax booth. In addition, even though we do not hear Jesus exhort Levi to "fish" for people as Jesus does with Peter, James, and John in 5:10, Levi nevertheless casts a wide net when he invites his fellow tax collectors to dine with Jesus in his own home, presumably at his own expense (5:29). Furthermore, Levi now falls within a stream of repentant and faithful tax collectors in Luke's Gospel. Tax collectors, as opposed to the religious elite, responded favorably to John the Baptist's call for repentance in 3:12-13. Jesus reminds John's messengers of this same juxtaposition between the repentant tax collectors and the unyielding Pharisees again in 7:29-30. Similarly, Jesus will describe a contrast between repentant tax collectors and unrepentant Pharisees in 15:1-2 and 18:10-14. Finally, in 19:1-10, Zacchaeus, a chief tax collector, will exhibit a response similar to Levi's. In short, when Levi encounters Jesus, he repents. His newfound loyalty to Jesus manifests itself when he both walks away from his tax booth and throws a great banquet so that others can encounter Jesus as well. Levi simultaneously clings to Jesus while loosening his grip on his money and possessions. Without a doubt, Luke lifts up Levi as an ideal disciple.

Of course, Luke paints a picture of the Pharisees throughout his Gospel that is almost as negative as the portrait of Jesus is positive. For instance, Luke has already provided a clear and highly negative characterization of the Pharisees by 5:27-39, even though it is only the second time that Luke has specifically mentioned the Pharisees. In particular, in 5:27-39 Luke demonstrates that the Pharisees opt to separate themselves from sinners whereas in 5:27 Jesus seeks out sinners like Levi (5:31-32). The Pharisees elect to avoid sinners in an effort to achieve and to maintain holiness. Jesus, on the other hand, adopts a new approach as his parable in 5:36-39 further illustrates. As the Holy Spirit-empowered Son of God, Jesus seeks out sinners in order to call them to holiness by means of repentance (5:31). Luke's readers quickly learn that Jesus not only has the authority and power to heal withered hands (5:17-26) but also has the authority and power to transform sinners, even tax collectors, into servants of God and faithful disciples who point others to Jesus. Of course, the Pharisees in 5:27-32 are not persuaded. They will continue to complain about Jesus' practice of eating with tax collectors and sinners throughout this Gospel (e.g., 15:1-2).

(4) Luke 6:1-11. Twice before, Luke has mentioned that Jesus performed a miracle on the Sabbath, but no one objected (4:31-37, 38-39). In Luke 6:1-11, however, the Pharisees, Jesus' burgeoning foils, again challenge his actions and those of his disciples primarily because their activities take place on the Sabbath. It should also be noted that Luke 6:1-5 and 6:6-11 function as the third and fourth of four consecutive controversy stories in 5:17–6:11 in which the Pharisees serve as an impediment to Jesus' ministry.

First, in 6:1-5 Jesus' disciples pluck some grain, rub it together, and eat it on the Sabbath. The Pharisees contend, however, that the disciples' actions violate the Mosaic Law (e.g., Exod 20:8-11; 34:21). The Pharisees relied not only on the written form of the Mosaic Law to guide their actions but also on the oral interpretation of the law that had purportedly been handed down from the time of Moses.

By means of both 6:1-5 and 6:6-11, however, Luke establishes that Jesus as the Son of God possesses the authority to interpret Scripture and to govern Sabbath observances. For instance, in 6:3-4, Jesus references 1 Sam 21:1-10 when David fled from the wrath of Saul, who wanted to kill him. In desperate need of provisions, David stopped and demanded that Abimelech, the priest, give him and his men bread. The only bread available was the holy bread, which was made each Sabbath as an offering to the Lord and which only the priests were to eat (Lev 24:5-9). Regardless, David accepted the holy bread, which presumably sustained him and his men as they fled from Saul.

By citing David's example, Jesus demonstrates that he has the authority to interpret the Scriptures. Moreover, Luke's readers can see that Jesus' interpretation of Scripture is more faithful than that of the inquisitorial Pharisees or the scribal tradition. David was God's anointed one (Acts 13:11). It was right and proper that God's own holy bread sustained God's servant in this exceptional situation. The same is true for Jesus, his disciples, and the heads of grain. Jesus and his ministry represent an exceptional situation. Furthermore, because Jesus is the Son of God (1:32, 35; 3:22; 4:41), the Sabbath now serves Jesus just as it does the Lord. Jesus concludes by saying, "The Son of Man is lord of the Sabbath" (6:5). The Sabbath not only serves Jesus; Jesus also governs its proper observance (Caird, *Saint Luke*, 99).

Similarly, in 6:6-11, the Pharisees watch Jesus, fearing that he might heal a man with a withered hand on the Sabbath. In response, Jesus quizzes the Pharisees. He asks whether the Mosaic Law and the Sabbath were intended to bring about good or harm, to save (Gk. *sōzō*) or to destroy life (6:9). As the one who has the authority both to interpret Scripture and to govern the Sabbath, he restores the man's hand. As only someone empowered by God could (5:17), he enables the man's hand to function as hands were always intended to function since the beginning of creation. In the process, for the first time in this Gospel, Jesus utilizes the Greek verb *sōzō*, which means "to rescue" or "to save" (6:9). Jesus rescues this man by healing his withered hand.

Furthermore, Jesus performs this act of restoration by merely speaking three imperative commands (6:8, 10). Ironically, while the Pharisees expect to see Jesus exert too much physical energy on the Sabbath, Jesus does not use any physical action when he heals the man with the withered hand. Instead, he simply speaks commands that lead to the man's healing (Wolter, *Gospel According to Luke*, 1:257). Here, perhaps, Luke wants his readers to realize that the same God who commanded creation into being in Gen 1 is now working through Jesus to restore creation (5:17). As a result, Jesus' actions imply that it is both fitting and faithful to the Scriptures for God's restoring and saving work to take place on the Sabbath (5:10). In response, Jesus' opponents grow increasingly angry at Jesus (6:11), much as we first saw at the synagogue in Nazareth (4:28-29).

Authority to Call Disciples (6:12-16)
Jesus not only has the authority to heal, cleanse, forgive, save, interpret Scripture, and govern the Sabbath but also has the authority to select twelve apostles from among his disciples (cf. Matt 10:2-4; Mark 3:16-19; Acts 1:13). Jesus first calls Peter, James, and John to follow him as disciples in 5:1-11. By 6:12, however, Jesus has far more than twelve disciples. In 6:17, Luke refers to a great crowd of disciples, though he does not tell his readers exactly how many disciples are present. By 10:1, we know that at least eighty-two disciples are following Jesus. Regardless, in 6:13, Luke's main point is that Jesus selects twelve of the disciples (followers who travel with and learn from Jesus) to serve as apostles (disciples who are sent out by Jesus to carry out his ministry and message).

Beyond his main point that Jesus appoints twelve apostles in 6:12-16, Luke also highlights two other details in this pericope. First, Jesus spends the entire night in prayer to God before he makes this critical decision (6:12). Luke never portrays Jesus as being independent of the Father. Rather, Jesus as the Son of God relies on the Father for both guidance and power throughout this Gospel (3:21-22; 5:17). Jesus' regular practice of prayer (5:16), which Luke highlights more than any other Gospel writer, best illuminates this intimate relationship between Jesus and the Father.

Only Luke informs his readers that Jesus prays prior to the Spirit's descent at the baptism (3:21), before selecting his apostles (6:12-13), prior to Peter's confession (9:18), prior to the transfiguration (9:28-29), and before teaching his disciples how to pray (11:1-2). Only Luke includes Jesus' parable of the unjust judge and persistent widow (18:1–8) and his parable of the Pharisee and tax collector (18:9-14), both of which Jesus tells in order to teach about one's proper disposition during prayer. Finally, Jesus prays on the night of his arrest both as he is on the Mount of Olives alone with his disciples and as the crowd arrives to arrest him (22:39-53).

In short, Luke repeatedly shows Jesus praying at decisive points in his life and ministry. As a result, Luke assures his readers that Jesus is fully in line with the Father's wishes and the overarching work of God in the world known as salvation history. Moreover, prayer in Luke's writings has a revelatory function (Crump, *Jesus the Intercessor*, 21). God's will and the Holy Spirit's power are most clearly known and experienced by means of and as a result of prayer. This reality is true for Jesus in Luke's Gospel, and it is it equally true for Luke's readers.

Second, it is of great importance that Jesus selects twelve apostles from among his disciples. For instance, Luke names Judas Iscariot as one of the apostles in 6:16, but due to his betrayal of Jesus and apparent apostasy, Luke no longer lists Judas among the apostles in Acts 1:13; there he only names eleven apostles. Peter, however, then guides the believers to select a twelfth apostle prior to Pentecost (Acts 1:15-26). All of Jesus' disciples gathered that day seem to agree that the cadre of apostles must be restored to a total number of twelve. As a result, Luke seems to indicate to his readers in both Luke and Acts that the number twelve is symbolically and theologically important to Jesus.

Almost certainly, Jesus selects twelve apostles because the number twelve corresponds to the twelve tribes of Israel. By selecting twelve apostles to represent his ministry and proclaim his message in Luke's writings, Jesus appears to see the apostles as a foretaste of "the restored Israel." The image of "the restored Israel," as embodied by the apostles, then provides the foundational identity for the church in Acts (Walton, "Calling the Church Names," 105).

Authority to Teach Disciples (the Sermon on the Plain) (6:17-49)

Matthew clusters many of Jesus' teachings together in a three-chapter unit in his Gospel known as the Sermon on the Mount (5:1–7:27). Luke shares many of these same teaching materials with his readers, but he spreads them throughout his Gospel. Nevertheless, the teaching section that Luke recounts in Luke 6:17-49 corresponds with a significant portion of Matthew's Sermon on the Mount. Luke's abbreviated version is frequently referred to as Jesus' Sermon on the Plain. Whereas Jesus goes up onto a mountain in order to teach in Matt 5:1-2, in Luke 6:17 Jesus comes down off of a mountain to a flat place or plain in order to teach among the people (6:12-13, 17).

(1) Luke 6:17-19. Three groups of people gather around Jesus. First, Jesus brings his twelve apostles with him as he descends from the mountain (6:17). Next, additional disciples congregate. By this point, the number of disciples has grown large enough that Luke refers to these additional disciples as a great crowd. Finally, a great multitude of other people (literally "the people") has come from all over. This third group, the multitude, has come from territories that Jesus has not even visited up to this point. Moreover, they are coming from both predominantly Jewish territories to the south and predominantly Gentile cities to the north. Though "the people" is Luke's standard phrase for Jewish adherents (Tannehill, *Narrative Unity of Luke-Acts*, 1:143–44), the geographical breadth represented in 6:17 nevertheless highlights the swelling reach of Jesus' ministry.

Furthermore, these crowds gravitate toward Jesus for three reasons. They want to hear him teach, they want him to heal their diseases, and they want him to cure them of unclean spirits (6:18). These are the same types of activities that Jesus first mentioned in his inaugural sermon in the synagogue at Nazareth (4:18-19). Here Luke shows his readers that Jesus remains faithful to God's original calling and that Jesus' words are truthful.

Notably, Luke also informs his readers that the one who has been empowered by (3:21-22) and filled with (4:1, 14) the Holy Spirit now exudes that same power: the power of God is literally radiating from him (6:19). Luke portrays Jesus as the one who is so full of God's power by this point that he overflows with it. As that divine power spills out of him, it heals and restores those with whom it comes into contact (cf. 5:17). Furthermore, Luke uses this information to set the stage for Jesus' teachings in 6:20-49. The same divine power that enables Jesus to heal and restore will likewise inspire and empower Jesus to form and to shape his disciples through his teachings (Talbert, *Reading Luke*, 71).

(2) Luke 6:20-26. It is important to notice that when Jesus begins to teach in 6:20, he specifically addresses his disciples as opposed to the

multitude (Talbert, *Reading Luke*, 71). His comments in the Sermon on the Plain (6:20-49) are not tailored to the general audience who gather to be healed of infirmities or even an audience of curious investigators who have not yet made up their minds about Jesus. Rather, in the Sermon on the Plain Jesus primarily speaks to those who have already left everything to follow him (6:20). As a result, Jesus' remarks do not serve as an introduction to Jesus' ministry or his message. Instead, first and foremost, his remarks aim to comfort, guide, and form those who are already following Jesus: "This sermon teaches not what must be done to *enter* the kingdom of God, but what is expected of one who is already *in* the kingdom" (Craig Evans, *Luke*, 107). Of course, if "the people" overhear Jesus' words, they will get a glimpse of what following Jesus entails. Here, however, Jesus primarily aims to mold his disciples more closely into his image. Jesus does not set out a soteriology based on works or liberation in 6:20-49. Instead, he sets out a lifestyle of discipleship for members of the believing community.

In 6:20-23, Jesus begins his sermon by announcing the beatitudes, or statements of congratulation and approval based on "an awareness of the ultimate outcome of history" (Talbert, *Reading Luke*, 72–73). Whereas Matthew includes nine beatitudes in Matt 5:3-12, Luke only includes four. By means of these beatitudes, Jesus affirms that God's favor is upon the poor, hungry, grief stricken, and reviled, despite what their outward circumstances may suggest. As Luke relays Jesus' teachings, however, he accents particular aspects of Jesus' remarks. All four of the conditions that Jesus mentions—poverty, hunger, grief, and rejection—were well-known hardships that Israel encountered in a variety of OT contexts. For instance, postexilic writers especially refer to Israel as the poor and oppressed in contrast to their enemies (e.g., Isa 61:1; 66:2; Ps 9:9, 18; 25:16; 40:17; 70:5; 86:1-3; 109:22). Furthermore, this terminology frequently referenced both economic and spiritual conditions simultaneously. Devout but impoverished Jews in a postexilic context sought to place their hope solely in God. They believed their difficult circumstances strengthened their religious commitment. To give attention exclusively to either the physical realm or the spiritual realm would miss the point. As a result, it is doubtful that ancient exegetes would have drawn sharp distinctions between Matthew's "poor in spirit" (Matt 5:3) and Luke's "poor" (Luke 6:20) as contemporary scholars often do (Levin, "Poor in the Old Testament," 260–70). Rather, postexilic Jews often considered themselves to be God's faithful servants precisely because they were solely dependent on God (Talbert, *Reading Luke*, 73–75). They were both physically poor and spiritually poor, which in turn aided their quest for righteousness (e.g., Isa 29:18-19; 61:1; *Pss. Sol.* 10:7.)

Regardless, Jesus personalizes his message for his disciples. He does not utilize third-person plural pronouns as we see in Matt 5:3 ("theirs"); he does not speak abstractly about some group of people in the past or the present who may be poor, hungry, grieving, or rejected. Rather, in Luke Jesus utilizes the second-person plural pronouns ("you all"). Jesus speaks directly to the conditions that his followers are currently experiencing, and he speaks a personal word to them. What has been true of God's care for Israel in the past—despite unpleasant circumstances—is now true for "you all" (Jesus' disciples) in the present. Furthermore, Jesus contrasts their present state of suffering and hardship with both a present and future hope that accompanies the inaugurated but not fully realized kingdom of God (5:20-23).

Jesus also takes the time to expound on the rejection that his disciples are experiencing, and in turn he guides them toward proper responses in 6:22-23. Regardless of the prejudice or persecution that his followers experience as a result of following the Son of Man (cf. Acts 6–7), Jesus assures his disciples of God's approval and future blessings. Already at this point in Luke's Gospel, we see the apocalyptic belief in the separation of people in the afterlife based on their earthly actions. Jesus' parable of the rich man and Lazarus in 16:19-31 will further illustrate this concept (Henning, *Educating Early Christians*, 122–26). Regardless, Jesus casts the harassment and persecution of the disciples in a distinctive light. Previous generations mistreated God's prophets in the same ways that this generation is mistreating Jesus' disciples (6:23). Given that Luke goes out of his way to depict Jesus as a prophet throughout this Gospel (e.g., 4:14-30), it is not surprising to see him also characterizing Jesus' followers as mistreated prophets of God.

As stated above, unlike Matthew, Luke only includes four beatitudes in the Sermon on the Plain; also unlike Matthew, Luke then pairs those beatitudes with a parallel set of woes in 6:24-26. In contrast to Jesus' encouragement of the poor, hungry, grieving, and rejected, Jesus now issues woes for the rich, well fed, laughing, and embraced. Just as Jesus pronounces a reversal of fortunes for those who are currently struggling, so also Jesus pronounces a reversal of fortune for those living in ease and abundance. Similar to our discussion of the poor, Luke connects the physical realm with the spiritual realm when discussing the rich. Mary's Magnificat weds together the rich, powerful, and proud (1:51-53). "The rich" in Luke's writings refers both to a physical state and a spiritual state (Tiede, *Luke*, 141–42). Regardless, Jesus speaks directly and personally to those standing nearby who may fall into these categories. For instance, he again uses the second-person plural pronoun ("you all"). In addition, Jesus points to both present and future consequences for those who fall into these traps. The people who currently trust in their earthly resources and status will ultimately discover that those resources cannot support them in the age to come.

Finally, Luke accentuates the prophetic theme in his Gospel to an even greater extent when he shows Jesus wedding together woes with his beatitudes. The eighth-century prophets like Isaiah, Amos, and Micah did not exclusively speak words of comfort. Rather, they frequently warned their audiences to repent. Jesus resembles the great prophets when he pairs his words of comfort with his words of warning. Jesus declares the Lord's comfort to those in need, but he likewise calls on those in the lap of luxury to repent. Notice also that Jesus concludes his woes in a manner similar to that of his beatitudes. Whereas previous generations mistreated the faithful prophets of God (6:23), those same people unfortunately honored and rewarded false prophets (6:23, 26). As a result, Jesus sketches "two ways" or two paths for his disciples. He encourages them when they function as faithful prophets of God, but he censures them when they function as false ones.

(3) *Luke 6:27-36*. After pronouncing four woes against the rich and privileged, Jesus again turns his attention to the apostles and the crowd of disciples (6:27). In contrast to those about whom everyone speaks well (6:26), Jesus instructs his disciples about how to respond to the maltreatment they are experiencing. First and foremost, Jesus teaches his disciples to love their enemies (6:27, 35). This teaching is the core principle that he seeks to develop in his followers. More than simply wanting the disciples to do good, bless, and pray for their enemies, Jesus teaches them that all of these actions must be motivated by love—the kind of love that God himself has shown to humanity (6:36).

Jesus then provides four illustrative examples of times when his disciples may encounter their enemies. In addition, Jesus describes ways in which his disciples may respond to those enemies with love as opposed to hatred and retribution. The four scenarios are (1) a person strikes you on the cheek (6:29a), (2) a person takes your outer garment (6:29b), (3) a person begs for help from you (6:30a), and (4) a person takes your goods or belongings (6:30b). Jesus is not limiting his overarching message about love to these four scenarios. Rather, Jesus hopes his disciples will utilize these examples as templates as they respond to their own life situations.

Notably, in each instance the principle of reciprocity and a desire for self-protection would have guided most people in Jesus' day (6:32-34) (van Unnik, "Die Motivierung der Feindesliebe," 284–300). Jesus, however, challenges this principle of reciprocity that guides one to return hatred with hatred and favor with favor. Regardless of whether people mistreat his disciples or ask them for favors that can never be repaid, Jesus substitutes the

Golden Rule (6:31), which is based on love (6:35), in place of the principle of reciprocity (Tannehill, *Luke*, 118–19). Jesus is not advocating "passivity in the face of aggression" but rather is requiring his disciples to take loving action. One must actively "find the good not only for oneself but for the enemy" (Tannehill, *Luke*, 118).

Furthermore, the love of the enemy that Jesus describes does not grow out of self-advancement even in one's relationship with God. Rather, Jesus calls his disciples to be merciful by means of showing love, doing good, and lending to those in need because God is merciful (6:36). Jesus mentions that those who live by the principle of love, rather than reciprocity, will receive a future reward, but Jesus also pairs his statement about a future reward with a statement about becoming the children of the Most High. It is precisely as Jesus' followers imitate the works of God that they most fully reflect God and are therefore most clearly God's children (6:35). Gratitude for God's love and mercy in the past, present, and future provides the true motivation for showing God's love and mercy toward one's enemy.

(4) Luke 6:37-42. In 6:37-42 Jesus transitions from speaking about interactions with enemies to addressing how his disciples should interact with one another. For instance, four times in 6:41-42 Jesus uses the term "brother" (Gk. adelphos), a term the NRSV translates as "neighbor." Luke and most other New Testament (NT) writers, however, generally employ the word "brothers" to denote fellow disciples or Christians, which seems to be the case here in 6:37-42. Whereas Jesus dealt with external relations in the previous unit, now Jesus deals with internal relations among his disciples.

Jesus continues to group his comments in clusters of four in 6:37-38. In this instance, he discourages judging and condemning while he fosters forgiving and giving. In each case, Jesus describes the natural corollary that accompanies those actions. Jesus then tells a parable in 6:39-42 that further illustrates these instructions about how to treat one's fellow disciples. In hyperbolic fashion, Jesus employs a series of metaphorical images: a blind guide, a disciple who presumes to know more than the teacher, a speck in one's eye, and a log in the other's eye.

Ultimately, Jesus informs his disciples that they themselves must experience God's transformation before they can properly direct others toward that same transformation (6:42): "In the NT period new Christians learned the meaning of the Christian way from observation of those who were already Jesus' followers. This is why Paul could speak about his converts' imitating him (1 Cor 4:15-17; 11:1; Phil 3:17; 2 Thess 3:7)" (Talbert, *Reading Luke*, 78). Here in Luke 6:37-42, Jesus likewise acknowledges this need for new followers to learn by imitation of more experienced disciples. Yet if the guides have not yet experienced transformation from their old ways to the ways of the teacher (6:40), then their judgments and condemnations will be no better than a blind person leading a blind person. Disciples cannot surpass the teacher (Jesus), but they should increasingly become more like the teacher (6:40) (Tiede, *Luke*, 145). Disciples, however, cannot be beneficial tutors who guide, correct, and extend mercy until they have first tackled their own hypocrisy (6:42) and become "fully qualified" by being more like the teacher (6:40).

Jesus is not saying that his disciples should allow immoral behavior or wrongheaded ideas to go unchallenged. He is not suggesting that the disciples turn a blind eye to serious moral failings and harmful practices among the community of followers. Rather, he is saying that his disciples must first judge themselves and expunge their own immoral practices before evaluating others (Danker, *Jesus*, 89).

(5) Luke 6:43-49. After having shaped the disciples' mental and spiritual outlook in regard to both external and internal relations, Jesus begins to sum up his comments by means of two units. First, Jesus uses agricultural imagery to describe the transformation or lack thereof among those who are drawn to him. He will utilize this type of agricultural imagery again in the parable of the sower (8:5-15) and the parable of the unfruitful fig tree (13:6-9). In each of these instances, though especially in 6:43-45, Jesus depicts a scenario that alludes to more than merely human willpower and effort. Rather, the good and the evil trees are recognized by their fruit. No one implores them to be good or even better trees. The fruit simply reveals the true nature of the trees.

Similarly, Jesus locates the core essence of a person in the heart (6:45). Beyond the various teachings in this sermon about turning one's cheek (6:29) or giving to others in need (6:38), the heart serves as the ultimate foundation from which love flows. If God has transformed one's heart, then one will be able to bear the good fruit of God's love (6:27, 35). If not, then the evil fruit of reciprocity (e.g., retribution and selfish lending) will be the result.

Finally, Jesus concludes his sermon by illustrating the wisdom of those who hear and obey the word of the Lord as God's prophet proclaims it versus the foolishness of those who hear the word of the Lord and ignore it. Much like the author of James (1:22-25), Jesus explains that it is wise both to hear and to act upon good teaching. Jesus desires for his disciples to hear and to act in light of the overarching work of God in the world.

Jesus' Prophetic Ministry in Capernaum and Nain (7:1-50)

Jesus returns to Capernaum in 7:1. He then moves on to Nain in 7:11 and appears to remain there until 8:1. In the literary unit that runs from 7:1 to

7:50, Luke begins by pairing together two healing stories that further illustrate Jesus' identity as a faithful prophet of God. In addition, as we have seen in a variety of locations in Luke's Gospel, Luke once again pairs together two stories that feature a leading male character and a leading female character (Wolter, *Gospel According to Luke*, 291). For example, Zechariah and Mary both receive an angelic visit and sing hymns of praise in Luke 1. Similarly, Luke tells us about both Simeon and Anna's reactions to the Christ child in 2:21-38. Here in 7:1-17, Luke narrates Jesus' healing of the centurion's slave (7:1-10) followed by Jesus' healing of the widow's son (7:11-17). In short, Luke routinely makes a concerted effort to show how both men and women are recipients of and participants in God's redemptive work in the world. In this instance, Luke highlights a Gentile soldier and a Jewish widow.

In Luke 7:18-50, Luke places John and Jesus side by side once again, much as he did in Luke 1–3. First, Luke revisits the ministry of John the Baptist in 7:18-35. In doing so, Luke resumes his depiction of John the Baptist as a prophet of God. Then Luke segues to a story about Jesus in the house of a Pharisee in 7:36-50. Here also, Luke portrays Jesus as a prophet of God who faces criticism and opposition. Indeed, Luke binds all of Luke 7 together using images and vocabulary related to John and Jesus functioning as prophets of God. For instance, Luke employs the word "prophet" (Gk. *prophētēs*) on four occasions in this chapter (7:16, 26ab, and 39). In addition, Jesus raises a man from the dead in 7:11-17; up to this point in the Scriptures, only Elijah (1 Kgs 17:17-24) and Elisha (2 Kgs 4:32-37) have performed similar miracles. Without a doubt Luke depicts both John and Jesus as prophets of God in this Gospel. Jesus, however, is unquestionably the greater prophetic figure. As we saw from the beginning, Luke makes it crystal clear that a new day has dawned with the arrival of Jesus. Even though John is a great prophet, "the least in the kingdom of God is greater than he" (7:28).

(1) Luke 7:1-10. The encounter between Jesus and the centurion in Luke 7:1-10 enlightens Luke's readers on at least two major fronts. First, Luke further highlights Jesus' authority in this pericope. Jesus has returned to Capernaum (cf. 4:31) on the Sea of Galilee. Shortly thereafter, Jesus has a significant exchange with a Roman centurion, a military officer who oversees an 80-soldier unit. Luke first provides the backdrop to this exchange in 7:2. The centurion has a dying slave whom he values highly. As a result, the centurion wants Jesus to restore his slave to health.

To communicate with Jesus, the centurion sends a group of Jewish elders to make the case on his behalf. Perhaps the centurion reasons that Jesus will respond better to a request from his fellow countrymen than a request from a Roman soldier. The Jewish elders validate this impression when they inform

Jesus of all the reasons that he should assist the centurion. Notably, in the process, the elders voice concern only for the well-being of the centurion, not for the centurion's slave. The elders confidently inform Jesus that the centurion is worthy (Gk. *axios*) of Jesus' assistance for two reasons: he loves the Jewish people, and he personally funded the construction of the synagogue in Capernaum (7:4-5). Jesus, in turn, agrees to accompany the Jewish elders to the centurion's house.

At that point, the centurion sends a second delegation of his friends to communicate with Jesus (7:6). His message suggests that the Jewish elders went beyond what the centurion had originally intended. By means of his friends, the centurion now contradicts the claims of the Jewish elders and says to Jesus, "I am not worthy (Gk. *hikanos*) to have you come under my roof." He clarifies that he also has avoided meeting with Jesus face to face out of respect for and deference to Jesus. He merely wants Jesus to heal his slave by declaration.

Throughout Luke's Gospel, Jesus exhorts those around him to learn about the kingdom of God from their everyday circumstances. Here, the centurion makes the same theological move without being prompted by Jesus to do so (Caird, *Saint Luke*, 108). The centurion reasons that as a Roman soldier, he is under the authority of his superiors, and he in turn has authority over those beneath him in the military hierarchy. Each person simply follows orders. Likewise, the centurion is simply asking Jesus to give an order. He is not requesting Jesus to divert his time or attention to the centurion (7:8).

Jesus responds by pointing out the tremendous faith of the centurion (7:9). The whole pericope functions as a pronouncement story. The scene builds until it reaches an apex that consists of Jesus' pronouncement. Jesus declares that this Gentile's faith exceeds the faith of those "in Israel." The faith of this Roman soldier exceeds the faith of the Jewish elders who so confidently approached Jesus in the beginning and made judgments about worthiness.

Consequently, the startling turn in this pericope takes place when the centurion derives theological insight and truth from everyday occurrences. He works by way of analogy. He knows what it is like to be under the authority of a superior and to act with authority over others. The centurion's comments suggest that Jesus holds a similar position. Jesus clearly possesses the authority to heal the centurion's slave even from a distance simply by speaking. At the same time, the centurion seems to sense that Jesus' power derives from God's own authority (Marshall, *Luke*, 282). As a result, the centurion's faith rests on his conviction that the almighty God is at work in Jesus. He believes that God has granted Jesus authority over sickness and disease.

Second, Luke narrates 7:1-10 in such a way that it prepares Luke's readers for the overarching narrative of Luke and Acts. The centurion in Luke 7 and another centurion in Acts 10 share many commonalities. Cornelius, the centurion in Acts 10, is also a God-fearer who worships the God of Abraham and participates in the traditional acts of Jewish piety even though he has never converted to Judaism (Acts 10:2, 22). For example, Cornelius gives alms, or financial assistance to the poor, and he prays constantly to God (Acts 10:2, 4, 31). Akin to the centurion in Luke 7, Cornelius initially communicates with Peter in Acts 10 via a delegation. Finally, much like the centurion in Luke 7 who works to prevent Jesus from coming under his roof, in Acts 10:38 Peter indicates that both he and Cornelius know the Mosaic Law prohibits a Jew from visiting the home of a Gentile (Acts 10:28; cf. *m. Oholot* 18:7).

Of course, the theological landscape changes between Luke 7 and Acts 10. Whereas Jesus never enters the centurion's house or even meets face to face with the centurion in Luke 7:1-10, Peter elects to meet with Cornelius, enter his house, and accept hospitality from his Gentile counterpart in Acts 10:48 (cf. Acts 11:2, 12) (Arterbury, *Entertaining Angels*, 153–66). The parallel stories about Roman centurions in Luke 7 and Acts 10 help to illustrate the dramatic shift of the ages that takes place with the arrival of the kingdom of God that Jesus ushers in. The story about Cornelius, the first Gentile convert in Luke's writings, marks the beginning of the mission to the Gentiles in the early church. From Luke's perspective, the Abrahamic covenant, which includes a blessing for the entire world, finds its ultimate fulfillment in the Gentile mission (1:72-73, 2:32; cf. Gen 12:1-3). Even though Jesus' positive reference to Naaman, the Syrian general (2 Kgs 5:1-14), in Luke 4:27 and his healing of the centurion's slave in Luke 7:1-10 both foreshadow this future development, Luke will not officially group Gentiles among God's people in his writings until after Jesus' ascension into the heavens and the arrival of the Holy Spirit (Acts 1–2). For Luke, who vowed to write an orderly account in 1:1, the two centurions in Luke's writings help illustrate the chronological and theological order that takes place in the unfolding redemptive work of God in the world.

(2) Luke 7:11-17. After leaving Capernaum, Jesus travels southwest and arrives at the Galilean village of Nain (7:11). As Jesus approaches the gate of the town, a funeral procession carrying a young man exits the town, likely walking to a nearby cemetery. The man's death creates an especially tragic situation for his mother. The deceased youth was her only son, and her

husband had previously died (7:12). As a result, going forward the widow has no predictable means of economic support. Not surprisingly, Luke points out to his readers that Jesus has great compassion for this woman who is in dire straits (7:13). In response, Jesus raises the young man from the dead (7:14-15). The crowds around Jesus then proclaim him to be "a great prophet" (7:16).

Since Jesus' inaugural sermon in Nazareth (4:16-27), Luke has been systematically demonstrating to his readers how Jesus' ministry fulfills the words of Isaiah that Jesus read in the synagogue that day. For example, in this literary unit Jesus brings good news to the poor (cf. 4:18). At the same time, Luke has been establishing Jesus' prophetic identity throughout Luke 4–7. Regardless, Luke 7:11-17 provides undeniable proof for Luke's readers that Jesus is indeed a prophet of God. Notably, Luke alone includes this story in his Gospel.

Apart from Jesus' own bodily resurrection (24:1-12), this pericope constitutes only the third recorded instance within the Scriptures of a person being resurrected from the dead. (Three subsequent resuscitation accounts can also be found in John 11, Acts 9:36-42, and Acts 20:7-12.) More precisely, the OT contains only two instances of a person being raised from the dead: Elijah raises a young man from the dead in 1 Kgs 17:17-24, and Elisha raises a young man from the dead in 2 Kgs 4:32-37.

Luke apparently alludes to these two miraculous events that predate Jesus while narrating Jesus' raising of the widow's son in Luke 7:11-17. For instance, one can detect numerous parallels and echoes among the three passages (i.e., 1 Kgs 17:17-24; 2 Kgs 4:8-37; Luke 7:11-17). In 1 Kgs 17:17-24, a widow from Zarephath's only son becomes sick and dies; Elijah cries out to the Lord; the child is revived; Elijah takes the child, presents him to his mother, and declares that the child is alive; and the woman concludes that Elijah is a man of God. In 2 Kgs 4:8-37, a Shunammite woman likewise concludes that Elisha is a holy man of God; her husband is old and her only son dies; Elisha prays to the Lord and lays upon the child; the child is revived; and Elisha presents the living child to the mother. Finally, in Luke 7:11-17, the widow from Nain's only son dies; Jesus comforts the mother and commands the young man to arise; Jesus presents the revived youth to the mother; and all the people conclude that Jesus is a great prophet. Luke even uses the exact same Greek phrase in 7:15 ("presented him to his mother") as is found in 1 Kgs 17:23 LXX (Johnson, *Luke*, 119). Furthermore, the village of Nain was in close geographical proximity to the ancient village of Shunem. Without a doubt, Luke hoped his readers would notice the numerous similarities between the mighty deeds of Elijah and Elisha and the ministry of Jesus.

Fundamentally, in these early sections of his Gospel and most definitely in Luke 7:11-17, Luke is showing his readers that Jesus is the long-expected prophet like Moses who will lead God's people (Deut 18:15) and know God face to face (Deut 34:10). For instance, in Peter's second sermon in Acts, Peter makes the connection explicit between Jesus and the often-cited prophecy from Deut 18 (Acts 3:22-23; cf. Acts 7:37). Jesus is the prophet like Moses. Nevertheless, observant readers of Luke's Gospel and especially Luke 7:11-17 should have anticipated Peter's remarks in Acts. Jesus has just performed an act that was exclusively associated with God's great prophets. Luke shows his readers that Jesus has power even over death, but he also shows them that Jesus is the "prophetic Messiah" whom they have anticipated for generations (Johnson, *Luke*, 119–20). As a prophet of the Lord, Jesus now speaks and acts for God (4:24, 24:19).

(3) Luke 7:18-23. Luke informs his readers in 3:18-20 that Herod Antipater (or Antipas), the Roman-appointed tetrarch of Galilee and Perea, has imprisoned John the Baptist. Antipas became angry when John rebuked him for divorcing his Nabatean wife in order to marry Herodias, his niece. To make matters worse, Herodias had previously been married to Herod II, Antipater's half-brother, whom she divorced (Josephus, *Ant.* 18.5.4). Eventually, Luke indicates that Herod Antipas beheads John, but Luke does not narrate the event (9:7-9).

In between John's initial arrest (3:22) and his execution (9:9), John's disciples converse with John, presumably while he is still incarcerated (7:18-23). His disciples provide a report to John about Jesus and his activities (7:18). In response, John sends two of his disciples to ask Jesus about his identity (7:18b-19). In particular, John wants to know whether Jesus is "the one who is to come" (7:20).

Even though Luke indicates that the mothers of John and Jesus are relatives (1:36), Luke never specifically says that John and Jesus encountered one another after their births, not even at Jesus' baptism (3:21-22). As a result, John's questions appear to be natural. John has previously proclaimed that "one who is more powerful than I is coming" (3:16), but Luke never suggests that John had identified Jesus as the coming one prior to 7:18-23. So now that John has heard the reports of Jesus' miraculous deeds, John seeks clarity from Jesus himself about Jesus' identity. At the same time, Luke likely included this passage in his Gospel because the exchange between John and Jesus will also aid Luke's own readers in their quest to understand Jesus' identity clearly.

In response to John's question (7:20), Jesus simply lists the kinds of things he has been doing. Jesus chronicles the ways in which he has been healing the blind, disabled, and diseased. He mentions having raised the dead, which he just accomplished (7:11-17), and claims that "the poor have good news brought to them" (7:22; cf. 4:18, 6:20). Notably, John's disciples do not merely rely on Jesus' oral testimony. Presumably they witness some of these miraculous events in person (7:20-21).

While clarifying his identity for John's disciples, Jesus invokes language and images found in Isa 29:18-19, 35:5-6, and 42:18—passages that refer to the one who will come and help the blind, diseased, and deaf. In addition, and perhaps even more important, Jesus once again alludes to Isa 61:1, which he previously quoted in the synagogue at Nazareth (4:18-19). In essence, Jesus demonstrates that he has accomplished the very things that many in Israel expected God to accomplish through the long-anticipated prophet of God (cf. John 6:14). Furthermore, Jesus demonstrates that he continues to fulfill the words of Isa 61:1 as he first claimed in his inaugural sermon at Nazareth (4:16-21). This development further reveals and clarifies Jesus' identity as an authentic, truthful, and reliable prophet.

Finally, by providing a convincing answer to John and his disciples about Jesus' status as the long-anticipated, messianic prophet, Jesus implicitly offers an invitation to John's disciples to begin to follow Jesus now. John spoke of the coming one, who would be greater than himself (3:16-17). Jesus' answer illustrates that "the greater one" has arrived. If John's disciples truly believed John's message in the past, then they should now become disciples of Jesus in the present. As he moves forward in his writings, Luke will return to this subject. For instance, in the book of Acts, Luke continues to speak of John's disciples and their transition from following John to following Jesus. When Paul passes through Ephesus in Acts 19:1-7, he encounters twelve of John's disciples who were previously baptized with John's baptism of repentance. Paul, however, reminds them that John spoke of the coming one (Acts 19:4; cf. Luke 3:16-17; 7:20). Paul then clarifies that Jesus was the expected Messiah for whom John prepared. As a result, these former disciples of John become Jesus followers. Those whom John had previously baptized are now "baptized in the name of the Lord Jesus," and they receive the Holy Spirit (19:5-6). In short, in Luke 7:17-35 Luke lays the groundwork for an ongoing transition from following John to following Jesus.

(4) Luke 7:24-35. Once John's emissaries depart, Jesus takes the opportunity to provide additional clarity about John's identity, just as he provided clarity about his own identity in 7:18-23. Jesus addresses the crowds directly with a series of three rhetorical questions about John (7:24-26.) Jesus first

asks two rhetorical questions about John that presume a negative answer. By means of these questions, Jesus essentially claims that John was a strong and courageous man of humble status. He was not a flimsy reed, and he did not dress in soft or luxurious clothes (7:24-25). Instead, by means of a third rhetorical question in which Jesus presumes a positive response, Jesus claims that John was a prophet of God (7:26). John, however, had a unique role as a prophet. Malachi prophesied that God would send a messenger before the day of the Lord to help the people repent. Jesus cites Mal 3:1 and claims that John was the Elijah-like prophet who preceded God's anointed one (7:27). In essence, John was not just any prophet. He was among the greatest of God's prophets. Jesus claims that no human who had ever been born was greater than John (7:28).

Jesus then takes a significant turn as he seeks to illustrate the work of God before and after Jesus' arrival. With Jesus' appearance, the kingdom of God has broken into the earthly realm. Whereas John is equal to the greatest in the age before the Messiah, Jesus claims that now even "the least in the kingdom of God" are greater than John (7:28). Now even the most insignificant disciples will be greater than the greatest OT prophet. Just as Mary signaled in the Magnificat, God is now functioning as "Savior," not only for Israel but also for an unsuspecting young woman (1:46-55). Now, in the kingdom of God, even those with little or no status are highly valued servants (1:47-48).

In the immediate context of 7:29, Luke then singles out the repentant tax collectors around Jesus as examples of "the least" in the kingdom of God. Shockingly, the tax collectors were among those who elected to praise God and seek John's baptism of repentance in 3:10-14. Equally surprising, the Pharisees and lawyers rejected God's call for repentance from the beginning of this Gospel (7:30), and they fail to acknowledge "the justice of God" (7:29). Rather than welcoming God's emissaries, they first criticized John for his austere approach to life and ministry, and now they criticize Jesus for being too carefree (7:31-34). In particular, they criticize Jesus for being a friend of tax collectors and sinners (7:34). The Pharisees and lawyers fail to realize that "the least in the kingdom of God" are greater even than John. The fruits of their failures to perceive the in-breaking of God's kingdom will eventually prove Jesus' point (7:35). On the other hand, Jesus' claims about the great worth of repentant sinners are verified, at least for Luke's readers, in the subsequent pericope about the woman who bathes Jesus' feet with her tears and anoints them with ointment (7:36-50).

(5) *Luke 7:36-50.* The Lukan story of the woman who anoints Jesus' feet with ointment must be read within its immediate literary context. For Luke,

this event further illustrates Jesus' comments about the importance of John the Baptist in 7:24-35. From a literary-critical perspective, it is unhelpful, if not impossible, to harmonize Luke 7:36-50 with Mark 14:3-9, Matt 26:6-13, or John 12:1-8. If one attempts to read the final form of the text, one must simply set aside the other three canonical accounts of a woman who anoints Jesus and deem them to be completely separate events. For instance, the other three pericopes narrate events near the end of Jesus' life after he has arrived at Bethany, which is in Judea rather than Galilee. In Matt 26:6-13, Mark 14:3-9, and John 12:1-8, Jesus claims that the anointing prepares him for burial. Narratively speaking, Luke is nowhere close to depicting Jesus' death and burial in Luke 7. Furthermore, all three of the non-Lukan passages feature a foil who criticizes Jesus for allowing a woman to waste valuable financial resources as she anoints Jesus. In Luke 7, the criticism levied against Jesus pertains to his willingness to associate with sinners and tax collectors. Of course, even beyond these similarities, it remains difficult even to reconcile the differences between the unnamed woman who anoints Jesus' head in Simon the leper's house in Matthew and Mark's Gospels and Mary the sister of Lazarus who anoints Jesus' feet in her brother's home in John's Gospel. Luke's story about a sinful woman who anoints Jesus' feet in the house of Simon the Pharisee must be interpreted within the context of Luke's Gospel, which depicts it as an independent event.

Within Luke 7:24-50, Luke continues to substantiate his case for Jesus' identity as a prophet of God. In the process, Luke weds Jesus' comments about John's ministry (7:24-35) together with Jesus' visit in the home of Simon the Pharisee (7:36-50) in a chiastic manner. Notice the literary logic:

(a) Jesus describes John as a prophet (7:26-28).
   (b) Thankfully, the tax collectors and others recognized God's righteousness, or justice, when John exposed their sin and demanded their repentance (7:29; cf. 3:7-9).
      (c) Unfortunately, the Pharisees and lawyers dismissed God's critique and rejected God's call to repentance through John's proclamation (7:30; cf. 3:10-14). Instead, they criticized John's asceticism, believing that he was demon possessed (7:33).
      (c') These same Pharisees and lawyers now criticize Jesus for being a friend of tax collectors and sinners (7:34). Simon the Pharisee's actions further depict the manner in which the Pharisees fail to recognize Jesus as God's prophet. Simon hosts Jesus in an inadequate, inhospitable, and socially offensive manner (7:36). He does not clean Jesus' dusty feet, greet him properly

with a kiss, or put oil on his head to counteract the effects of the sun as meritorious hosts did for their guests (7:44-46) (Arterbury, *Entertaining Angels*, 137–39).

(b') Instead, a "sinful" woman of the city hears a report about Jesus, enters the house, and finds Jesus reclining at the table. At that point, she not only carries out the expected duties of a meritorious host—those that Simon the Pharisee failed to perform—but also, by using her own tears, kisses, and costly ointment to welcome and care for Jesus, she far surpasses typical hospitality expectations (7:37-38). Furthermore, like the tax collectors, she performs actions that illustrate her willingness to repent due to her encounter with God's prophet.

(a') Simon then concludes that Jesus cannot be a prophet. If Jesus were a prophet, he would know that the woman is a sinner and would prohibit her from caring for him (7:39).

To counteract Simon the Pharisee's final verdict that Jesus cannot possibly be a prophet of God, Jesus tells the parable of two debtors (7:41-42). One man owes a debt roughly equivalent to five hundred days' worth of wages for a common laborer. The other owes a debt roughly equivalent to fifty days' worth of wages for a common laborer. Unfortunately, neither man is able to pay back their debts. They are both in a hopeless situation, even though one is in a hopeless situation ten times more severe than the other. After informing Simon that the fictive creditor absolves both men's debts, Jesus asks which one will love the forgiving creditor more—which one will be more grateful to the gracious creditor. As one would expect, Simon picks the one who owes the creditor more, or the one who receives more grace or favor (Gk. *charis*), and Jesus indicates that Simon has "judged rightly" (7:43).

Jesus then draws obvious connections between the two debtors and the two hosts (Simon the Pharisee and the sinful woman). In particular, Jesus compares the sinful woman to the debtor who cannot repay the debt of five hundred denarii. The creditor in the parable released the debtor from circumstances that would have resulted in lifelong servitude. As a result, the debtor will fervently love the gracious creditor. Similarly, the sinful woman who has been forgiven from her many sins has shown great love to Jesus through her tears, kisses, and ointment (7:47a). She appears to do the very things that the Pharisees and lawyers fail to do. She acknowledges "the justice of God," accepts "God's purposes," and loves God deeply (7:29-30, 47). Jesus informs her that her sins have been forgiven (7:48). Her faith in Christ, her recognition of his identity as one who speaks for God, has saved her (Gk. *sōzō*).

Unfortunately, Simon the Pharisee has shown little love because he does not recognize his own indebtedness or sinfulness (7:47b). Like the Pharisees before him, he cannot recognize God's prophet and refuses to conform to God's purposes (7:29-30). As a result, Jesus assesses Simon the Pharisee's response negatively. Jesus' declaration about Simon the Pharisee is perhaps the most biting, though not the only, critique of the Pharisees in Luke's Gospel. Jesus said the Pharisees and lawyers previously failed to acknowledge God's righteous verdicts (7:29) and consequently "rejected God's purpose for themselves" (7:30). Now, Jesus adds to his portrait of the Pharisees. In short, he says they are not able to love God deeply enough. They cannot love God properly because they do not recognize the magnitude of their own sinfulness, largely because they have rejected the words of God's prophets—John in the past and Jesus, the messianic prophet, in the present.

Jesus and His Followers (8:1-21)

In 8:1-21 Luke begins to focus more of his attention on Jesus' disciples. Through the birth narrative, Jesus' preparation for ministry, and the beginning of Jesus' ministry in Luke 4:14-7:50, Luke has thoroughly established the identity of Jesus. Now in Luke 8–9, Luke will likewise establish the identity of the disciples before Jesus and his followers embark on the journey to Jerusalem beginning in 9:51. In this particular unit (8:1-21), Luke bookends Jesus' parable of the sower (8:4-18) with a story about Jesus' surprising benefactors beforehand (8:1-3) and his true family afterward (8:19-21). The unit's structure highlights the notion that "the good soil" includes those who respond appropriately to Jesus. Regardless of one's inherited earthly status, those who listen to Jesus and respond appropriately become his true followers and family members.

(1) Luke 8:1-3. When Jesus moves on from Nain, Luke indicates that his itinerant travels take him to a variety of cities and villages in Galilee. As he goes, he announces the good news about the arrival of the kingdom of God. In addition, Luke notes that the twelve apostles and some other disciples are traveling with Jesus (8:1). In the process, Luke briefly comments on an extraordinary development in Jesus' ministry. Well beyond the cultural expectations of Jesus' day, many female disciples have joined Jesus' entourage (Bauckham, *Gospel Women*, 112–13). Luke indicates that Jesus has cured them of "evil spirits and infirmities" (8:2). Consequently, they enlist as his disciples out of gratitude and loyalty. They closely resemble the repentant woman who anoints Jesus' feet with ointment in the previous unit (7:36-50).

Altogether, Luke names three specific women: Mary Magdalene, Joanna, and Susanna.

By spotlighting these women, Luke makes a clear statement to his readers that Jesus incorporated women into the inner circle of his disciples. By adding this information about the female disciples as early as 8:1-3, Luke prepares his readers to understand better the angels' post-resurrection comments in 24:6-7 to the women who had followed Jesus all the way from Galilee to Jerusalem (see 23:55–24:10). Significantly, the two angelic figures remind the women about a passion prediction found in 9:18-24 that Jesus spoke exclusively to his disciples, which suggests that the female disciples are present in 9:18-24 as well. Furthermore, Luke goes on to indicate that many women, including the three who are named, financially support Jesus' ministry on an ongoing basis, thereby assisting him in his work (8:2-3) (Garland, *Luke*, 341–42). In short, these female disciples are both recipients and benefactors of Jesus' endeavor to bring good news about the kingdom of God to the people.

Notably, while introducing the female disciples in 8:2-3, Luke not only names Joanna but also makes note of Joanna's spouse (though it is not entirely clear whether her husband is living or deceased at this point). Joanna was the wife of Chuza, who served as a steward for Herod Antipas—likely managing one of Herod's royal estates or serving as his "finance minister" (Bauckham, *Gospel Women*, 137). At the least, Luke's comments about Chuza and Joanna suggest that they had significant interactions with Herod, the tetrarch over their region. If indeed Chuza was a prominent official in Herod's court as the vocabulary suggests (Gk. *epitropos*; Bauckham, *Gospel Women*, 135–36), then Chuza and Joanna would have enjoyed an elevated social status and generous income.

At that point, Joanna's discipleship adds to and interacts with some pre-established themes in Luke's Gospel. For instance, Luke dedicates his Gospel to "Theophilus," who was most likely a person of elevated rank (1:4). Whereas Luke frequently shows Jesus welcoming the downtrodden into his fold of disciples, here we see Jesus likewise welcoming and valuing those of high social rank who follow him and use their resources to further the expansion of the kingdom of God.

In addition, Luke has already shown his readers that conflict exists between Herod Antipas and the work of God in the world. For example, John the Baptist rebuked Herod Antipas (3:18-20), much like the prophet Nathan challenged King David in 2 Sam 12:1-15. Throughout the remainder of Luke and Acts, Luke will continue to demonstrate that rulers like Herod are frequently at odds with Jesus, his mission, and his followers (e.g., 9:7-9;

13:31; 23:11; Acts 4:27; cf. Acts 12:1). Ironically, here in 8:2-3, a person from within Herod's own household is following Jesus. Even more, Joanna, one of Jesus' benefactors, is financially supporting Jesus' ministry with resources that ultimately derive from Herod's own household. In short, the kingdom of God is not only expanding but is also claiming the territory and realm of earthly kingdoms and rulers without those rulers even realizing it.

(2) *Luke 8:4-15.* As noted above, Luke creates a distinct literary unit in 8:1-21 when he places Jesus' parable of the sower (8:4-15) in between Luke's comments about Jesus' female benefactors (8:1-3) and his true family (8:19-21). Consequently, Luke maintains a singular aim for the entire unit that runs from 8:1-21. Luke demonstrates that regardless of one's inherited earthly status, those who listen and respond properly to Jesus become his true followers, the "good soil," and his true family members. As a result, even though the parable of the sower remains largely consistent with the same parable in Mark 4:1-20 and Matt 13:1-17, the context of the parable of the sower in Luke's Gospel accentuates the need to hear and to respond properly to Jesus—no matter one's station in life.

Luke narrates Jesus' parable of the sower briefly and straightforwardly (8:4-8). Jesus, while addressing a crowd, speaks of a sower who spreads seed. In the process, the seed falls on four types of soil, three of which result in negative outcomes and one of which results in a positive outcome. In the first three instances, the seed is thwarted when it lands along the path, on the rock, and among the thorns (8:5-7). The seed produces a miraculous yield of a hundredfold, however, when it lands on the good soil (8:8).

Jesus' disciples, as opposed to the crowd, then ask for further clarity about the meaning of Jesus' parable (8:9). Remarkably, despite the fact that the agricultural situation Jesus describes is a typical scenario for his day, the disciples remain uncertain of the lesson that Jesus is teaching them. They therefore ask Jesus to explain. In response, Jesus begins by stating that he reveals "the secrets of the kingdom of God" to his disciples by means of parables. These same parables, however, prevent the casual members of the crowd from understanding Jesus' spiritual lessons. Jesus proclaims the parable to the entire crowd, but he only gives the explanation of the parable to those who seek understanding.

By way of explanation, Jesus cites Isa 6:9-10. Notably, in Acts 28:26-27, Paul also quotes the entirety of Isa 6:9-10 to the Jewish leaders in Rome in an attempt explain the difference between Jewish believers and Jewish unbelievers (Acts 28:17-29). In essence, Jesus compares his parables to prophetic speech, which at times Israel heeded and at times Israel rejected. The key to comprehending the parable of the sower rests with the receptivity of the listeners toward Jesus. Parables provide either an opportunity for Jesus' audience to dig deeper in order to "find the real meaning" of his proclamation or an opportunity for them "to turn a blind eye and a deaf ear" to Jesus' words (Marshall, *Luke*, 323).

When Luke narrates Jesus' explanation of the parable, he again opts for a straightforward, brief style. The seed is the word of God, which the prophet Jesus proclaims (8:11). The word of God is spread widely to all types of people. The people—represented by the pathway, the rocky soil, and the thorny soil—all share the same fundamental problem. They fail to "hear" or respond properly (8:12-14). In particular, they all hear the word of God, but each group fails to produce fruit (8:14). Consequently, the different types of soil correspond to the different obstacles that prevent each group from listening well and producing the kind of fruit that God desires. For instance, the pathway suffers from demonic distraction and defeat (8:12). The rocky soil responds poorly to harassment and persecution (8:13), and the thorny soil is thwarted by love of riches and life's pleasures (8:14). Regardless, the common denominator for all three groups of people is the failure to hear and to respond properly, which includes producing fruit. Luke alone records Jesus saying that the end result for these groups of people is an absence of belief and salvation (Gk. *sōzō*) (8:12).

Alternatively, the good soil represents those who, no matter their inherited station in life, "hear the word, hold it fast in an honest and good heart, and bear fruit with patient endurance" (8:15). Here, Luke makes sure to capture the fullness of Jesus' point. Those who listen and respond properly are those hear the word of God, treasure it through wholehearted belief, and respond with enduring obedience. These are the ones who—despite the hardships presented by evil, persecution, and austere conditions—opt to follow Jesus anyway as one his disciples.

John the Baptist was the first person in Luke's Gospel to call his fellow Jews to bear the kind of fruit that matched their religious pedigree as God's people (3:8-9). In this pericope also, Jesus indicates that those the good soil represents will distinguish themselves by bearing fruit: "If one keeps Jesus' parable in its original context, one will recognize that most everyone in Jesus' audience thought they were among God's people. Jesus is challenging that notion by insisting that only those who bear fruit, fruit which other parables will define as hearing and obeying his words (see esp. Matt 7:24-27; Luke 6:46-49), can qualify for that label" (Blomberg, *Interpreting the Parables*, 294).

(3) Luke 8:16-18. Without a break in logic, Jesus then seeks to reinforce his fundamental point about proper listening by using the metaphor of a

lamp. A proper response to Jesus' preaching involves a public response (8:18). The people the rocky soil represents in the parable of the sower respond unhelpfully when they encounter testing or trials (8:13). They fold when a public response is required. Similarly, Jesus argues that a lamp is no good if it is hidden, thereby preventing it from shedding light on its surroundings. Proper listening includes hearing, believing, and obeying with endurance in a public manner (8:15-17). Those who respond to Jesus' preaching properly become his disciples and begin to function as a lamp that shines light to others in an obvious manner. Disciples, who function as lamps, will make known to others the secrets of the kingdom of God that have been entrusted to them (8:9-10) (Nolland, *Luke*, 1:392).

(4) Luke 8:19-21. Whereas Mark places Jesus' interaction with his family prior to the parable of the sower (Mark 3:31-35), Luke places it afterward. More important, Luke creates a tightly knit unit in Luke 8:1-21, which emphasizes that regardless of one's sex (8:2), income (8:3), life circumstances (8:11-15), religious heritage (8:15; cf. 3:7-9), or familial relationships (8:19-21), Jesus invests most deeply in those who listen and respond to his proclamation about the kingdom of God. Luke's narration about Jesus' interaction with his family of origin clearly illustrates these ideas, which consequently makes this episode a fitting conclusion to the literary unit that runs from 8:1-21.

Jesus' mother and brothers arrive to visit with Jesus in 8:19. Luke has already introduced Mary as the mother of Jesus (1:26–2:52; Acts 1:14), but he does not provide specific names for Jesus' brothers (cf. Acts 1:14). In Acts, Luke refers to James but not to their fraternal relationship (Acts 12:17; 15:13; 21:18). Mark, on the other hand, names four of Jesus' brothers and mentions some sisters (Mark 6:3). Regardless, in 8:19, Luke simply informs his readers that Jesus' mother and brothers arrive to visit with Jesus.

When Jesus is informed that his biological family has arrived, Jesus radically redefines family for his audience. He now claims that those who hear the word of God and do it are his true "mother and brothers." Those who believe the word of God that Jesus proclaims and obey it are Jesus' closest relatives (8:21; cf. 8:12). Here, Jesus redraws the hierarchy of relationships within the lives of his disciples. Following Jesus' lead, early Christians likewise adopted this familial language to refer to their fellow believers as brothers and sisters.

Jesus' Power over Nature, Demons, Disease, and Death (8:22-56)

Luke has previously demonstrated that Jesus has power over demons, disease, and death, but Luke seeks to reinforce and expand the conversation about Jesus' power in this final literary unit prior to the commissioning of the twelve apostles in 9:1-6. Here, Luke seeks to show that Jesus possesses the divine power of Yahweh. This divine power is most evident when Jesus calms the sea storm and directs an entire army of demons. Following these two miracles are another resuscitation miracle and a healing miracle. All four feats firmly establish Jesus' divine status before the narrative shifts toward his journey to Jerusalem in 9:51.

(1) Luke 8:22-25. When Jesus calms the sea amid a windstorm in 8:22-25, it further reveals the divine power of God at work in Jesus. Matthew (8:23-27) and Mark (4:35-41) also include this dramatic story, though Luke's narration has more in common with Mark than with Matthew.

The pericope begins when Jesus seeks to cross the Sea of Galilee with his disciples (8:22). After Jesus falls asleep, a severe windstorm creates a perilous situation for the boat and the crew (8:23). Luke underscores the severity of the situation when he says that Jesus and the disciples "were in danger." In response, the disciples frantically wake Jesus. They address Jesus using the deferential title of "Master" or "Commander" (Gk. *epistatēs*) (8:24). Jesus, in turn, wakes and immediately rebukes (Gk. *epitamaō*) "the wind and the raging waves." Here Luke employs the same vocabulary that we saw in 4:35, 39, and 41 when Jesus rebuked demons and diseases. Consequently, it appears that Jesus rebukes the evil forces at work in the wind and sea in the same way that he rebukes the demons.

After calming the waters, Jesus then turns to his disciples in a teachable moment and asks, "Where is your faith?" (8:25). It is difficult to know the tone with which Jesus speaks to his disciples at this precise moment. Was it an angry tone or a compassionate one? Regardless, the next time Jesus uses that phrase ("Where is your faith?") with his disciples, Jesus is teaching them in 12:28. In the latter instance, Jesus' question is clearly a rebuke for failing to place their trust in God. As a result, our best evidence suggests that Jesus was irritated with the disciples in 8:25 as well.

Finally, the disciples respond to Jesus with fear and amazement (8:25; cf. 8:35, 37). Fear, in particular, is a common—and indeed the proper—reaction of humans to a manifestation of God in their midst. This can be seen in numerous texts in the OT and NT (see e.g., Gen 26:24; Exod 3:6; Luke 1:12; 2:10; 8:35, 37). Here in Luke 8:25, Jesus has given his disciples reason to believe that they have just witnessed a manifestation of the divine in their midst. For instance, this is the first occurrence in Luke's Gospel in which Jesus demonstrates his power over the natural elements. The import of this miraculous event is that from the beginning of creation, God alone has been the one who commands the wind and sea (Gen 1:6-10). God alone is the one who orders creation. Many portions of the OT then reinforce this belief (see

Jesus' Galilean Ministry

e.g., Ps 89:9; 107:28-30; Job 26:12). In 8:22-25, when Jesus commands the wind and sea as only Yahweh can, it reinforces the unique identity of Jesus as the Son of God (cf. 8:28; also 1:32, 35; 3:22; 4:41). Consequently, the disciples are left asking, "Who then is this, that he commands even the winds and the water, and they obey him?" (8:25). The implied answer is "The Son of God."

(2) Luke 8:26-39. In 8:26-39, Luke narrates the exorcism of the Gerasene demoniac (cf. Matt 8:28-34; Mark 5:1-20). While doing so, Luke continues to construct an impressive four-fold set of miracles in 8:22-56 that demonstrates the breadth of Jesus' power as the Son of God. Obviously, by including this exorcism account Luke seeks to show his readers that Jesus' power greatly exceeds that of the demonic realm.

According to the best manuscripts, just after Jesus and his disciples cross the Sea of Galilee, they arrive in the region of the Gerasenes (8:26). The city associated with the Gerasenes is Gerasa, which is about thirty miles southeast from the Sea of Galilee (or Lake Gennesaret) in the Transjordan. Some confusion exists, however, among other ancient manuscripts about the proper name of the region that Jesus visits. For instance, some manuscripts refer to the region of the Gadarenes, which corresponds to Gadara. Origen even suggested that the Gospel writers were referring to the region of the Gergesenes, which corresponds to Gergesa, a seaside town. Fueling this debate is the pig stampede in 8:33. The story suggests that the swine are somewhat near the lake into which they run. Regardless of the specific city, Luke makes it clear that Jesus is on the east side of the Sea of Galilee, which would have been predominantly populated by Gentiles, and that the man and the herd of pigs were in the countryside well outside the city where the townspeople lived (see e.g., Craig Evans, *Luke*, 137–38).

As soon as Jesus arrives on the east side of the Sea of Galilee, he is met by a demon-possessed man from Gerasa. Luke paints a horrific portrait of the torment that this man has long endured as a result of his demon possession (8:27, 29). In addition to having no clothes and no home, the man lives among the tombs, which makes him perpetually unclean in the eyes of the Jews (e.g., Num 19:11, 16). Jesus then commands the evil spirits to come out of the man (8:29). They respond by causing the man to fall down before Jesus and shout, "What have you to do with me, Jesus, Son of the Most High God? I beg you, do not torment me" (8:29). This reaction echoes a variety of previous passages in Luke's Gospel. For instance, God's own voice first identifies Jesus as God's son at the baptism (3:21-22). Additionally, Luke narrates Jesus' first exorcism in 4:31-37, where the demons also identify Jesus as "the Holy One of God" (4:34). In the previous story, Jesus calms the sea as only

God can do (8:24-25). Finally, here in 8:29 the demons once again recognize Jesus as "the Son of the Most High God." As a result, Luke further reinforces Jesus' unique identity and divine power while narrating Jesus' encounter with the Gerasene demoniac.

At that point, Jesus asks the Gerasene man his name, and the man answers, "Legion," a name that refers to the many demons that possess him. The implications of the man's response are significant. Previously, Jesus exorcised multiple demons from one man (4:31-37) and seven demons from Mary Magdalene (8:2), but now the number of demons is astronomically large. The word "legion" technically refers to a division of the Roman army numbering between four and six thousand soldiers. In essence, here in 8:26-39, Luke depicts Jesus as being in a showdown with an army of demons. Even when the ratio is six thousand to one, however, the demons are no match for Jesus. His divine power as the Son of God is so great that no demonic force can ever defeat him.

Admitting defeat, the demons beg Jesus a second time in 8:31-32. They ask that he not send them into the abyss. Numerous Jewish and Christian texts around the time of Jesus spoke of the expectation that God would eternally banish the demons to a bottomless abyss at the final judgment (see e.g., Rev 9:1-11; 11:7; 17:8; 20:1-3; *1 En.* 16.1; *Jub.* 10.5-11) (Craig Evans, *Luke*, 137). The fact that Jesus does not send them directly to the abyss suggests that it is not yet time for the final judgment. Nevertheless, the outcome of the demons in this story clearly foreshadows what the future holds for them. Jesus sends the army of demons into a large herd of swine, which were deemed unclean for the Jews (Lev 11:7; Deut 14:8) but not for the Gentiles who populated this region. Immediately, the demons control the herd of pigs as evidenced by the destructive outcome (8:33).

After the swineherds report the event to the people throughout the region, many come and investigate (8:34-35). Notably, they find the formerly possessed man "sitting at the feet of Jesus, clothed and in his right mind" (8:35). Luke now depicts the man as one who wants to be a disciple of Jesus. Later, Luke will depict Mary (10:39) and Saul (Acts 22:3) in the same manner—sitting at the feet of their teacher. The eyewitnesses then relay to the Gerasene people how Jesus has healed, or saved (Gk. *sōzō*), the man from the demons. The people respond with great fear (8:35, 37) just as the disciples had done when Jesus calmed the sea storm (8:25). As noted in the previous pericope, fear is the typical response in the biblical texts to a manifestation of God's power. The people are so afraid that they ask Jesus to leave their region. Due to this unforgettable display of divine power, the people desire to rid themselves of Jesus. Of course, after the destruction of a large

Jesus' Galilean Ministry

herd of swine, it is also clear that Jesus and his power had a negative impact on their local economy.

Jesus cooperates with the request of the Gerasenes. He gets into the boat in order to return to Galilee (8:37). Before he departs, however, the formerly possessed man begs (Gk. *deomai*) Jesus (8:38), just as the demons had initially begged (Gk. *deomai*) Jesus (8:28). The demons begged Jesus not to torment them. The healed man begs that he might be with Jesus, just like the other disciples (8:38; cf. 8:1). Surprisingly, instead of calling this man to follow him as he did with Peter, James, and John (5:1-11), Jesus commands the former demoniac to return to his home in a predominantly Gentile region (8:39). Furthermore, Jesus instructs him to declare "how much God has done" for him. The man obeys by proclaiming throughout Gerasa "how much Jesus has done" for him (8:39).

Luke accomplishes at least two objectives by means of the ending of this pericope. First, Jesus' instructions to the former demoniac, who lived in a Gentile region, lays additional groundwork for the Gentile mission that begins in Acts 10. Between the centurion who had faith in 7:1-10 and the restored demoniac who desires to be a disciple in 8:26-39, Luke has highlighted the embryonic role of two Gentiles within his Gospel. While these two Gentiles who demonstrate their faith in Jesus do not directly follow Jesus and are not fully incorporated into Jesus' ministry, both foreshadow the inclusion of the Gentiles that will take place after Jesus' resurrection and ascension. Most important, Jesus' receptivity to both men helps to provide the warrant that will be needed later to justify the declaration of God's favor upon both Jews and Gentiles who believe in Jesus and respond appropriately.

Second, Luke further intertwines the work of God and Jesus by means of the conclusion to this encounter. After Jesus orders the demons to depart, thereby healing (or saving) the man (8:36), Jesus then commands the man to declare what "God had done" (8:39). In response, the man obeys, but as he does so he declares what "Jesus had done" (8:39). In effect, Jesus' accomplishments are God's accomplishments and vice versa. Both God and Jesus, as the Son of God (8:28), bring about salvation and restoration for humanity. Luke wants his readers to realize that the work of God and the work of Jesus are one and the same. They cannot ultimately be separated.

(3) *Luke 8:40-56.* To complete the set of four miracles in 8:22-56 that climactically illustrate Jesus' power over all realms as well as his status as the Son of God, Luke narrates the last two miracles in a parallel fashion. Mark frequently intertwines two narratives. In this instance, Luke follows his source and retains Mark's sandwiching effect. In this intercalation, Jesus heals a woman who has been bleeding for twelve years (8:42b-48), and he

raises a twelve-year-old girl from the dead (8:40-42a, 49-56). The story of the bleeding woman is imbedded in the story of the twelve-year-old girl. Luke desires his readers to read and interpret the stories together.

In the process, Luke's readers can discern a variety of commonalities between the two miracles, as well as some similarities with the previous two miracles. For instance, Luke continues to rely heavily on theological terms like faith or belief (Gk. *pistis*) to describe an appropriate human response to Jesus (8:48, 50) and terms like saved or salvation (Gk. *sōzō, sōtēria*) to describe how Jesus aids the afflicted (8:48, 50). Furthermore, Jesus continues to disregard the Jewish purity laws as we saw in the previous unit (8:26-39). Both the bleeding woman (Lev 15:25-32) and the dead girl would have been considered unclean (Culpepper, "Luke," 9:191). Nevertheless, Jesus comes into contact with both of them without worrying whether he himself will become unclean.

Additionally, Jesus continues to show compassion for both those of high status (8:41; cf. 8:2-3) and those of low status (8:43; cf. 8:26-39), both the clean and the unclean. On the one hand, Jairus provides leadership for the worshiping community. On the other, the woman is prevented from participating in worship whatsoever due to her flow of blood. Jesus responds empathetically to both. While Jesus' compassion for the poor and disenfranchised sets him apart from most in his day, he does not disregard the pleas coming from the well respected in his day such as Jairus. Finally, Jesus' mighty acts continue to go well beyond mortal capabilities. Rather, Luke continues to exhibit Jesus' divine power by means of the miracles that he is performing.

In the narrative itself, when Jesus traverses the Sea of Galilee from the Transjordan back to Galilee, a large crowd welcomes him (8:40). In particular, Jairus, the leader of the synagogue, approaches him, falls down before him, and begs Jesus to come to his house and heal his only daughter who is dying (8:41-42). Notably, aspects of Jairus's actions may remind Luke's readers either of people whom this Gospel has portrayed positively—the demoniac who falls down before Jesus (8:28, 38) or the woman whose only son dies (7:11-17)—or of those whom the Gospel has portrayed negatively—the inhospitable Pharisee who invites Jesus to his home (7:36-50). Here, however, Luke clearly portrays Jairus in a positive manner. Like the Roman centurion who has faith in Jesus' ability to heal (7:1-10), Jairus's actions also reveal his faith. He fully trusts that Jesus can help his twelve-year-old daughter who is dying.

At that point, Luke temporarily leaves the narrative about Jairus and his daughter hanging in midair. In the meantime, Luke turns his readers'

Jesus' Galilean Ministry

attention to a woman who has had a flow of blood for twelve years—a possible reference to an atypical menstrual cycle (8:42b-43a). Consequently, she has been considered ritually unclean and unable to worship God with the rest of the people for over a decade. Due to her state of uncleanness, she has been sequestered in a manner that prevents her from physically touching others. Otherwise, they also will be rendered unclean (Lev 15:25-32). The flow of blood has further victimized this woman because she has spent all her money on physicians. Yet none of them have been able to heal her (8:43b).

Attempting to keep her actions a secret, she stealthily touches the fringe of Jesus' clothing, and immediately she is healed (8:44, 47). Jesus, sensing that the power of the Holy Spirit has again been at work through him, asks who touched him (8:45-46; cf. 3:22). In a respectful manner, Peter addresses Jesus as Master and reminds him of his crowded context (8:45; cf. 8:24). At that point, however, the woman realizes that she cannot keep her desperate actions a secret any longer. Akin to Jairus, she fearfully falls at Jesus' feet, publicly admits that she touched him, and testifies that touching Jesus immediately healed her (8:47).

Luke builds a moment of suspense for his readers. The unclean woman has touched Jesus, which should render Jesus unclean according to the Jewish ritual laws. Moreover, when Jesus inquires about who touched him, the woman fearfully confesses. Perhaps Luke's first readers wondered if Jesus might respond with anger. Instead, Jesus addresses her as "Daughter," thereby reaffirming her status as a Jewish woman among God's people. His address places her back among the people from whom she has been separated. Finally, he claims that her faith has healed or saved her (Gk. *sōzō*), and he tells her to "go in peace" (8:48).

Luke shows his readers that God's power is at work in Jesus to redeem and to save God's people—collectively and individually. What her money cannot buy and what no human can do, not even multiple physicians, Jesus does. Jesus does not worry about her uncleanness contaminating him. As Son of God (8:28), he has the power to heal her disease, to make her clean, to restore her to her community, and to grant a life of peace to her. In short, Jesus saves this woman from her life of torment and publicly affirms her spiritual identity in the presence of a great crowd.

At that point, Luke resumes the story of Jairus and his dying daughter. Unfortunately, while Jesus' attention is focused on the bleeding woman, Jairus's daughter dies (8:49). In response, Jesus commands Jairus just as Jesus has commanded the storm (8:24), the demons (8:29), the former demoniac (8:39), and soon Jairus's daughter (8:54). He commands Jairus not to fear, but rather to believe or have faith (Gk. *pistis*). Jesus announces that Jairus's daughter will be saved or rescued (Gk. *sōzō*) just as the hemorrhaging woman has been rescued (8:50).

From that point on, Jesus' actions again resemble those of the great prophets, Elijah (1 Kgs 17:17-24) and Elisha (2 Kgs 4:32-37). Just as he raised the widow's only son from the dead in 7:11-17, so also Jesus will raise Jairus's only daughter from the dead in 8:51-56. When Jesus arrives at the home, the grieving has already begun (8:52). Jesus tells those gathered that the girl is sleeping, a term that can refer to literal sleep or death in antiquity (cf. 1 Thess 4:13). The mourners laugh at Jesus, assuming he is referring to literal sleep. Their laughter, however, reinforces the main point, which is that the girl has died (8:52-53). In a private gathering of Peter, James, and John along with the girl's parents, Jesus commands the dead girl to get up. Consequently, her spirit returns to her. Jesus has resurrected her. In addition, the girl eats food, which verifies that she is a human being as opposed to a vision or an angel (cf. 24:36-43; *Tob.* 12:19) and that she is fully alive in her body and not only her spirit (8:54). Notably, Jesus, who publicly announced the healing of the hemorrhaging woman to the crowds in 8:48, here seeks to keep this resurrection of the dead girl a secret. From Luke's perspective, raising her from the dead foreshadows Jesus' own resurrection, but it is not yet time for Jesus to talk openly about the events that will occur at the end of his life.

In sum, Luke has impressively highlighted the divine power of Jesus as the Son of God in 8:22-56. Before Jesus' first commissioning of the apostles in 9:1-6, Luke has sought to summarize definitively Jesus' authority over nature (8:22-25), the demonic realm (8:26-39), disease (8:42b-48), and death (8:40-42a, 49-56). Moreover, Jesus possesses this authority because he is "the Son of the Most High God" (8:28). He brings salvation, restoration, and wholeness to those who exhibit faith. The Spirit of God is at work in him to bring about God's kingdom on earth.

Commissioning the Twelve (9:1-9)

Throughout the second large division in Luke's Gospel (Luke 4:14–9:50), Luke has sought to establish the identity, character, message, and power of Jesus. As we near the end of this narrative unit, Luke continues to enhance our understanding of Jesus while also beginning to shift the reader's focus toward the disciples, whose character development will provide the focus in the third narrative division of Luke's Gospel (9:51–19:27). Thus, in Luke 9:1–50 Luke reveals highly important information about the identity and mission of both Jesus and his disciples. This dual emphasis on both Jesus and

Jesus' Galilean Ministry

the disciples can easily be observed in Luke 9:1-6, the commissioning of the twelve apostles.

(1) Luke 9:1-6. We first learn of Jesus' authority and power at the beginning of Luke's Gospel. The birth narrative discloses Jesus' divine origins (ch. 1–2), and God's declaration about Jesus at the baptism (3:21-22) reveals Jesus' authority and power. Then in the course of his public ministry (4–8), Luke chronicles events that demonstrate Jesus' power over every realm—nature, demons, disease, and death. Now, however, we learn something remarkable about Jesus. Not only does Jesus possess authority and power, but we see that Jesus is capable of giving his authority and power over demons and diseases to his disciples (9:1). It is one thing to possess power, but Luke shows his readers that Jesus has ultimate command of his power to the point that he is able to share it with his followers at will. God's Spirit empowers Jesus, and now Jesus empowers his disciples.

Similarly, we learn a great deal about the identity and work of the twelve apostles in Luke 9:1-6. Notably, Jesus empowers them and commissions them to do the same types of things that Jesus himself has already been doing. Jesus commissions them to bring wholeness to people's lives through exorcisms and healings, and Jesus tells them to proclaim the kingdom of God (9:1-2). These twin tasks of restoring wholeness and preaching the kingdom are the same prophetic tasks that we see Jesus repeatedly engage in throughout Luke 4–9. Robert Tannehill further claims that these twin activities of healing and exorcism are "indications of the reign of God" breaking in (*Luke*, 151). In essence, the apostles' miraculous actions substantiate their message about the arrival of the kingdom of God.

In the process, Jesus prepares the apostles for rejection (9:5). From the beginning, Jesus discloses that his apostles will encounter the same types of responses that he himself has received. Nevertheless, despite this gloomy forecast, Jesus requires his disciples to depend on the hospitality of potential guests as they go about their mission. He requires them to travel as typical first-century Mediterranean people would have done. Jesus provides them with power and authority over demons and diseases (9:1), but he does not supply them with physical provisions. He does not grant them financial or provisional independence from those to whom they will minister. Instead, Jesus' instructions mean that the apostles will both minister to others and be dependent on others. As they set out with the knowledge that Jesus has empowered them to preach God's kingdom and to heal the afflicted, they cannot go with a sense of superiority or preeminence over those to whom they are sent given that they will simultaneously be begging for food from those same people (Arterbury, "Entertaining Angels: Hospitality in Luke and Acts," 20–26).

(2) Luke 9:7-9. After embarking, Luke indicates that the apostles faithfully carry out Jesus' commission (9:6). Their faithfulness in carrying out Jesus' ministry of preaching the kingdom and healing the afflicted creates such a widespread commotion that even Herod, the tetrarch over Galilee and Perea, hears about it. Yet Herod is not sure what to make of the reports he receives. Noticeably, however, Herod's questions center on Jesus rather than the disciples (9:7-9). Herod asks, "Who is this?"—the same question that has been voiced about Jesus in Luke 5:21, 7:49, and 8:25.

The activities being reported to Herod remind him of John the Baptist's ministry. John, Jesus, and now the apostles all resemble the great prophets from the OT. For example, Elijah and Elisha both perform miracles and proclaim God's word. Consequently, some around Herod suggest that Elijah, who never died but instead rode a chariot directly to heaven, has returned (9:7-8). Others suggest to Herod that this new prophetic teacher (Jesus) may be John or another ancient prophet who has been raised from the dead.

While Luke does not narrate the event like Mark does (Mark 6:17-29), Luke nevertheless informs his readers that Herod previously beheaded John (9:9; cf. 3:18-20; 7:18-23). Notably, if Luke had a copy of Mark as most scholars believe, it means that Luke intentionally omitted Mark's narration of John's death from his Gospel. Perhaps Luke thought the story about John's death would distract from the narrative's current focus on Jesus and his disciples; or perhaps Luke elected to maintain a singular focus on the martyrdom of Jesus in his writings. For instance, over the course of the first three chapters of this Gospel, Luke deliberately compares John and Jesus in a parallel format using an ancient rhetorical technique known as *synkrisis*. Luke shows how John and Jesus are similar while also demonstrating how Jesus is far greater than John. Luke compares the announcement of their births, the prophecies about their future ministries, their births, and even their time spent in the wilderness. Yet Luke does nothing more than allude to John's tragic death whereas he makes Jesus' death his central theme for the last division of this book. Similarly, it should be noted that Luke likewise does not narrate the death of Peter or Paul in the book of Acts (though debate exists about whether Luke knew of their deaths). Ultimately, we can see that Luke develops a unique focus on Jesus' death in the sweep of God's salvation history as depicted by the books of Luke and Acts.

Feeding the Five Thousand (9:10-17)

As they traveled, the apostles proclaimed the arrival of God's kingdom, healed diseases, and exorcized demons. Many of those whom their ministry impacted have followed them to Bethsaida where the apostles reunite with Jesus. Moreover, Luke once again shows us that the work of the apostles is simply an outgrowth of the work of Jesus. Notice Jesus' response to the crowds in Luke 9:11. He speaks to the crowds about the kingdom of God, and he heals those in need—the same two activities that Jesus commissioned the apostles to do in Luke 9:2.

Jesus' response to the crowds in Luke 9:10-17, however, differs significantly from that of the apostles. When Jesus commissioned his disciples, he required them to be dependent on the hospitality of gracious hosts as they traveled (9:3-15). In Bethsaida, the tables have turned. Jesus not only serves as teacher and healer to the crowds but also serves as gracious host to them (Tannehill, *Luke*, 154). We first catch a glimpse of his role as host in 9:11 when he welcomes the crowds, but Jesus' hospitality is most clearly seen when the day draws to a close (9:12). The apostles encourage Jesus to dismiss the multitude that includes five thousand men (9:14). The disciples believe the multitude needs to disperse so that the crowds can seek hospitality among various hosts throughout the region.

Jesus has other plans. He opts to meet the needs of this throng of people. Interestingly, however, he begins by commanding his apostles to care for the enormous crowd. In essence, the Lukan feeding of the five thousand narrates an alternative type of apostolic commissioning. With an emphatic second-person plural pronoun, Jesus says, "*You* give them something to eat" (9:13). Of course, the disciples object while noting that their resources are woefully insufficient. They only have five loaves of bread and two fish. Yet just as Jesus had empowered his apostles to carry out his ministry and message in 9:1-2, here again Jesus enables his apostles to feed the people. Just as Elijah miraculously supplied food for the widow at Zarephath (1 Kgs 17:8-16) and Elisha fed a hundred men with twenty loaves (2 Kgs 4:42-44), so also Jesus miraculously multiplies the loaves and fish like a great prophet. The difference being, of course, that Jesus feeds far more people with even fewer provisions.

Through this scene, Luke places the apostles in both a positive and negative light. On the one hand, the apostles do what Jesus tells them, and the multitude is fed. On the other hand, the apostles appear to possess severely limited understanding and faith. They just returned from a journey in which they healed diseases and exorcized demons, but now it does not occur to them that they—let alone Jesus—can feed a multitude. As a result, the feeding of the five thousand serves as another important teaching moment for the apostles. They are learning how Jesus wants to utilize them as an extension of his own ministry and message, but this work can only take place under the power and authority of Jesus. Notably, at the end of the meal, the apostles collect twelve baskets of leftovers. In essence, each apostle now has a basket with food to offer those in need (Tannehill, *Luke*, 155).

Finally, it is important to notice that this pericope simultaneously points backward and forward to rich theological motifs. On one hand, the feeding of the five thousand shares numerous overtones with typical Jewish expectations about the banquet the Messiah will host upon his arrival. The vision of the long-awaited messianic banquet includes an abundant supply of food in which everyone has more than enough to eat (e.g., Isa 25:6-10a; *1 En.* 60.24; Luke 13:29). On the other hand, Jesus' words and actions point forward. In Luke 9:16 Jesus takes the loaves and fish, looks up to heaven, blesses and breaks them, and gives them to the disciples. The same set of actions and the same vocabulary reemerge at the Last Supper (22:19) and during Jesus' encounter with the men on the road to Emmaus (24:30). In addition, the echo of Jesus' actions with the bread and loaves even carries over to the communal meals of the Christians in the book of Acts (e.g., Acts 2:42, 46; 4:34).

Peter's Confession and Jesus' Transfiguration (9:18-36)

(1) Luke 9:18-20. Among the Gospel writers, only Luke tells us that Jesus was praying just before he questions his disciples about his identity in 9:18-20. As we have seen before in this Gospel, Luke greatly accentuates the role and the importance of prayer. In addition, we have seen a strong correlation between prayer and revelation (e.g., 3:22-23; 6:12-16). Up to this point when Jesus prays, he appears to gain greater clarity about the Father's will. In this section, though, we see that prayer not only leads to greater clarity about God's will for Jesus but also prepares Jesus' disciples for God's revelation (Crump, *Jesus the Intercessor*, 21). For example, up to this point, Luke has exclusively portrayed Jesus as praying alone. In 9:18 Jesus again prays by himself, but for the first time his disciples are near him.

Even more important, for the first time in this Gospel a disciple recognizes Jesus as "the Messiah of God" or God's "anointed one" (Gk. *christos*) (9:20; cf. Acts 2:36, 38). Peter is the first person in Luke's Gospel to attribute the title of Messiah or Christ to Jesus. The angel of the Lord proclaims it in 2:11. Luke as the narrator informs his readers that Jesus is the Christ in 2:26, and the demons know Jesus is the Christ in 4:41. Peter, however, is the first person in the story to understand this point, and it comes directly after

Luke refers to Jesus' time of prayer in the presence of the disciples. In short, prayer provides the doorway for what appears to be God's revelation (cf. Matt 16:17), which enables Peter to proclaim that Jesus is the Messiah.

Furthermore, unlike Mark's Gospel where the multiplication of the loaves takes place in Mark 6:30-44 and Peter's great confession takes place in Mark 8:27–9:1, Luke does not separate these two events. Rather Luke places the feeding of the five thousand (9:10-17) back to back with Peter's identification of Jesus as God's Messiah (9:18-27). As a result, a couple of observations are in order. First, Luke crafts his narrative so that overt questions about Jesus' identity appear both directly before and after the miraculous feeding of the multitude in 9:10-17. Herod raises questions about Jesus' identity in 9:7-9, and Jesus asks his disciples questions about his identity in 9:18-20. This arrangement suggests that Luke wants his readers to pay special attention to the questions about Jesus' identity throughout Luke 9:7-27.

Second, by placing the two stories back to back, Luke may provide his readers with an explanation for Peter's newfound awareness about the identity of Jesus. Luke's unique chronology forces us to ask whether Jesus' actions at the feeding of the five thousand provide the catalyst for Peter's fresh enlightenment. In other words, while Peter's understanding of Jesus' identity as God's anointed one was likely growing from their first encounter, Luke frames 9:7-27 in such a way that we must ask whether the multiplication of the loaves provides Peter with a clarifying moment. Robert Tannehill argues that it does, and he writes, "Only when understood as an anticipation of the eschatological banquet would this meal lead to the conclusion that Jesus is the Messiah" (*Luke*, 154). Jesus supplies abundant provisions in a context of scarcity. In the process, he provides a foretaste of what faithful Jews had long anticipated—a future golden age of abundance that God's Messiah would introduce.

(2) Luke 9:21-27. Of course, Jesus says much more about his own identity in the subsequent discussion. Immediately after Peter correctly identifies Jesus as the Christ (or Messiah), Jesus forbids the disciples from telling anyone. Jesus first opts to define the role of the Messiah properly before he allows his disciples to speak about it. In particular, Jesus teaches the disciples that he must "undergo great suffering, and be rejected by the elders, chief priests, and scribes, and be killed, and on the third day be raised" (9:22). Up to this point in Luke's Gospel, we have learned a great deal about Jesus. We learned in 2:30-32 that he would bring salvation to both the Jews and the Gentiles. We learned in 4:18 that he is the herald of the good news to the poor. We learned that he is a great prophet. Now, however, Jesus adds the necessity (Gk. *dei*) of his suffering. Robert Brawley argues that Luke designed

"a progressive discovery" in his Gospel of what it means for Jesus to be God's Messiah (Brawley, *Centering on God*, 44–51). Jesus' words in 9:23-27 add significantly to that discovery process. We learn that any conception of Jesus as the Messiah that fails to incorporate suffering into the role of the Messiah will be insufficient. At the end of the Gospel, on the road to Emmaus, Jesus will once again openly teach about his role as the Messiah (or Christ), but when he does so he again intimately connects the title of Messiah with suffering (24:26, 46; cf. Acts 3:18).

Unlike Matthew and Mark, Luke does not include Peter's rebuke of Jesus or Jesus' rebuke of Peter (9:21-22; cf. Matt 16:22-23, Mark 8:32-33). Rather, Luke's focus remains exclusively on Jesus' radical call of discipleship to his followers. If anyone elects to follow Jesus, who himself must suffer (9:21-22), then she or he should anticipate the real possibility that she or he will also suffer (9:23). Even more, Jesus' foreboding words are intensely personal. Jesus employs singular pronouns. He is speaking directly to each of his disciples as individuals. Each hearer will need to set his or her course. No one else can do it for them. Notably, though, this path of self-denial and suffering is not a one-time decision in Luke's Gospel. Rather, the decision to "take up one's cross" must be made on a daily basis (9:23).

(3) *Luke 9:28-36.* Much like Moses' transcendent encounter with Yahweh on Mount Sinai (see esp. Exod 24:12-18; 34:29-35), Jesus likewise encounters the presence of God on a mountain in Galilee, and his appearance is temporarily altered (9:29). Apart from other indicators, Luke assures his readers of God's presence when God speaks directly to the disciples who accompany Jesus—Peter, James, and John (9:35). Notably, we only hear the voice of God twice in Luke's Gospel. God speaks to Jesus at the baptism in 3:22, and now God speaks directly to these disciples at the transfiguration. Previously, at the baptism, God elected to provide Jesus with unequivocal clarity about God's approval and Jesus' identity and empowerment just before Jesus began his ministry (3:21-22). Now, at the transfiguration, God communicates these same sentiments about Jesus to the disciples just before Jesus' journey to Jerusalem.

The reason behind God's decision to speak directly to the disciples at this particular point in time is perhaps less clear. Why does God opt to intervene at this moment as opposed to an earlier point or a later one? The answer appears to be found in the previous section (9:18-27). For the first time, a human has declared Jesus to be God's Messiah (9:20). Yet Jesus orders his disciples not to tell anyone and immediately begins to describe the necessity (Gk. *dei*) of his suffering (9:21-22). Counter to common expectations in a first-century Jewish context, Jesus shockingly claims that the Messiah has been anointed to suffer. God then speaks directly to the disciples in the next scene and commands them to "listen" to Jesus (9:35). In essence, God endorses the astonishing teaching of Jesus (9:21-22) and directs the disciples to adopt Jesus' teaching as well (9:35). The disciples will experience confusion and lapses at other points in Luke and Acts, but at least for Luke's readers God's directive prevents any confusion on this fundamental point—that it is necessary for Jesus, the Messiah, to suffer (9:22).

Among the Gospel writers, Luke alone points out the importance of prayer at Jesus' transfiguration. For instance, in 9:28-29 Luke twice emphasizes that Peter, James, and John are praying. In the process, Luke continues to link prayer with God's revelation. Luke has now placed two pericopes back to back (Peter's confession in 9:18-20 and the transfiguration in 9:28-36) in which prayer leads to increased insight about Jesus' role in God's overarching redemptive work in the world. Furthermore, both Moses and Elijah appear and converse with Jesus on this illuminating occasion. In part, they function as witnesses to and representatives of God's salvific work prior to the time of Jesus. In particular, both Moses and Elijah served as God's primary spokesperson at critical points in salvation history as the Law and the Prophets chronicle. As a result, we begin to observe a strong correlation in Luke's writings between Scripture, prayer, and God's revelation of God's own salvific plan (cf. Luke 24:27-32; 24:44-47; Acts 10:1-48). Luke also informs us that Moses and Elijah primarily speak with Jesus about his forthcoming departure (or his "exodus") in Jerusalem. Echoing the departure of the Hebrews from Egypt, the conversation in Luke 9:30-31 foreshadows Jesus' crucifixion, resurrection, and ascension.

Luke is not only the sole author who tells us that the disciples are praying prior to Jesus' transfiguration (9:28-29) but also the only Gospel writer who tells us that Peter, James, and John fall asleep at the transfiguration (9:32). Literally, they "had been weighed down by sleep." As a result, it is not until they are "fully awake" that they can behold Jesus' glory along with Moses and Elijah. In many respects, the Lukan transfiguration scene foreshadows the future struggle of the disciples at the Mount of Olives in 22:39-46. In both texts the disciples are praying just prior to a pivotal event in Jesus' life and ministry, and in both texts falling asleep has a negative connotation. Apart from physical rest, Luke frequently refers to falling asleep at the wrong time as a type of spiritual laxity in Luke and Acts (e.g., Acts 20:7-12; Arterbury, "The Downfall of Eutychus," 201–21). Moreover, Jesus frequently instructs his disciples to stay awake and alert (12:35-38; 21:34-36). Perhaps the greatest temptation the disciples face throughout Luke and Acts is not the temptation to apostatize but rather the temptation to fall asleep. Here in the Lukan transfiguration scene, Luke establishes two distinct paths for the disciples (9:32). They must choose between sleep and wakefulness. They only recognize and experience God's revelation and the glory of Jesus when they are fully awake.

The Disciples' Inadequacies (9:37-50)

In this concluding section of the second major division in Luke's Gospel, which chronicles Jesus' ministry in Galilee (4:14–9:50), Luke accentuates the shortcomings of the disciples. While Luke will ultimately illustrate the growth of Jesus' disciples over the narrative sweep of Luke and Acts, at this point their weaknesses outweigh their strengths. In fairly brief fashion, Luke walks us through three consecutive types of failures to which the disciples are still susceptible in 9:37-50. They fail to exorcise a demon (9:37-43a), they fail to understand Jesus' passion prediction (9:44-45), and they desire the wrong things like honor and power (9:46-50). Despite witnessing the mighty works and teachings of Jesus on a daily basis during his Galilean ministry, the disciples' faith and spiritual maturity remain in their infancy. Jesus' words and miraculous deeds alone are not potent enough to transform these flawed human beings. Their maladies will require an even greater remedy.

First, in Luke 9:37-43a, the weak and confused disciples are unable to exorcise a demon from a young boy. Previously, Jesus commissioned the disciples and gave them power over demons (9:1). Now, however, Luke shows us that the disciples are helpless without Jesus' empowerment. Just as Moses encounters confusion and faithlessness among the Hebrew people when he descends from Mount Sinai in Exod 32:15-24, so also Jesus descends from the mountain after the transfiguration and hears of his disciples' failures (9:37-41). Without their leader, the disciples are impotent. Subsequently, Jesus sends for the young boy afflicted by the demon, rebukes the unclean spirit, heals him, and returns him to his father. What was an impossible undertaking for the disciples now appears as little more than a menial task for Jesus. In the end, all are astounded "at the greatness of God" as revealed in Jesus' actions (9:43a).

Second, the disciples fail to understand Jesus' forecast about his impending suffering and death. Jesus predicts his suffering and death on three occasions in Luke's Gospel (9:22; 9:44; 18:31-33). Luke 9:44 represents the second of these passion predictions. According to Luke, the disciples cannot perceive the meaning of Jesus' prophecies about his death until it is revealed to them (9:45; 24:16), and the first glimpses of that understanding do not surface among the disciples until two of them encounter Jesus after the resurrection on the road to Emmaus (24:32).

Finally, Luke shows us that at this point in time the disciples still aim for the wrong goals and objectives. For example, Jesus' disciples argue among themselves "as to which one of them is the greatest" (9:46). The disciples are steeped in an honor versus shame culture. Not surprisingly, Jesus' disciples want to be praised and esteemed by their contemporaries. Jesus, however, provides a different example for his followers. He embraces a small child as an object lesson for his embryonic pupils. In antiquity, children possessed little, if any, honor, authority, or status (Betsworth, *Children*, 123–24). Despite that cultural norm, Jesus claims that even a child who represents Jesus, or associates herself with Jesus, should be received, welcomed, and cared for as if Jesus or God the Father had just approached (9:48) (Fitzmyer, *Luke*, 1:817). Cultural status provides no assistance when one seeks to understand how God measures greatness among humans. The only criterion that matters is whether one recognizes Jesus' identity as the Son of God and responds accordingly.

Immediately thereafter, John's response in 9:49-50 both reinforces Jesus' previous words from 9:48 and portrays the disciples as people who cannot yet understand Jesus' teaching. John recalls when he and some fellow disciples sought to stop someone who was doing the work of Jesus (e.g., expelling demons) and identifying with Jesus. He says, "we saw someone casting out demons in your name" (9:49). Contrary to what Jesus just said about a child who comes in the name of Jesus, here the disciples disregard a disciple whom they have never met. In essence, John suggests that this unknown disciple does not have the proper credentials or the desired status because he does not travel with Jesus and the twelve. Jesus' response, however, echoes his previous comment about children in 9:48. He says, "whoever is not against you is for you" (9:50). Despite saying something that will sound different in 11:23, here John has already identified the exorcist as one who works in Jesus' name (9:49). As a result, Jesus is teaching his disciples to accept, welcome, care for, and esteem other disciples who likewise associate themselves with the name of Jesus regardless of their cultural status or pedigree.

Jesus' Journey to Jerusalem

Luke 9:51–19:44

Introduction

Luke elongates and carefully crafts the pivotal middle section of his Gospel to resemble the great epics that were so familiar to his Greco-Roman readers (e.g., Homer's *Odyssey* and Virgil's *Aeneid*). Akin to Odysseus and Aeneas, Jesus embarks on a journey in 9:51 from Galilee to Jerusalem that will fulfill his destiny and forever shape the identity of his followers. A journey motif likewise dominates the book of Acts as Luke traces the movement of the gospel and the spread of Christianity from Jerusalem to Rome.

Compared to Mark, Luke greatly supplements and enhances this relatively short period of Jesus' life and dedicates nine and a half chapters to Jesus' journey to Jerusalem. From a source-critical perspective, many argue that Luke drew primarily upon a sayings source (Q or Matthew) as well as special Lukan material (L) when he augmented the brief travel narrative that he inherited from Mark. Regardless, in his Gospel, Luke has greatly accentuated the literary emphasis on Jesus' journey toward Jerusalem by dedicating one third of his Gospel to this period in Jesus' life. Indeed, Luke has so emphasized Jesus' journey to Jerusalem that he makes it "the central part" of his Gospel (Koester, *Ancient Christian Gospels*, 343).

Despite repeated rejection, Jesus teaches and transforms his disciples in the midst of the journey. Rather than primarily seeking to establish Jesus' identity, which the first nine chapters of Luke's Gospel have largely accomplished, the journey narrative more clearly establishes the identity of those who wish to follow Jesus. Complete devotion to God, mercy, prayer, and generous stewardship are just a few of the characteristics of Jesus' true disciples as evidenced by his tutoring of the disciples while journeying from Luke 9:51–19:44. The disciples must be formed and prepared before they arrive in Jerusalem. Jesus must shape them prior to his death. In the end, careful readers may realize that the author likewise invites all readers of this

Gospel to journey with Jesus on a similar, formative trek while reading Luke 9:51–19:44.

Rejected by Samaritans (9:51-62)

Similar to the beginning of Jesus' public ministry in Galilee, Luke provides his readers with another starting point in Luke 9:51-62. These verses serve as the introduction to the third major division in Luke's Gospel, which consists of the pivotal journey narrative in Luke. Moreover, Luke crafts the beginning of Jesus' journey in 9:51–62 to resemble and echo Jesus' proclamation and actions in the synagogue in Nazareth, which served as the introduction to Jesus' public ministry—the second major division in Luke's Gospel. In essence, Luke thematically and stylistically links the beginning point of Jesus' journey (Luke 9:51-62) with the beginning point of his ministry in Galilee (Luke 4:14-30).

(1) Luke 9:51-53. Luke starts by noting a dramatic shift in Jesus' geographic location and his activities in 9:51. "The days drew near" for Jesus "to be taken up." As a result, Jesus sets his face to go to Jerusalem (9:51; cf. 9:31). In this short verse, Luke indicates that time journeys on and so must Jesus. In the process Luke uses two phrases that derive from the Hebrew Scriptures. First, in 2 Kgs 2:9-10 LXX, Elijah is taken up (Gk. *analambanō*) in a fiery chariot. Using a related word, Jesus forecasts his own "up-taking" (Gk. *analēmpsis*) (Luke 9:51). Of course, even though the language harkens back to Elijah and thereby identifies another similarity between Jesus and the prophet Elijah, the language most clearly points forward to the end of the Gospel of Luke. In particular, Jesus will be taken up at his ascension (Luke 24:50-52; cf. Acts 1:6-11). Here in 9:51, however, Jesus' words appear to foreshadow the entire passion narrative, which will conclude with Jesus' ascension or "up-taking."

Second, Luke uses a Hebrew idiom when he portrays Jesus as "setting his face" to go to Jerusalem. The same phrase is utilized in Ezek 6:2; 13:17; 14:8; 15:7; and Isa 50:7 to connote actions of taking a firm stand or strengthening one's resolve to accomplish a difficult or unpleasant task. Here, Jesus "sets his face to go to Jerusalem," the place where he will be arrested, tried, beaten, and killed. Jesus is aware of the foreboding nature of his trip to Jerusalem, and yet he firmly resolves to make the trip anyway.

As distinct from Matthew (19:1) and Mark (10:1), Luke not only notes Jesus' departure from Galilee but also, and alone among the Gospel writers, mentions Jesus' precise destination. Jesus will journey *to Jerusalem*, which Luke repeatedly characterizes as a menacing destination for any prophet and especially for Jesus (9:51). In particular, the Lukan Jesus characterizes

Jerusalem as the city that kills God's prophets (Luke 13:33-34; 17:11). As a result, Luke portrays Jesus as the one who elects to follow the difficult path of the Father's will despite the persecution and hardships that he knows he will encounter on that path.

Immediately thereafter in 9:52-53, Luke illustrates the rejection that Jesus must face on this hazardous trek to Jerusalem. Only Luke informs his readers about the maltreatment that Jesus experiences as he travels through Samaria. Jesus sends his messengers ahead of him to prepare the way and to make hospitality arrangements, yet an entire village of Samaritans refuses to welcome Jesus and his fellow travelers. In the process, those who associate with Jesus are now beginning to experience the same type of rejection that he has already encountered since 4:14-30.

The precise reason for the Samaritans' inhospitality remains unclear. Perhaps the Samaritans feel that hosting Jesus and his disciples will require too much expense and personal sacrifice, or perhaps these Samaritans reject all Galilean pilgrims who travel through Samaria on their way to Jerusalem. For instance, these Samaritans might assume that these Galilean pilgrims aim to worship at the Jerusalem temple, which the Samaritans reject. Samaritans contend that Mt. Gerizim is the proper place to worship God. On the other hand, these Samaritans might reject any Jew who ventures into their territory after centuries of tension between the two people groups and especially after John Hyrcanus I destroyed the Samaritan temple on Mt. Gerizim during the Hasmonean dynasty in 128 BCE (Josephus, *Ant.* 13.9.1; *J.W.* 1.2.6).

Regardless, the Samaritans refuse to receive or host Jesus (9:53). Luke suggests that the rejection of Jesus is ultimately a by-product of Jesus having already set his face toward Jerusalem and the path of suffering (9:53). The Samaritans' rejection of Jesus at the beginning of his journey to Jerusalem is, however, paradigmatic. It foreshadows the rejection that will characterize the rest of Jesus' life. It also illustrates for Luke's readers that both Galileans (4:14-30) and Samaritans (9:51-53) participate in the rejection of Jesus. Of course, once Jesus arrives in Jerusalem, Judean Jews will likewise participate in his maltreatment.

(2) Luke 9:54-56. James and John react strongly and adversely to the Samaritans' rejection of Jesus. They ask Jesus whether he wants them "to command fire to come down from heaven and consume" the Samaritans. Apparently, James and John are becoming increasingly aware that Jesus has imbued them with power and authority (cf. 9:1). As a result, much like Elijah called down fire on the military force sent by King Ahaziah in 2 Kgs 1:1-16 (see textual variant for Luke 9:54), James and John believe it is proper to punish their enemies who reject God's prophet.

Jesus, however, rejects the vengeance that James and John propose. Unlike Matthew (16:22-23) and Mark (8:32-33), Luke does not narrate Jesus' rebuke of Peter after Jesus' first passion prediction (9:21-27). Rather, the only rebuke of the disciples that Luke narrates in his Gospel is his rebuke of James and John in 9:55, and Luke is the only writer who mentions this rebuke. Matthew and Mark show Jesus rebuking Peter for failing to understand the necessity of Jesus' suffering, but Luke shows Jesus rebuking his disciples for desiring vengeance and attempting to misuse the power and authority he had given them. In 9:1 Jesus gave his disciples the power to heal diseases and cast out demons. In 9:12-17 Jesus instructed the disciples to participate with him in the miraculous feeding of the five thousand. Here in 9:53-54, however, Jesus rebukes his disciples for judging the Samaritans and desiring retribution. Jesus, instead, opts for restraint and mercy.

At this point, it is worth noting the numerous similarities between the beginning of Jesus' Galilean ministry (4:14-30) and the beginning of Jesus' Samaritan ministry (9:51-62). In both contexts, Elijah's prophetic ministry is cited as an example (4:25-26; variant of 9:54). Likewise, both passages depict Jesus as a great prophet (4:24; 9:51) whom the people ultimately reject (4:28-29; 9:53).

Similar to Luke's comparison between John the Baptist and Jesus in the opening chapters of this Gospel, however, Jesus resembles and yet far surpasses Elijah and his prophetic ministry. Whereas Elijah called down fire on his enemies, Jesus calls for restraint and mercy in both passages. Jesus simply walks away from the crowd at Nazareth (4:30), and in Samaria he simply elects to travel on to the next village. Finally, just as Jesus does not allow the murderous mob at Nazareth to prevent him from teaching and ministering among Galileans, so also great hope still remains for Samaritans in Luke's writings well after the people's rejection of Jesus in Luke 9:51-53. For example, Jesus tells the parable of the good Samaritan in Luke 10:29-37. Only one leper returns to thank Jesus for his healing in Luke 17:11-19, and he happens to be a Samaritan. Finally, Luke narrates the spread of the good news about Jesus throughout Samaria in Acts 8. In essence, by opting for mercy and restraint rather than vengeance and punishment like the prophets of old, Jesus establishes a longer arc of ministry that allows those who initially reject him to reconsider their decisions at other points in time. By employing restraint and mercy, Jesus leaves open the possibility of a more positive reception in the future.

(3) Luke 9:57-62. In the wake of the Samaritan rejection of Jesus and his disciples, Luke tells us about three "would-be" followers of Jesus. After hearing Jesus' rebuke of James and John, three more people vow their loyalty

to Jesus. These "would-be" followers of Jesus do not struggle with external rejection as James and John did. Rather they struggle with divided loyalties. Jesus' responses, however, highlight the absolute demand of following him.

The first "would-be" disciple promises to follow Jesus anywhere. Jesus, however, highlights the extreme cost of discipleship. Even foxes and birds experience the comforts of home more than Jesus does (9:57-58). The same will be true for his followers.

Jesus calls the second man to follow him, but the man attempts to delay his response. He indicates that he wants to follow Jesus, but he wants to wait until after he buries his father—after his father dies. We see a similar phrase in Chariton's ancient Greek novel *Chaereas and Callirhoe* 3:5:1–2. Even though Chaereas's elderly father, Ariston, begs him to wait and "to bury" him first before he embarks on a dangerous mission to rescue Callirhoe, his abducted wife, Chaereas departs anyway. Chaereas's friend, Polycharmus, similarly wants to help, but he is not as resolute. At first, he claims he cannot leave his parents before they die, though he changes his mind at the last second and boards Chaereas's ship as it departs from the harbor. Here in Luke 9:60, however, Jesus prioritizes the proclamation of the kingdom of God. Jesus' ministry and message clearly take precedence. Neither Jesus' journey to Jerusalem nor God's overarching redemptive work (or "salvation history") can be postponed in order to accommodate this man's individual plans. Jesus' face has already been set for Jerusalem (9:51), and any of those who wish to follow him must do the same.

The demands of the kingdom of God are so great that Jesus will not even allow a third man to delay long enough to say goodbye to those in his household (9:61-62). Here again, Jesus' words and actions resemble those of Elijah in 1 Kgs 19:19-21 when Elijah calls Elisha but first allows Elisha to say goodbye to his parents. Jesus, however, possesses an even greater urgency, and he demands even more from his disciples. It appears that this particular juncture in salvation history—or God's redemptive work in the world—is of supreme importance.

Commissioning the Seventy-two (10:1-24)

The negative outcome of Jesus' interactions with the three would-be disciples in 9:57-62 may have tempted Luke's first readers to conclude that only a select few are capable of following Jesus in the manner in which he demands. In Luke 10:1-24, however, Luke supplies a far more optimistic portrait of those who wish to follow Jesus (Culpepper, "Luke," 9:219). Those who follow Jesus in 10:1-24 are portrayed as positively as the would-be disciples were portrayed negatively in 9:57-62.

Unlike Matthew and Mark who narrate two feeding stories (e.g., feeding the five thousand and feeding the four thousand) and two stories about Jesus healing blind men, Luke only includes one example of each—the feeding of the five thousand (9:12-17) and the healing of the blind man alongside the road (18:35-43). Luke typically eliminates doublets, or stories that feature similar circumstances; notably, though, the only doublet that Luke incorporates into his Gospel involves a pair of commissioning stories. Like Matthew and Mark, Luke narrates Jesus' commissioning of the twelve apostles in Luke 9:1-6. Unlike Matthew and Mark, Luke then introduces Jesus' commissioning of the seventy-two in 10:1-24. Consequently, Luke's editorial decisions suggest that Luke intends to place a high degree of emphasis on Jesus' commissioning his disciples. Furthermore, when one considers additional passages that are unique to Luke's writings and that focus on Jesus' commissioning of his disciples in some form (e.g., Luke 22:35-38; 24:36-49; Acts 1:6-8), Luke's attention to Jesus' commissions becomes a major theme in this Gospel.

On the other hand, when we place the commissioning of the twelve (9:1-6) side by side with the commissioning of the seventy-two (10:1-24), we can detect some noticeable differences. First, Luke dedicates four times as much space to the commissioning of the seventy-two as he does the twelve.

Second, Jesus informs the twelve from the outset that he has empowered them to heal diseases, cast out demons, and proclaim the kingdom of God (9:1-2). Jesus does not share that same information with the seventy-two other disciples. Instead, they joyfully report to Jesus that they cast out demons in his name, and at that point Jesus clarifies that he gave them power over adversarial spiritual forces (10:17-20). In essence, the seventy-two embark with greater uncertainty, and they must discover the resources with which Jesus has gifted them as they go about fulfilling Jesus' commission.

Third, in 10:2-16 (cf. 9:3-5), Luke provides the seventy-two with a more comprehensive set of instructions. On the one hand, Jesus outlines the urgent need for "laborers" and for haste (10:2-9). For example, Jesus prohibits the seventy-two from even greeting anyone on the way lest those acquaintances deter them from their mission (10:4; cf. 2 Kgs 4:29). On the other hand, Jesus also provides the seventy-two with a heightened expectation of rejection (10:10-16).

Finally, unlike his response to the twelve (9:10), Jesus reacts joyfully and elaborates extensively after hearing the successful report of the returning disciples in 10:17-24. Collectively, these observations suggest that Luke intentionally lays far more emphasis on Jesus' commissioning of the seventy-two than he does on the twelve. So we must ask what additional insights Luke hoped his first readers would gain by reading 10:1-24, which only appears in Luke's Gospel.

The earliest Greek manuscripts that include 10:1-24 are evenly divided between the number of unnamed, commissioned disciples being either seventy or seventy-two (10:1, 17) (Metzger, "Seventy or Seventy-two Disciples?" 299–306). As a result, the first edition of Luke's Gospel may have included either number. Translators and scholars who are forced to decide between the two numbers tend to rely on literary or theological arguments to make a final decision about which number to publish since the manuscript evidence is so evenly weighted. Furthermore, most scholars believe that the numbers of disciples in both Lukan commissioning stories likely carry symbolic importance. For example, the consensus opinion is that when Jesus appoints twelve apostles in Luke 9:1-6, he does so because it creates a correlation with the twelve tribes of Israel as seen in the OT. By appointing twelve apostles, the apostles take on symbolic significance as the restored or reconstituted Israel.

It is perhaps more challenging to determine the symbolism that Jesus' commissioning of the seventy or seventy-two unnamed disciples in 10:1-24 evokes. In addition, because the Greek manuscript tradition about the number of disciples in 10:1-24 is so evenly divided, many scholars conclude that Luke's first readers likely connected Luke's intended symbolism with both numbers. In other words, scholars frequently ask the following question: "What OT symbolism might Luke's readers have associated with both numbers—seventy and seventy-two?"

Given the criteria mentioned above, two main options rise to the fore as answers to this question. First, Moses selects seventy elders of Israel to help him guide and direct the people in Exod 24:9. Notably, Moses then adds two additional elders in Num 11:16-25. As a result, Luke's first readers may well have discerned a symbolic correspondence between the seventy or seventy-two elders of Israel and the seventy or seventy-two unnamed disciples of Jesus. If so, the imagery correlates nicely with the Jewish imagery of Jesus' ministry and the twelve apostles. Furthermore, Jesus ministers within a Jewish context throughout the entirety of his ministry.

Alternatively, others point to Gen 10:2-31 and the so-called "table of nations." The author of Genesis chronicled all seventy of the existing nations in the world at the time that Genesis was written. Much later, when the Hebrew Bible was translated into Greek in a collection of manuscripts known as the Septuagint (or LXX), the editors added the names of two additional nations to Gen 10, perhaps to correspond to the world as they knew it. As a result, Luke's first readers may well have discerned a symbolic correspondence between the seventy or seventy-two nations of the world (or the Gentiles) and the seventy or seventy-two disciples that Jesus commissions in Luke 10. If so, the imagery nicely anticipates the Gentile mission, which does not officially begin until Acts 10 but which is frequently foreshadowed throughout Luke's writings, including as early as 2:32.

Quite honestly, Luke may have intended either image, but if Luke also wrote the book of Acts, as many believe, then I am inclined to lean toward the latter suggestion. In part, Luke's decision to include the commissioning of the seventy-two unnamed disciples helps to prepare his readers for the ministry of the early church (Culpepper, "Luke," 9:219) and perhaps for the literary arc of the book of Acts. For example, the eleven apostles, minus Judas, will continue to play important roles in the period after Jesus' ascension, but by no means are they the only important followers of Jesus at the end of Luke or in the book of Acts.

By means of 10:1-24, Luke shows his readers that there are many other fully equipped disciples whom Jesus has commissioned to carry out his ministry and teachings beyond simply the twelve apostles. Luke does not name names in chapter 10, but by not citing specific names he prepares his readers to revere any disciple who will faithfully carry out Jesus' ministry and message with power after he is gone—people like Stephen, Philip, Paul, Barnabas, Lydia, and Priscilla. To buttress further the argument that Luke 10 foreshadows the ministry of the disciples in Acts, a variety of other clues can be garnered. Luke 10:1-24 is set in Samaria, outside of Judea or Galilee. Furthermore, Tyre and Sidon, Gentile cities, are placed in a positive light (10:13). When Jesus instructs his Jewish disciples traveling in Samaritan territory to "eat what is set before you" in 10:8, he lays the groundwork for the later conclusion that God has set aside the OT food laws for Gentile converts in Acts 15. Finally, Jesus requires his disciples to depend on the custom of hospitality as they depart in Luke 10, and the custom of hospitality is integrally connected to the church's Gentile mission that begins in Acts 10 (Arterbury, *Entertaining Angels*, 153–81).

Last, it is important to take note of Jesus' comments in 10:18-19. Jesus indicates that he saw a vision as the seventy-two disciples faithfully carried out their mission. In particular, Jesus says that he was watching (imperfect tense) "Satan fall from heaven like a flash of lightning," and he claims that those whom he has commissioned have authority over the enemy. Here Luke "depicts an unabashedly apocalyptic scene in the midst of a document not usually considered to be 'apocalyptic'" (Garrett, *Demise of the Devil*, 46). Citing a prophecy about the king of Babylon in Isa 14:1-27 (Luke 10:15), Jesus now envisions "a dramatic reduction of Satan's dominion" after which

Jesus' disciples will no larger be controlled by or vulnerable to the enemy (Garrett, *Demise of the Devil,* 50). Just as the king of Babylon was dethroned, so also Satan will suffer the same fate.

Perhaps the more difficult question relates to the timing of this overthrow. Susan Garrett argues that Satan's definitive defeat takes place during Jesus' resurrection and ascension. The point at which Jesus is "exalted to the position of judge and intercessor at God's right hand (the same position often thought to have been occupied by Satan)" marks the ouster of Satan from the heavenly court, never to return again (cf. Job 1:6-12; Zech 3:1; John 12:31; Heb 2:14; Rev 12:7-11) (*Demise of the Devil,* 51). Consequently, the victorious images of the seventy-two disciples in Luke 10:1-24 appear to prefigure the work of the church in Acts after the dramatic reduction of Satan's dominion.

Loving Neighbor and Loving God (10:25-42)

Jesus' parable of the good Samaritan and Jesus' encounter in the home of Martha and Mary are discreet pericopes. The parable is a fictive narrative whereas Jesus' visit with Martha and Mary is best described as historiography. Luke places the two pericopes together in one literary unit, despite the fact that their theological trajectories appear to move in opposite directions. As a result, it appears that Luke hoped his first readers would read the parable of the good Samaritan and Jesus' visit with Martha and Mary as complementary aspects of a larger discussion about loving God and loving neighbor.

(1) Luke 10:25-28. The unit begins when a lawyer, or an expert in the Mosaic Law, asks Jesus an important question (Danker, *Jesus,* 220). Luke, of course, already informs us that the lawyer aims to test or tempt (Gk. *ekpeirazō*) Jesus (10:25a). The lawyer asks, "Teacher, what must I do to inherit eternal life?" (10:25b). This question is an important question in Luke's Gospel and in particular during Jesus' journey to Jerusalem. For example, the lawyer asks his question near the beginning of Jesus' journey, but a rich ruler will ask the exact same question near the end of it (18:18). With this narrative structure, Luke seems to depict the lawyer's question as a significant one that needs to be addressed by Jesus on more than one occasion. Perhaps Luke hoped to show his readers multiple aspects of Jesus' overarching answer to this weighty question.

Upon hearing the question, Jesus redirects the lawyer back to the Scriptures and back to the lawyer's own area of expertise (10:26). Jesus knows that the lawyer can offer an excellent answer to his own trap question. The lawyer answers his own question by quickly citing well-known directives from the OT to love God (Deut 6:5) and to love one's neighbor (Lev 19:18). The lawyer clearly understands the intent of the Scriptures (10:27). As a result, Jesus affirms the teaching of Scripture, and therefore the man's answer, as a reliable guide for one who is seeking eternal life. Jesus simply says, "do this, and you will live" (10:28).

(2) *Luke 10:29-37*. The lawyer, still attempting to gain the upper hand, asks a follow-up question: "And who is my neighbor?" (10:29). Jesus replies by telling the parable of the good Samaritan. He begins by describing a well-known scenario for travelers in antiquity. Robbers ambush, strip, beat, and abandon a severely injured man along a sparsely populated, eighteen-mile stretch of road between Jerusalem and Jericho (10:30). Anyone who happens along and helps this man will be seen as a heroic figure.

Notably, the first two people who traverse that way elect to pass by the "half dead" man without rendering aid. Both the priest, a member of the highest religious order, and the Levite, a lay associate of priests, choose not to help the man in dire straits (10:30-32). Without a doubt Jesus exposes the priest and the Levite as misguided foils.

The narrative logic of the parable, however, suggests that these two figures likely relied on the Torah's teachings about cleanness and uncleanness to justify their decisive inactivity. For instance, in Num 19:11-13 we read that anyone who touches a dead body will be considered unclean for seven days, which prevents that person from participating in the religious activities of the tabernacle. In addition, Lev 21:1-3 and 21:10-11 specifically exempt priests from burying their deceased relatives in an effort to avoid uncleanness (Talbert, *Reading Luke*, 130). Consequently, the priest and Levite likely prioritize remaining "clean" and carrying out their priestly duties over discerning whether the man alongside the road is dead or "half dead." In the end, few of Luke's first readers were likely surprised by the priest's and Levite's misguided priorities and their failure to love their neighbor.

Shockingly, Jesus then introduces a Samaritan as the hero of the parable. Even if some of Luke's readers were unaware of the disdain that many first-century Jews held for Samaritans as far back as the exilic and the postexilic reconstruction periods (e.g., 2 Kgs 17; Ezra 4; Neh 2:19; 4), all of Luke's readers would at least recall that an entire village of Samaritans recently rejected Jesus and his emissaries in Luke 9:51-56. James and John were so offended by the inhospitality of the Samaritans that they wanted to call down fire and destroy them. Yet here, forty-one verses later, unlike the priest and Levite, the Samaritan sees the injured man, has pity on him, and begins to care for him in dramatic ways. Unlike the priest and Levite who fail "to do" (cf. 10:25, 28) anything that the Torah prescribes, Jesus chronicles numerous ways in which the Samaritan cares for the needy stranger (10:33-35). The Samaritan goes above and beyond the mandates of the law.

At the completion of the parable, Jesus asks the lawyer a leading question (10:36). He essentially asks which one of the three passersby carried out the Torah's instructions to love one's neighbor (Lev 19:18), and of course the lawyer points to the Samaritan who showed mercy or pity (10:37). At that point, Jesus takes the discussion back to where it began. The lawyer initially asked what he must *do* to inherit eternal life (10:25). In response, Jesus told the lawyer to *do* what he knows to do based on the Torah (10:28)—a directive that the lawyer resisted. Now, Jesus instructs the lawyer to "go and *do*" as the Samaritan has done (10:37).

(3) Luke 10:38-42. Just as the parable of the good Samaritan reorders expectations and priorities, Jesus' visit in the home of Mary and Martha does as well. After Luke's readers have read about dramatic instances of inhospitality by the Samaritans (9:51-56) and the fictive priest and Levite in the parable of the good Samaritan (10:29-37), Martha's exemplary hospitality stands out as ideal. She is not merely talking about religious aims and goals. She is *doing* something, much like the Samaritan in Jesus' parable. Martha welcomes Jesus (10:38) and busies herself with the normal duties associated with hosting a traveler in an ancient context (see e.g., Gen 18:1-22).

Martha, however, becomes frustrated with her sister Mary, who neglects the duties of hospitality while sitting at Jesus' feet and listening to him (10:39-40). At that point, Jesus' words again likely shocked Luke's first readers. Jesus declares that Martha is distracted whereas Mary has chosen the "better part." Mary has elected to do the only thing that is necessary (10:41-42). Surprisingly, Mary takes on the disposition of a disciple in 10:38-42 (cf. 8:35; Acts 22:3) (Talbert, *Reading Luke*, 132). She focuses her attention on Jesus, listens to his teachings, and desires to learn from him. Jesus essentially suggests that if Martha, an ethical host engaging in exemplary hospitality, neglects to take advantage of the opportunity to be with Jesus and to listen to his words attentively, her oversight will cancel out the benefit of her meritorious actions.

(4) Luke 10:25-42. Perhaps the most challenging question relates to how the entire unit from Luke 10:25-42 hangs together. How can Jesus' parable of the good Samaritan be read back to back with Jesus' visit in the home of Mary and Martha? Jesus lifts up the Samaritan as an exemplar when he provides care for the half-dead traveler along the road, but Jesus does not praise Martha for her meritorious actions when she cares for him—another traveler—as a guest in her home.

Ultimately, Luke 10:25-42 should be read as a collective unit that utilizes a chiastic structure. The lawyer asks Jesus, "What must I do to inherit eternal life?" in 10:25. Then, due to Jesus' prompting, the lawyer answers his own question by citing the Torah's instructions to love God and to love neighbor (10:27). Interestingly, when the lawyer asks a follow-up question, he only asks Jesus about the identity of his neighbor (10:29). He assumes he knows who God is and how to love God. Jesus' parable of the good Samaritan then provides an answer to the lawyer's second question about the identity of his neighbor. Of course, Jesus does not directly answer the lawyer's question. The lawyer asks about "who," whereas Jesus teaches about "what." Jesus makes it difficult for the lawyer to cull anyone out using a narrow definition of "neighbor." Instead, Jesus shows that one *neighbors*, even to a perceived enemy, when one acts with pity and mercy.

By means of the Mary and Martha pericope, however, Luke continues the conversation. In Luke 10:38-42, Luke portrays Jesus as more than a neighbor. If Jesus is merely a neighbor, then Martha's actions are above any form of reproach. Instead, Martha errs in failing to recognize the identity of her guest. She fails to perceive the importance of being with, attentively listening to, and learning from Jesus, whom Luke has already identified for his readers as Savior, Christ, and Son of God (e.g., 2:11; 3:22). Conversely, Mary's discernment about Jesus' identity—as one uniquely connected to God—leads her to an appropriate reaction to Jesus. Mary provides an example of how one loves God (Talbert, *Reading Luke*, 132). Consequently, this rhetorical unit falls into a chiastic pattern. The lawyer introduces (a) loving God and (b) loving neighbor in 10:27. The good Samaritan then models (b') the love of neighbor in 10:29-37, and Mary models (a') the love of God in 10:38-42. As a result, all of 10:25-42 must be read as a collective response to the lawyer's initial question about experiencing "eternal life" (10:25).

Teaching about Prayer (11:1-13)

Unlike Matthew, who locates the Lord's prayer (Matt 6:9-13) and Jesus' comments about "asking, seeking, and knocking" (Matt 7:7-11) in the Sermon on the Mount, Luke combines these conversations along with a parable and places them in the journey section of his Gospel. By means of this three-part conversation (Luke 11:1-4, 5-8, 9-13), Jesus seeks to shape the content and the disposition of his disciples' prayers.

(1) Luke 11:1-4. The context for this three-part conversation on prayer is found in 11:1. Jesus is praying. When he finishes, a disciple asks Jesus to teach the disciples to pray. Notably, Jesus, the Son of God, repeatedly prays

to the Father in Luke's Gospel. Throughout Luke's Gospel, prayer serves as an avenue of revelation whereby God makes his will known to his people, even to the Son of God (cf. 3:21-22). The disciples now seek to engage faithfully in the same types of activities as Jesus—including prayer.

Jesus begins by providing a model prayer that perhaps resembles the prayer he just prayed (11:2-4). In the process, Jesus' prayer shares many elements in common with Jewish prayers of his day (Werline, *Pray Like This*, 86–87). He refers to God as "Father"—a position of power and authority in Roman antiquity (Werline, *Pray Like This*, 88–89)—and praises God's name. Thereafter, Jesus prays for the arrival of God's kingdom, food, forgiveness of sins, and divine direction, which leads away from trials or temptations (the Greek word, *peirasmos*, can refer to either, and Luke seems to imply both meanings). Rodney Werline has shown that Mark routinely places prayer and demons in opposition to one another in his Gospel (*Pray Like This*, 102–11), and a similar dynamic seems to be present in Luke's Gospel. Jesus not only prays about avoiding physical, earthly hardships, but also simultaneously prays for pathways that lead away from spiritual conflict and struggle.

In short, Jesus coaches his disciples to pray for God's will to be done, for mandatory provisions, for right relations with God and others, and for God's safeguarding from physical and spiritual threats. Jesus does not disclose magic words that will allow his disciples to control any and all situations. Rather, he offers them a model that illustrates the types of topics, words, and requests that characterize faithful prayers.

(2) Luke 11:5-8. Next, Jesus tells the parable of the friend at midnight (11:5-8). The parable functions as the second part of a three-part conversation on prayer. The logic of the parable rests on the ancient custom of friendship. Friendship in antiquity primarily revolved around an implied agreement to reciprocate generously whenever one's counterpart needed assistance (Parsons, *Luke*, 183–85). In essence, within a reciprocal relationship, one friend was obligated to assist the other friend because the latter had already assisted the former.

In Jesus' parable, a man is caught between two friends. First, a friend arrives at midnight at the main character's house (11:6). The main character is obligated to host his friend, but he has no bread. (Notably, Jesus prayed about bread in the previous passage, Luke 11:3.) So the host goes to a second friend at midnight and requests that the second friend loan him three loaves of bread (11:5). Despite cultural expectations that come with friendship, the second friend is unwilling to help because he and his household are already in bed (11:7). In this instance, the implied duties of a reciprocal friendship do not outweigh the man's desire for sleep. Nevertheless, Jesus concludes that the man will eventually get up and give bread to his friend due to the persistent knocking rather than the moral obligations that accompany friendship (11:8).

Some may be tempted to conclude that the response of the uncooperative man who only helps his friend due to the persistent knocking resembles God's response to those who pray, but this flawed interpretation misses the rhetorical argument of Luke 11:1-13. For instance, Jesus first described the subject matter about which one might pray in 11:1-4. Here in 11:5-8, however, Jesus describes the proper disposition of those who pray. The parable is far less about God and far more about those who pray. Jesus does not provide his disciples with a magical incantation in 11:1-4 that the disciples can now expect to recite quickly on a single occasion whenever they want God to do a favor for them as a friend might. Instead, just as we see Jesus praying on numerous occasions in Luke's Gospel, so also the disciples must persistently engage in the activity of prayer, perhaps at times with desperation. In essence, by means of the parable, Jesus tutors his disciples to cultivate the proper disposition in prayer (11:5-8) to accompany the words, ideas, and topics that he has already mentioned (11:1-4).

(3) Luke 11:9-13. In the third part of this three-part discussion of prayer, Jesus moves back to direct exhortation. In addition, whereas the parable builds upon "friend" language, Jesus now returns to "Father" language as we first saw in 11:2. In the process, Jesus sets up a contrast between human friends and the "heavenly Father." If 11:1-4 introduces the proper subject matter for prayer and if 11:5-8 describes the ideal human disposition of persistence during prayer, Jesus now discusses God's disposition toward those who offer prayers in 11:9-13.

Jesus encourages his disciples to ask, seek, and knock with confidence (11:9-10). Their confidence, however, does not lie in the hope that God will reciprocate for past favors like a human friend. Rather, their confidence rests on the nature and disposition of the God to whom they pray (11:11-13). The heavenly Father responds to the prayers of Jesus' disciples like a compassionate father who cares for his children. Importantly, though, Jesus claims that the heavenly Father gives the Holy Spirit to those who ask (11:13). Above all else, Jesus promises that God will share God's own redemptive and empowering work in the world with those who ask for it through prayer.

Dialoguing with Disciples and Adversaries (11:14–13:9)

(1) Luke 11:14-26. After Jesus exorcises a demon from a mute man, the man begins to speak (11:14). This miraculous act amazes the crowds and leads them to expound upon Jesus' miraculous powers. Some in the crowd theorize

Jesus' Journey to Jerusalem

that Jesus possesses the authority to direct the demons precisely because he is empowered by the ruler of the demons, Beelzebul, whose name derives from Baal, the Canaanite fertility god (cf. 2 Kgs 1:2-3). Jesus, however, explains that his authority to command demons must come from God rather than Satan. Satan would never harm his own agents by casting them out of the mute man. Otherwise, Satan's kingdom would be divided against itself and would quickly crumble from within (11:17-18).

Alternatively, Jesus casts out demons by the authority of God. As a result, the crowds should acknowledge the arrival of God's kingdom among them. Just as Pharaoh's magicians concluded that "the finger of God" was at work to perform God's mighty deeds through Moses and Aaron in Exod 8:19 (cf. Exod 31:18), so also the crowds should now observe these mighty deeds and once again conclude that "the finger of God" is at work through Jesus (11:20). Moreover, the crowds should recognize that the power of God easily overpowers the power of Satan (11:21-22).

Finally, Jesus previously spoke inclusively about all those who associate with his name (cf. 9:49-50). Some of the twelve disciples sought to prevent a man from casting out demons in Jesus' name in Luke 9 because he did not travel along with Jesus and the twelve. Here in Luke 11, however, Jesus speaks not about inclusivity but about division. Now, rather than a context where a variety of people seek to identify with Jesus, the context revolves around the contrasting realms and authority of Satan and God. Given this context, Jesus says, "Whoever is not with me is against me, and whoever does not gather with me scatters" (11:23). Jesus, as the harbinger of God's kingdom on earth, seeks inclusivity among his adherents (9:49-50), but he draws a stark contrast between those associated with God versus those associated with Satan (11:23).

(2) Luke 11:27-36. In response to Jesus' remarkable words and deeds, a woman in the crowd praises Jesus' mother and ultimately his ancestry. Jesus, however, shifts the focus away from his ancestry and heritage toward a focus on the word of God. He declares, "Blessed rather are those who hear the word of God and obey it!" (11:27-28).

As the crowds increase, Jesus then illustrates this same dynamic (the greater importance of hearing and obeying the word of God as opposed to relying on one's ancestry and heritage) in Israel's history (11:29-32). For instance, Jonah declared the word of God to the Ninevites and functioned as God's sign to them (11:30; cf. Jon 3:4-10). Shockingly, the Ninevites heard and obeyed the word of God despite the fact that they were pagans (or Gentiles) by ancestry and heritage. Similarly, the queen of Sheba, another Gentile, traveled a great distance (likely from the southern-most part of Arabia) to hear the word of God as communicated via the wisdom of Solomon (11:31; cf. 1 Kgs 10:1-10; 2 Chr 9:1-9). As a result, despite having questionable pedigrees, the Ninevites and the queen of the South both exemplify what it means to hear and obey the word of God.

In the process, Jesus declares that he, as the Son of Man, now embodies and articulates the word of God to an even greater degree than Jonah or Solomon did in the past. He notes that some among the Jewish crowd demand signs to verify that Jesus speaks and works on God's behalf (cf. 11:16). They will soon realize that the Son of Man (the apocalyptic judge who brings God's judgment and reign to the earth; cf. Dan 7:13-14) provides the most important and clearest sign for which anyone could hope. In particular, the Son of Man's presence and ministry will provide a far greater sign than the sign that Jonah's ministry provided (11:30, 32). Furthermore, Jesus declares that his proclamation of the word of God to the Jewish crowds is far greater than the words Solomon spoke (11:31). The Jewish crowds should not, therefore, rely exclusively on their heritage. Rather, they should hear the word of God as embodied and proclaimed by Jesus and repent if they wish to be prepared for the judgment (11:32). In addition, they should function as brightly burning lamps that enable others to see (and to hear) God's revelation (11:33-36).

(3) Luke 11:37-54. Once again, a Pharisee invites Jesus to dine with him in his home only to become offended by what he perceives as a lack of religious piety on Jesus' part (cf. 7:36-50; 14:1-24). The Pharisee's critique of Jesus then provides Jesus with an opportunity to reframe his host's understanding of authentic devotion so that it will more accurately reflect God's character. Though impossible to know for certain, the repetition of this scenario in a Pharisee's home suggests that at least some Pharisees were naturally drawn to Jesus and his ministry even if they ultimately found themselves at odds with Jesus. As a result, Luke, by means of Jesus' encounters with the Pharisees, systematically illustrates for his readers the places where Jesus and his followers significantly diverge from the Pharisaic tradition (cf. 5:17–6:11; 14:1-24; 15:1-2; Acts 15:5).

In this instance, the Pharisee takes offense at Jesus' decision not to wash ritually before eating a meal. In Exod 30:17-21, God instructed Aaron and the priests to wash their hands and feet before entering the tent of meeting or offering incense on the altar. Centuries later, the Pharisees sought to live out these same temple regulations within their homes as an act of devotion to God.

In response, Jesus differentiates between external and internal piety, between two types of cleansing. Much like the eighth-century prophets (e.g., Amos 5:21-24; Mic 3:9-12), Jesus does not condemn visible acts of worship and devotion like tithing (11:42). He does, however, criticize his host (11:39-41), the Pharisees as a sect (11:42-44), and the lawyers (11:45-52) for neglecting the internal dispositions and ethical actions that God's covenant with the Hebrew people also prescribed. They are seeking to honor God in the present while neglecting many of God's directives from the past. Jesus condemns the Pharisees and lawyers for embracing greed, wickedness, and the love of public adulation while neglecting almsgiving, justice, and the love of God (11:41-42).

In essence, Jesus, as a great prophet, now condemns the Pharisees and lawyers for failing to heed all of God's word, which was previously announced through the Law and the Prophets. With their hypocrisy (11:42; cf. 12:1), the Pharisees and lawyers have repeated the mistakes of their preexilic ancestors. As a result, they also share responsibility for the death of God's messengers (11:47-51)—prophets like Zechariah (2 Chr 24:20-22). Even worse, the scribes and the Pharisees are in the process of rejecting Jesus' prophetic announcement of God's word in the present and are already "lying in wait" for him by the end of this encounter (11:53-54)—perhaps depicting the impending death of Jesus as another instance in which God's own people kill one of God's prophets (cf. 13:31-35).

(4) Luke 12:1-12. As Jesus departs the Pharisee's house (11:53) and begins to address his disciples directly (12:1), he expounds further upon the topics of the Pharisees' hypocrisy (cf. 6:6-11; 7:36-50; 11:37-34), impending judgment, alert waiting, and the need for repentance. This broad conversation ranges from Luke 12:1 to 13:9. In the process, Jesus both warns and encourages his followers. He instructs his disciples to fear God (12:5), and he instructs then not to fear for their lives (12:7). He explains that God is the one who has the power to banish people to hell (or *Gehenna*, a deep ravine near Jerusalem that was associated with eternal punishment; cf. Rev 9:1-2), and yet God also cares enough about them to count the hairs on their heads (12:5-7).

The line of demarcation between the ultimate mercy of God and the ultimate punishment of God hinges on how one responds to Jesus (12:8-12). Everyone who publicly confesses Jesus as the Son of Man—the apocalyptic judge who inaugurates God's reign upon the earth (cf. Dan 7:13-14)—will be welcomed by the angels of God, and those who do not openly acknowledge Jesus as the Son of Man will be rejected by him at the final judgment.

Jesus illustrates this point by referring to instances in which his disciples may be brought before "the synagogues, the rulers, and the authorities" at some point in the future. These instances provide the disciples with opportunities either to identify themselves as followers of Jesus or to deny that identity. Even then, the only unforgiveable action that Jesus specifically mentions is the attribution of Jesus' power to the work of something other than the holy power of God's own Spirit—the same mistake that some made when Jesus exorcised a demon from the mute man in Luke 11:14-15. If, however, one acknowledges that the "finger of God" empowers Jesus (11:20), then that same Holy Spirit will sustain that disciple during his or her trials and tribulations (e.g., Acts 4:5-12).

(5) Luke 12:13-34. Rather than acknowledging Jesus as God's ultimate king and judge, or "the Son of Man" (Dan 7:13-14), someone in the crowd asks Jesus to adjudicate a monetary dispute between him and his brother (12:13). In essence, the man requests that Jesus function as a type of judge, but one whose function is different from the role Jesus has just described (12:8-12). In response, Jesus warns the crowd against greed and an obsession with possessions (12:15). Thereafter, Jesus illustrates this warning by means of both the parable of the rich fool (12:16-21) and his comments about anxiety (12:22-34). Ultimately, Jesus sketches a stark contrast between the love of money and the love of God (12:33-34).

Jesus begins by telling the crowd a parable about a rich fool (12:13-21). The rich man is foolish because he gives great thought and effort to acquiring more possessions, but he does not give great thought or effort toward the riches found in a proper relationship with God (12:21). (Jesus diagnosed the Pharisees with the same plight in 11:39-40.) The man's land produces abundantly, and neither personal need nor generosity toward others who are in need motivates him. Rather, greed alone guides his efforts to build bigger barns and hoard more grain. He aims to depend exclusively on himself and his own resources while living a life of selfish leisure and abundance. Of course, Jesus quickly points out that his barns and crops will not assist him on the day of his death (cf. 16:19-31).

Next, Jesus again singles his disciples out from the crowd and specifically addresses them when he warns about a type of anxiety that fuels a fixation on material possessions (12:22-34). Here, Jesus further illustrates the same points that he made in the preceding parable. Ravens are not obsessed with storehouses and barns as the rich fool is (12:24; cf. 12:18). Likewise, lilies are not consumed with the type of clothes they will wear (12:27). Yet God graciously cares for both the birds and the flowers anyway. As a result, even though the Gentiles strive for monetary wealth and possessions in the Mediterranean setting of the first century (12:30), Jesus does not want his disciples to follow the lead of their cultural context.

Jesus' disciples should take comfort from the knowledge that God cares for them. As a result, they will be free to reserve their greatest energies and efforts for God's kingdom (12:31). Jesus wants his disciples to renounce greed, trust in God, and strive for his kingdom. He encourages them to foster faith rather than fear. He exhorts them to sell their extra possessions and give them to the poor as opposed to storing them up in barns as the rich fool needlessly desires to do (12:32-33; cf. 12:18-19). Trusting God and giving alms to the poor then become indicators that one's heart properly strives after God. In essence, Jesus suggests that "a strong interest in material possessions is not reconcilable with interest in God" (Brown, *Introduction*, 246). Striving for possessions and striving for God's kingdom are incompatible objectives.

(6) *Luke 12:35-48.* In conjunction with his warnings to avoid greed, self-sufficiency, and the desire to relax, eat, drink, and be merry (12:15, 19), Jesus now warns his disciples to invest their time and energies into watchful vigilance in Luke 12:35-48. In particular, he exhorts them to be alert. Rather than merely prohibiting unfruitful behavior like greed and laxity, Jesus urges his disciples to be proactive. In addition to giving alms to the poor (12:33), Jesus further illustrates what it means to be alert through a series of parables in 12:35-48.

First, Jesus reminds his disciples what it means for household servants to be alert and vigilant when their masters are away from the house attending a wedding banquet. Even after night has long since fallen, attentive and responsible servants do not extinguish the lights and go to bed before their master returns. No matter the hour of the night, responsible servants remain dressed, lamps lit, and waiting for the master's return (12:35-38). The language of "dressed for action" or having "your loins girded" echoes the Hebrew people who were expectantly awaiting their release from Egypt in the middle of the night by remaining dressed and ready to depart (Exod 12:11; Bovon, *Luke*, 2:231). Astonishingly, when servants display this type of vigilant dedication throughout the night, an appreciative master will begin to serve his servants upon his return to the house (12:37).

Second, Jesus illustrates vigilance using the metaphor of a homeowner and a thief. Attentive homeowners guard against thieves at all times, not just at one specific hour on one specific day. So also, Jesus' disciples should be perpetually prepared for the arrival of the Son of Man (12:39-40).

Finally, after Peter asks Jesus whether he is specifically addressing the twelve by means of these parables, a question that highlights the fact that Jesus is indeed addressing his disciples directly, Jesus tells a third parable in 12:41-48—though it may be a further expansion on the first parable about the master who is away at a wedding banquet while his servants remain at home (12:36-38). In particular, Jesus describes in 12:41-48 a spectrum of behaviors and dispositions among the servants who remain at home that range from industrious vigilance to ignorant inattention, along with a spectrum of reactions to those various types of servant behaviors on the part of the master. Despite the absence of one's master, servants who continue to work receive praise (12:43-44). Conversely, those who behave violently toward other servants or who indulge in food and drink rather than work while the master is away suffer punishment (12:45-46). In addition, more severe punishments are reserved for those who know what to do but elect not to do it, as opposed to those who fail to do what they should because of their ignorance (12:47-48).

Ultimately, throughout Luke 12:13-48 Jesus implores his disciples to practice faithful vigilance while they await God's decisive intervention in the world at Jesus' return (Carroll, *Luke*, 274). Jesus' comments in 12:13-34, however, should not be separated from 12:35-48. Jesus directly addresses his disciples in a singular setting throughout this unit even as the crowds listen in. In essence, in Luke's Gospel Jesus portrays vigilant disciples, who are awaiting the arrival of the Son of Man to usher in God's ultimate rule on earth (12:40; cf. Dan 7:13-14), as having a proactive stance toward both religious duties and economic resources. For instance, vigilant disciples who await the Son of Man properly carry out the work Jesus entrusted to them while also avoiding violence, greed, and overindulgence (12:15, 43-45; cf. Acts 1:8). Alert disciples place their trust in God for their provisions and give alms to the poor while waiting for the Son of Man's arrival (12:32-34, 37). Proper waiting for the Son of Man involves both attitudes and actions. It involves carrying out one's duties, but it also involves caring for the poor and warding off the accumulation of material possessions that aims to rely on oneself rather than to rely on God.

(7) Luke 12:49–13:9. Jesus continues his discussion about the arrival of the Son of Man from Luke 12:40 within the larger conversation that runs from 12:1 to 13:9. In addition, while scholars debate the precise meaning of "the Son of Man," in Luke 12 the term refers to God's royal emissary and judge who will appear in the end times just as Dan 7:13-14 prophesied (12:8, 10, 40).

Jesus clarifies that, as the Son of Man, he has come to bring fire (or purification; cf. 3:16; Mal 3:2) to the earth (12:49). Before judging the earth, however, he must first be baptized (or die; 12:50; cf. Mark 10:38). This fiery purification that accompanies the Son of Man does not and will not produce unity; it produces division and separation both in the present and in the future based on one's response to Jesus and his teachings (12:51-56).

Given that the Son of Man will soon judge the world (12:49), the best course of action in the present is to judge oneself now, thereby bringing oneself into alignment with the judge's wishes and assessments before the trial even begins. Proper repentance and purification in the present allow one to escape the future punishments that will be dispensed to those who are found wanting (12:57-59). Jesus illustrates this concept by setting up a fictive scenario in which the listener has been accused of a crime and is being taken to court for a trial. The wisest course of action, in light of the nearness of the impending trial, is to judge oneself quickly and settle the disagreement along the way before one ever appears before the magistrate.

In Luke 13:1-5 Jesus provides a second illustration of proper repentance in light of the nearness of future judgment. Here, Jesus cites two well-known examples of tragic deaths in Judea in Jesus' day. The Galileans died at the hands of Pilate—a harsh and violent Roman governor who intentionally harmed his victims—as they brought their sacrifices to the temple. The others died due to an unforeseen and unfortunate circumstance—the collapse of the tower at Siloam in the southern portion of Jerusalem—that was not the result of murderous human intentions. Regardless, while some in Jesus' day were inclined to label both tragic events as a manifestation of divine punishment due to human sinfulness, Jesus declares that the Galilean and Judean victims were no worse sinners than all of their Galilean and Judean neighbors or even those listening to him at that moment. He declares that all Galileans and Judeans will perish tragically as an act of divine punishment unless they, too, repent of their sinful ways.

Finally, in 13:6-9 Jesus concludes his prolonged comments about hypocrisy, judgment, vigilance, and the need for repentance that began in Luke 12:1. Once again he provides an illustration of proper repentance in light of the nearness of future judgment. In this third and final illustration, he tells the parable of the fig tree.

The fig tree has not produced any fruit over a three-year period. The landowner declares that its time is up. Judgment has arrived for the tree, and the landowner decrees that the gardener should punish the tree by cutting it down. The gardener asks for one more year. He essentially asks for a brief reprieve while hoping that with a little more cultivation the tree will finally "repent" from its unfruitful ways and begin to serve its God-intended purpose. Exemplifying mercy and patience, the landowner agrees, but the reprieve is indeed brief (Carroll, *Luke*, 279). The time of judgment remains close—only one more year before the landowner's judgment will be enacted.

Similarly, Jesus seeks to cultivate repentance in his listeners while knowing that both judgment and divine punishment are not far off. God's patience is growing thin. Similar to the one who attempts to settle accounts with his accuser prior to a hearing before the judge (12:57-59), immediate repentance constitutes the proper approach to the impending judgment of the Son of Man (12:49).

Healing and Parables (13:10–17:10)

Healing a Crippled Woman (13:10-17)

The canonical Gospels cite various sources of human suffering, sickness, and disability. At times, suffering, sickness, and/or disability are due to divine punishment in response to human sinfulness (e.g., Luke 1:20). At other times, no reason is given beyond natural causes (e.g., Luke 13:4; Mark 7:32). Finally, on other occasions, sickness, suffering, and/or disability are attributed to satanic or demonic affliction (Luke 11:14; Acts 10:38) (Talbert, *Reading Luke*, 141). The last explanation provides the context for the suffering of the bent-over woman in Luke 13:10-17. Jesus ultimately names "Satan" as the source of her eighteen years of disabling weakness (13:16; cf. 13:11). For eighteen years, she has been a walking illustration of how Satan's bondage shrinks and limits human life as God first created it.

It is equally important to note that, by this point, Jesus has already been engaged in a cosmic battle with Satan (Luke 4:5-13; 8:12; cf. 22:3, 31-32; Acts 5:3). And even though the battle has not yet reached its final resolution, Jesus has already assured his disciples that Satan will be defeated (Luke 10:17-18; cf. Acts 26:18). In particular, Jesus' healing ministry provides a foretaste of the coming disempowerment and defeat of Satan (Acts 10:38). Jesus' healing of the bent-over woman is no exception. With a simple declaration and touch of his hands, Jesus announces that the woman is free from the power that has oppressed her. Jesus' power to give life to this woman as God intended it easily overthrows Satan's power to reduce and cripple her life.

Of course, the fact that Jesus liberates the bent-over woman in a synagogue on the Sabbath should not surprise Luke's readers. During his first visit to a synagogue on the Sabbath in this Gospel, Jesus announced that God has anointed him to proclaim release to captives and freedom for the oppressed (4:16-19). Jesus' healing of the bent-over woman here in 13:10-17 merely invites the reader to recall Jesus' words from 4:16-21 (Garland, *Luke*, 546).

At the same time, Jesus' liberation of the crippled woman in the synagogue on the Sabbath produces a conundrum for those in attendance. Not surprisingly, the leader of the synagogue desires to uphold God's command to keep the Sabbath holy as Exod 20:9-10 and Deut 5:13-14 direct. Consequently, the synagogue official becomes incensed that Jesus has healed the woman on the Sabbath as opposed to another day of the week (cf. 6:1-11).

From the synagogue official's perspective, Jesus has violated the Sabbath by working rather than resting.

To defend his actions Jesus cites two important reasons for healing the woman on the Sabbath. First, Jesus exposes the hypocrisy of those in the synagogue by means of a scriptural argument. In Deut 5:14, while describing how God's people should observe the Sabbath, Moses mandates that the head of an Israelite household should not only observe the Sabbath himself but should likewise ensure that his children, servants, and livestock are able to rest—the type of rest that provides humans with an opportunity to worship God properly. Notice that in 13:15 Jesus specifically refers to the pastoral care of oxen and donkeys, both of which Deut 5:14 names. Jesus even points out that all of those in the synagogue are presently observing this teaching. Each one of them dutifully cares for his or her oxen and donkeys every Sabbath just as Moses commanded (13:15).

If Jesus had neglected to aid this bent-over woman on the Sabbath, however, he would have been neglecting to carry out the same teaching that they all seek to observe. If Jesus' audience cares for their animals on the Sabbath in keeping with Deut 5:14, why should he fail to care for this woman—who is far more valuable than their animals (12:7, 24; Carroll, *Luke*, 284)—on the Sabbath in light of the same commandment? By healing her, the Sabbath becomes not only a day of true rest for this previously afflicted woman but also a day of praise and worship for her (13:13). She can now fully celebrate the Creator just as God originally intended (Exod 20:9-10). Ultimately, Jesus' healing of this woman expands the praise and worship of God on the Sabbath (13:13); it does not diminish it in any way.

Second, and perhaps more important, Jesus does not first and foremost define this woman by her disability. Jesus does not refer to her as the "crippled woman" or the "bent-over woman." Jesus refers to her as "a daughter of Abraham" (13:16). Jesus points out to the synagogue leader and the others who are gathered that she is not somehow less human, less Jewish, or less important than they are. To neglect her well-being would be to neglect one's own family member in violation of the instructions in Deut 5:14. Having been oppressed and deformed by Satan for eighteen years, she may no longer resemble Abraham, but by the gracious and redemptive healing of Jesus she is enabled to straighten up and stand up into her true heritage and identity as a member of the people of God.

John the Baptist warned the Jewish crowds that if they continue to claim Abraham as their ancestor but fail to produce fruit worthy of repentance, God would "raise up" children to Abraham from the stones (3:7-9). Now John's words have begun to come true. The synagogue leader has not yet repented of his hypocrisy or begun to bear fruit as John commanded (cf. 6:1-11). Jesus, however, has just raised up one of Abraham's daughters (cf. 19:9).

The Kingdom of God (13:18-35)

Jesus' teaching in Luke 13:18-35 is bound together with the previous unit—the healing of the bent-over woman (13:10-17)—by means of "therefore" (Gk. *oun*) in 13:18. In general, both Jesus' teaching ministry and his healing ministry reveal and depict to Luke's readers the in-breaking of the kingdom (or reign) of God on earth (cf. 4:43). Consequently, in 13:18-35 Jesus now seeks to "interpret the preceding event as a symbolic enactment of God's rule" (Carroll, *Luke*, 286–87).

(1) Luke 13:18-21. First, in 13:18-21 Jesus elaborates on the nature of God's in-breaking kingdom through the parables of the mustard seed and the yeast. Both parables refer to the small beginnings of the kingdom's arrival, but in both instances those small beginnings eventually translate into momentous growth. The tiny mustard seed becomes a tree, and a little yeast leavens a large amount of flour. So it is with the kingdom of God, and so it is with the healing of the bent-over woman. At this point in time, Jesus' disciples are receiving a small sample or foretaste of what the kingdom of God will yield. Eventually, though, the kingdom of God's expansion will even overtake the domain of Satan (13:16; cf. 10:17-19) (Bovon, *Luke*, 2:297).

(2) Luke 13:22-30. Second, as Jesus continues his journey to Jerusalem, he answers a question about citizenship in God's kingdom. The specific question is, "Will only a few be saved?" (13:23). When Jesus addresses the question, he provides a two-part answer. In particular, he elaborates on both the "who" and the "when" of kingdom citizenship. Jesus suggests that the number of people included in the kingdom of God will be far fewer than the number who ultimately desire entry (13:24). As a result, Jesus instructs his audience to "strive to enter through the narrow door."

Jesus goes on to indicate that the timing of one's attempted entrance into God's kingdom is also vitally important. Throughout this Gospel, Luke places great emphasis on "today" as the desired and appropriate time for salvation (e.g., 4:21; 19:5, 9; 23:43). "Today" is the time to enter into and align with God's kingdom. Similarly, here in 13:25-27, Jesus indicates that once the door is closed it will not be reopened. Those who do not align themselves in the present with Jesus and his ministry as a harbinger of God's kingdom will experience future torment rather than future blessing. Implicitly, Jesus exhorts his audience members to affiliate with God's kingdom now, even as he journeys toward Jerusalem. Jesus encourages them to join his caravan as a foretaste of the kingdom.

Having just described the narrow doorway and the temporal limits of God's salvation in 13:24-27, however, Jesus then goes on to illuminate the remarkable breadth of God's kingdom in 13:28-30. Like the mustard seed and the yeast (13:18-21), the kingdom of God expands far beyond its small beginnings. For example, Jesus refers to those who aligned themselves with the God of Abraham, Isaac, and Jacob in ages past as full participants in God's coming kingdom (13:28). In addition, Jesus prophesies that God's rescue will extend far beyond the borders of Judea and Galilee. Those who have sought to worship and honor God in other lands likewise "will come" (cf. Ps 107:1-3; Isa 43:4-7) "to eat in the kingdom of God"—a phrase linked with God's salvation, protection, and provisions (13:29; cf. 14:15; 22:16, 29-30). In essence, those who align themselves with Jesus in the present will align themselves with God's salvific work throughout human history. In addition, those who align themselves with Jesus in the present will discover that they have been linked together with God's faithful servants from the past and in the future as fellow citizens in God's kingdom and fellow recipients of God's blessings (13:30). Not surprisingly, Jesus refers to the healed woman in the previous unit as a "daughter of Abraham" (13:16).

(3) Luke 13:31-35. Next, in 13:31-35 some Pharisees inform Jesus that Herod Antipas, tetrarch of Galilee and Perea, desires to kill him. After Jesus illustrated the in-breaking of the kingdom of God by releasing the bent-over woman from Satan's bondage in 13:10-27, and after Jesus expounded on the life-giving nature of the kingdom of God in 13:18-30, Luke now presents his readers with a vivid contrast in 13:31-35. Rather than life, these verses focus on death, particularly Jesus' death. Jesus restores life to the disabled woman and offers life to those who journey with him—both of which highlight the nature of God's kingdom—yet rulers like Herod Antipas serve a different kingdom and therefore a different purpose. Herod seeks to extinguish life rather than grant it. As an agent of the Roman government, Herod Antipas ultimately shows himself to be more aligned with the life-restricting work of Satan (13:16) rather than the life-giving work of Jesus (13:29).

Given that Luke has already portrayed Jesus as a faithful prophet of God (e.g., 7:11-17; 9:7-8), it is not surprising to see Jesus respond to Herod's threat in a manner that resembles the faithful responses of Israel's prophets to wicked kings (e.g., 1 Kgs 18). Jesus does not flee or hide. Rather, he prophesies boldly in the face of death. First, he informs Herod of the things that Luke 13:10-30 has just illustrated. Jesus' healing ministry and exorcisms are harbingers of the arrival of the kingdom of God. An immediate response to the in-breaking of the kingdom of God is required, however, because Jesus' earthly ministry will not last much longer (13:32). "On the third day"—a reference to Jesus' resurrection (24:6-7)—Jesus will complete, finish, or make perfect his work (13:32).

Furthermore, rather than flee to save his life, Jesus will journey on to Jerusalem because he "must" (Gk. *dei*) (13:33). Jesus willingly accepts the abuse and death that await him in Jerusalem because it is "necessary" within the framework of God's salvation history or God's overarching salvific work in the world. As a prophet who speaks and acts on God's behalf, it is unimaginable or near impossible for Jesus to die in any other place and in any other manner than as a rejected prophet of God in Jerusalem (13:33-35).

Conversing with Pharisees (14:1-35)

The Pharisees continue their love-hate relationship with Jesus in 14:1-6. For instance, at times the Pharisees listen to Jesus' teaching (e.g., 5:17), ask him to dine with them (e.g., 7:36-50; 11:37-54), and inform him about Herod Antipas's desire to kill him (13:31). Yet the Pharisees also question Jesus' teachings (e.g., 5:21), criticize his actions (e.g., 7:39), and seek to trap him (e.g., 14:1). These same dynamics are present in 14:1-24. For the third time in this Gospel, a leading Pharisee asks Jesus to dine with him. This influential host and his associates are, however, wary of Jesus. They watch him with great suspicion and pounce on him when the opportunity presents itself.

(1) Luke 14:1-6. In 14:1-6 the controversy surrounds a man with an abnormal retention of bodily fluid, or "dropsy," and whether or not Jesus will elect to heal him even though it is the Sabbath. We saw Jesus confront a similar situation in Luke 6:6-11 when Jesus healed a man with a withered hand on the Sabbath and in Luke 13:10-18 when Jesus healed the bent-over woman on the Sabbath. Throughout this Gospel, Luke has already established that Jesus possesses the authority to interpret Scripture and to govern Sabbath observances (e.g., Luke 6:1-11). Moreover, Luke has repeatedly shown his readers how Jesus fulfills the words he first spoke at the synagogue at Nazareth (4:14-21). When Jesus heals the man with a withered hand and the bent-over woman, he is releasing captives and freeing the oppressed (Garland, *Luke*, 567–68). Now in 14:1-6, Jesus once again uses his authority to restore the kind of health and wholeness to this man that God intended from the beginning of creation.

Consequently, much as he had done before, Jesus both heals the man with dropsy and addresses the scriptural debate that lies behind the Pharisees' disapproval of Jesus' actions. As "lord of the Sabbath" (6:5), Jesus heals the man with dropsy as a way of honoring rather than dishonoring God.

Furthermore, Jesus again echoes the teachings of Exod 20:8-11 and Deut 5:12-15 when he refers to children and oxen in 14:5 (cf. 13:14-16). The authors of both Exodus and Deuteronomy express explicit concern for children and oxen as a subsection of the command to keep the Sabbath holy (Exod 20:10; Deut 5:14). Thus, Jesus essentially reminds the Pharisees and lawyers that God's concern for children and oxen is well documented in the law (e.g., Deut 22:4). Similarly, Jesus announces and demonstrates that God is likewise concerned about men with withered hands, disabled women, and people with dropsy. Jesus heals them so that they, too, can honor God by resting and worshiping on the Sabbath. Jesus' healing actions expand, rather than diminish, reverence for God on the Sabbath.

(2) Luke 14:7-14. While still in the Pharisee's house, the banquet progresses according to typical banquet patterns in antiquity. Meals at banquets were served first, and a time of entertainment, conversation, or teaching followed the meal (see e.g., Talbert, *Reading Luke,* 169–70). For example, in Greco-Roman contexts, banquets served a vital function; they provided "the central arena for social, political, and religious interaction" (Shimoff, "Banquets," 441). Similarly, Jewish banquets appear to be sanitized adaptations of the Greco-Roman symposium that sought to avoid idolatry, illicit sexual activity, and excesses of food and drink. Unlike their pagan counterparts, rabbinic Jews and early Christians frequently appear to have utilized the second half of their ancient banquets to discuss the contours of covenant faithfulness, the Scriptures, and ethical conundrums (Shimoff, "Banquets," 444–47; Talbert, *Reading Luke,* 170).

Presumably after the meal, Jesus tells a parable that critiques the behavior of this elite group that has invited him to dine with them—both host and guests alike. In particular, Jesus notices the extent to which this group of lawyers and Pharisees embodies the pride and arrogance that are more characteristic of Hellenistic cultures. These Pharisees and lawyers appear to value societal status, honor, and prestige in a manner that resembles the honor/shame dynamics of their Greco-Roman counterparts. Jesus, however, narrates a parable that challenges their accepted practices from a profoundly countercultural viewpoint.

In his parabolic scenario, Jesus first depicts his fellow guests at the banquet as those who highly esteem and seek out societal prestige (14:7-11). With pride, they "sit down at the place of honor" when they are invited to a wedding banquet (14:8). But Jesus also points out the flaws in this type of hubris and vainglory. Societal admiration waxes and wanes. It cannot be perpetually controlled. "Hellenistic banquets," and presumably their Jewish adaptations, "were occasions for insulting people as well as honoring them.

Insult was achieved by assigning the intended victim a low-status place among the guests, and instructing the servants to be disrespectful to him. He would be served a poorer quality of food in a meagre quantity, far different from the extravagant array of food offered to other guests" (Shimoff, "Banquets," 443). In essence, guests at a banquet should not seek to elevate themselves because the honor ascribed to a guest by a host can be awarded or revoked on a whim. Societal honor accrued to one's account by his or her peers is a temporary and highly tenuous possession (14:8-9). In contrast to both the Hellenistic and rabbinic norms of banquets in his day, Jesus instructs his audience to seek and to embody humility rather than honor when they attend banquets (14:10-11; cf. Prov 25:6-7).

Having addressed his fellow guests, Jesus now aims to redirect his influential host in 14:12-14. Just as it is foolhardy for guests to seek social advancement and honor from their peers by posturing at banquets, so also it is wrongheaded for a host to plan a banquet with the express purpose of enhancing his or her social standing and reputation. To do so runs counter to the kingdom of God. Rather than using banquets and meals to cultivate reciprocity from and alliances with rich and influential friends as was common in Greco-Roman contexts, Jesus instructs hosts to embody generosity when giving banquets. Rather than seeking to benefit themselves, Jesus implores hosts to serve those in need—"the poor, the crippled, the lame, and the blind" (14:13). Jesus exhorts hosts to use their resources to aid others rather than themselves.

The benefit one gains from investing in the kingdom of God through acts of humility (14:10-11) and generosity (14:13) will result in an enduring blessing on the day of the Lord rather than the temporary honor or limited reciprocity that comes from seeking the favor of one's peers. In particular, unlike hosts and business associates, God's favor is not whimsical, conditional, or short-lived. Even more, humans cannot issue to one another the type of blessing that will be granted "at the resurrection of the righteous" (14:14). Only God can award unconditional approval and permanent benefit to humans.

(3) Luke 14:15-24. While still present at the banquet in the Pharisee's house (14:1) and in response to Jesus' previous statement about the future "resurrection of the righteous" (14:14), one of the other dinner guests provides additional commentary, if not an opposing word, about that future event. The dinner guest seems to assume that all those gathered for the banquet in the Pharisee's house will be included in "the resurrection of the righteous." The dinner guest proclaims, "Blessed is anyone who will eat bread in the kingdom of God!" (cf. Rev 19:9).

Notably, this guest's words supply further evidence that many Jews in the time of Jesus and beyond not only participated in a Jewish version of Hellenistic banquets as we see in 14:1-14 but also began to speak about the age to come as an eschatological banquet (Shimoff, "Banquets," 447). In particular, we see the kingdom of God increasingly depicted as a great banquet in the postexilic and intertestamental periods (e.g., Isa 26:6-8; 55:1-2; 65:13-14) (Bovon, *Luke*, 2:369). By Jesus' day, the phrase "eat bread in the kingdom of God" functioned synonymously with God's expected salvation (cf. 13:29; 22:16, 29-30). Not surprisingly, Jesus likewise portrays the coming kingdom of God as an eschatological banquet on a variety of occasions (e.g., 12:37; 13:29; cf. Rev 19:9).

It is within this context that Jesus tells the parable of the great banquet (14:16-24). Jesus responds to the comment of the anonymous dinner guest; in particular, Jesus responds to his fellow guest's expectations about the coming kingdom of God (14:15). Jesus begins the parable by speaking of a host who follows the conventions of his day. The host invites guests beforehand so that he can prepare appropriately for the banquet (14:16). Presumably, the invited guests then either accept or reject the host's offer at the time of the invitation. Hosts typically invited their guests many hours or even several days ahead of time so they knew how to prepare properly for the banquet (Bovon, *Luke*, 2:369). The host in this parable is no different. Having first established a guest list and then completed the preparations for the banquet, the host now sends his slave out a second time to announce that the time for the banquet has arrived (14:17).

Of course, the problem in the parable surfaces not in the invitation phase or the preparation phase but rather when it comes time for the guests to arrive at the banquet: "They all alike began to make excuses" (14:18). All of the guests back out at the last minute—after the host has already prepared. Furthermore, the excuses that the invitees offer for their absences are non-urgent in nature. None of the excuses constitute unavoidable circumstances or even activities that must take place on that particular day. The first wants to look at his newly purchased land. The second plans to work with his newly acquired oxen, and the third elects to skip the banquet because he desires to stay at home and enjoy the company of the wife he has recently married (14:18-20). In short, the allure of new properties, possessions, and pleasures prevents the guests from honoring their original commitment to the host. Here, the guests are depicted as those who prioritize the mundane over the urgent.

At that point, the host in the parable angrily invites those whom the prevailing culture of the day would typically overlook—people who would not normally make the invitation lists for Hellenistic-style banquets. Consequently, the host instructs his servant to go throughout the town seeking out and bringing back "the poor, the crippled, the blind, and the lame" (14:21). The banquet will still take place as planned, but the guest list will now look shockingly different than the host first envisioned.

Notably, just prior to telling this parable, Jesus sought to redirect his host—the Pharisee who hosted the banquet mentioned in 14:1. Jesus exhorted his Pharisee host to "invite the poor, the crippled, the lame, and the blind" when hosting banquets rather than those who are able to reciprocate his generosity and increase his honor in the community (14:13). Now, in 14:21, Jesus describes the host in the parable as doing the very thing that Jesus just instructed his own host to do in 14:13. After discovering the hard way that seeking to advance one's own social status by doing favors for one's fellow aristocrats is unpredictable and unreliable at best, the host in the parable now invites those in the streets and lanes of the city who cannot enhance his own standing within the community. The jilted host now opts to serve those in need rather than to serve himself.

When the servant informs the host in the parable that there is still more room, however, the host commands his servant to go beyond the boundaries of the town (14:22-23). He commands the servant to compel people who are traveling on the highways and those who are located beyond the walls of the town to join this banquet. Consequently, the banquet will now be filled with needy and disenfranchised locals as well as those from other regions. In essence, the host now uses his banquet to care for the needy and the stranger. His actions can now be characterized as genuine expressions of both charity and hospitality rather than self-serving politics.

Finally, Jesus switches from the singular "you" in 14:23 to the plural "you all" in 14:24a. Consequently, Jesus appears to conclude the parable of the great banquet in 14:24 while simultaneously returning his focus to his own host and fellow dinner guests in 14:24a. The words are both those of the host in the parable and the words of Jesus to his own host and fellow dinner guests (Bovon, *Luke*, 2:374). Recall that in 14:15, one of Jesus' fellow dinner guests appears to comment on "the resurrection of the righteous" by saying that everyone who eats bread in the kingdom of God will blessed (14:13, 15). His fellow dinner guest seems to assume that all of those in attendance at the Pharisee's banquet (14:1) will one day enjoy the feast in the kingdom of God. The Pharisee's banquet provides a mere foretaste of the unimaginable banquet God will host when God's kingdom arrives. Jesus and his parable have the last word, though. The last thing that Jesus says inside the Pharisee's house according to Luke is found in 14:24. Jesus concludes his parable, while apparently turning to his host and guests, and says, "For I tell you [all], none of those who were invited will taste my dinner."

Ultimately, in this final unit of Luke 14:1-24 Jesus responds to his fellow dinner guest's assertion that the coming kingdom of God will be like an extravagant banquet (14:15). By means of this parable, Jesus essentially affirms that this man properly understands the fundamental nature of the kingdom of God. It can indeed be compared to a great, eschatological banquet. Jesus, however, counters the man's expectations about who will participate in the banquet. Even though initially invited, many who are consumed with property, material possessions, and the pleasures of life will elect not to participate in the kingdom of God. They will be distracted precisely at the moment when it is time for the banquet to begin—a moment that is heralded by Jesus' presence among them in Luke 14:1-24.

In essence, Jesus suggests that his fellow dinner guest errs by assuming that God's kingdom will be heavily populated by the social elite and religious leaders of Jesus' day (14:15). Alternatively, Jesus depicts a banquet, and therefore the kingdom of God, as now being populated by two main groups: the needy from within the town and strangers from beyond its walls. Here, much as we see in the Gospel of Matthew and Paul's letter to the Romans, Jesus seems to suggest that God's invitation will be extended first to the descendants of Abraham and only later to the Gentiles. Yet, due to misplaced priorities, many among both groups will miss out on the eschatological banquet.

(4) Luke 14:25-35. In 14:25-35, Jesus resumes his journey to Jerusalem, but thematically Jesus' comments in this unit connect back to the preceding parable. In the previous section, Jesus' fellow dinner guest focused on the future blessings of God (14:15) while seemingly overlooking needy neighbors and strangers who surrounded him in the present (14:21-24). In response, Jesus told a parable about three people who are invited to a great banquet but who are ill prepared to attend the banquet when the time comes. All three tend to mundane matters (their property, their possessions, and the pleasures of life) rather than the urgent matter of a banquet that is now ready.

After resuming his journey, Jesus now warns the crowds around him to avoid the mistake of the three invitees in the parable of the great banquet (14:15-24). Jesus' presence, as the harbinger of God's kingdom, creates an urgent situation in the present that demands an immediate and unadulterated response. Those who wish to follow Jesus cannot elevate property, possessions, and family kinships (14:18-20) above the urgent and all-consuming call to follow Jesus. Disciples must devote themselves to the kingdom of God, which is now breaking in through the presence of Jesus. In particular, Jesus makes it clear that devotion to possessions and devotion to Jesus are incompatible with one another (14:33). True discipleship requires a singular commitment to Jesus.

More Parables and Teaching (15:1–17:10)

Next, Luke constructs a literary unit that runs from 15:1 to 17:10. Presumably, the Pharisees, scribes, tax collectors, sinners, and disciples all hear Jesus' remarks throughout this unit, which includes five noteworthy parables—the parables of the lost sheep (15:3-7), lost coin (15:8-10), lost son (15:11-32), dishonest manager (16:1-8a), and the rich man and Lazarus (16:19-31). Over the course of the unit, however, Jesus oscillates from one focal audience to another. Jesus begins by addressing the Pharisees and scribes directly (15:1), turns to speak with the disciples (16:1), returns to chastise the Pharisees, and concludes by providing some final exhortations to his disciples (17:1)—all in one setting. Throughout this unit, Jesus highlights the mercy of God, which in turn leads to the forgiveness of sin and the restoration of right relations with God and others. At the same time, however, Jesus also lifts up repentance as the proper human response to the arrival of God's kingdom. Just as God called his people to repent throughout the Jewish Scriptures in the past (16:16, 31), so also in Luke's Gospel both John and Jesus now beckon all to repent in light of God's coming salvation, which manifests itself through the forgiveness of sins (1:76-77; 3:3-14) and the kingdom of God (16:16).

Parables about "Lost" Things (15:1-32)

(1) Luke 15:1-2. The entirety of Luke 15 forms a sustained, four-part justification of Jesus' response to "tax collectors and sinners." Notice, for example, that Luke establishes the context for all of 15:3-32 in 15:1-2. Tax collectors and sinners come near to Jesus and listen to him, but the Pharisees and the scribes grumble about this dynamic. Astute readers should then be mindful of that contrast (tax collectors and sinners versus Pharisees and scribes) throughout Luke 15.

In short, the Pharisees and scribes consider Jesus' warm reception of the tax collectors and sinners to serve as proof that Jesus does not understand God or represent God in any way. In their thinking, if Jesus were from God, he would not allow the tax collectors and sinners to be near him. Luke's defense of Jesus on this topic unfolds as follows. Jesus narrates three consecutive parables on the same topic to address the doubts and criticisms of the Pharisees and scribes. He tells the parable of the lost sheep, the parable of the lost coin, and the parable of the lost son. Each parable drives home the same point. Yet the final parable has two distinct halves. The first half (15:11-24) coincides with the pattern and the point of the first two parables (15:3-7, 8-10), but the second half of the third parable (15:25-32) turns the conversation in a new direction.

(2) Luke 15:3-10. Jesus begins by narrating two fictive stories that establish his overriding response to the Pharisees' questions. First, he tells the parable of the lost sheep (15:3-7), and second, he tells the parable of the lost coin (15:8-10). Jesus invites his listeners to place themselves in both situations (15:4, 8). He assumes that anyone who loses a sheep out of a herd or a coin out of a collection will rejoice upon recovering it or finding it (15:6, 9). The stakes increase from the first story to the second story. In the first, the shepherd loses one hundredth of his flock. The woman, however, loses one tenth of her assets. In both cases, however, Jesus uses these fictive human experiences to create an analogy about how God cares for humans. In both cases, Jesus moves from the lesser to the greater. If a shepherd rejoices over a sheep that is found and if a woman rejoices over a coin that is found, how much more does God rejoice over a sinner who repents (15:7, 10)? Both parables end with a focus on God's celebration over repentant sinners.

(3) Luke 15:11-24. Jesus then ups the ante with his third parable. Here Jesus sustains the pattern he established in the first two parables, but he adds greater complexity into the mix. To begin with, the father loses far more than the shepherd or the woman. The shepherd lost one sheep out of one hundred and the woman lost one coin out of ten, but the father loses one out of his two sons. Even worse, neither sheep nor coins willfully lose themselves, but the lost son in Jesus' parable makes a conscious, calloused, and calculated decision to separate from his father, his family, and his homeland. He requests an early inheritance and relocates to a distant country (15:12-13). On top of everything else, the lost son squanders his resources and makes poor life choices (15:13-14). While neglecting adherence to the Jewish laws of purification (e.g., Lev 11:7; Deut 14:8), the man survives the abject poverty that was a natural consequence of his own decisions by tending pigs even as he longs to eat their slop (15:14-16) (Bock, *Luke*, 2:1311; Green, *Luke*, 580).

In essence, the father not only loses one of his two sons, but the son also knowingly rejects his father in the process (Bock, *Luke*, 2:1309–10). The son treats his father "as if he were dead" (Talbert, *Reading Luke*, 179). Jesus describes the younger son as both lost and prodigal. Moreover, the father is not positioned to correct the problem all by himself. The shepherd searches for his lost sheep, and the woman sweeps her house to find her lost coin, but the father of a rebellious son cannot act unilaterally. The father must first wait, watch, and hope for his son's return (15:20). It will do no good to search for and find a son who does not wish to return home.

Just as the causes and the predicament of the lost son are more complex than those of the lost sheep or the lost coin, the return of the lost son is also more complex. The son must participate in his own return; he must repent or change directions. Whenever the prodigal son concludes that it is both possible and wise to return home, he does so. He no longer expects to be regarded as a son, but he hopes to become one of his father's hired servants. Moreover, he approaches his father with humility and an admission of "sin" against both God and his father (15:17-19, 21). Whereas early on he acted out of defiance and rebellion, now, in the end, he opts for humble repentance.

The father likewise plays an instrumental role in the return of his son. The father sees him from far off as if the father has been actively looking and waiting for his return. Rather than treating him as an enemy, a stranger, or even as a servant, the father compassionately restores him to the status of treasured son complete with an expensive robe, sandals, and ring (15:20-22) (Danker, *Jesus*, 277; Green, *Luke*, 583). In short, the son repents and requests mercy, and the father responds far more graciously than the son had even hoped. Most important for Jesus' broader point in Luke 15:1-32, this parable ends with the father celebrating the return of his lost son. He throws a banquet and celebrates the son that was lost and is now found (15:23).

(4) Luke 15:3-24. At this point, the commonalities among the three parables (15:3-7, 8-10, 11-24) are pronounced. All three of the parables conclude with an emphasis on rejoicing when something or someone who was lost is found. In particular, the vocabulary present in the conclusions of the first two parables is sprinkled throughout the narrative flow of the third parable. In 15:7 and 15:10, Jesus says that there is "joy in heaven" (or God rejoices) when a sinner repents. In 15:18 and 15:21, the lost son refers to himself as a sinner. His return home portrays repentance (15:17-21), and the father's welcome illustrates what rejoicing and celebration look like in this particular setting (15:22-24). Neither Jesus nor Luke need to supply a concluding statement about heaven rejoicing over a sinner who repents in 15:17-24 as we saw in 15:7 and 15:10 because the pattern has already been established. Careful readers already know that Jesus has again explained why he "welcomes sinners and eats with them" (15:1-2). Jesus has convincingly demonstrated that God welcomes repentant sinners and tax collectors and rejoices over their desire to be in relationship with God. Jesus, as God's son, can do no different.

Jesus' Journey to Jerusalem

(5) Luke 15:25-32. The alternative group, however, consists of "righteous persons who need no repentance" (15:7)—a reference to the Pharisees and scribes who are present in 15:1-2. Consequently, Jesus will address God's reaction to this second group—the Pharisees and the scribes—throughout the rest of the narrative unit (15:25–17:10). Beginning in 15:25, Jesus maintains the same fictive context (the parable of the lost son), but he pushes on to teach an additional point, one that is different from the point he just established in 15:3-24.

After establishing that God welcomes repentant sinners and tax collectors and that Jesus is justified in doing the same, Jesus now appears to address the grumbling and the complaining of the Pharisees and scribes (15:1-2). Jesus does this by continuing the parable; he shifts the focus, however, to the older son. Jesus begins to illustrate what a "righteous person who needs no repentance," to which he alluded in 15:7, looks like. The elder son grumbles and complains while believing himself to be righteous and not in need of repentance. The elder son has remained with the father from the beginning, dutifully working in the fields (15:25, 29, 31). At first, he looks like the model son. Yet he cannot rejoice over the repentant return of his brother, nor can he himself repent of his failure to rejoice. Instead, he grows angry, refuses to celebrate, and resents his father's merciful response (15:28-30). The elder son will not even refer to his brother as such, only as his father's son (lit., "this son of yours") (15:30).

Ironically, the father did not search for the younger son in the far country, even though he longingly waited for his return. Now, however, the father searches for the older son just as the shepherd searched for his sheep (15:4) and the woman searched for her coin (15:8). The father values the older son so much that he leaves the celebration to find the older son and plead with him to join the party (15:28, 31-32). At this juncture, a careful reader may ask whether the older son is now likewise being depicted as "a lost son."

Jesus leaves this puzzle unresolved. When Jesus concludes the parable in 15:32, the younger son has been fully restored. In addition, the father eagerly offers mercy or forgiveness and restoration to the older son, but it remains unclear whether the older son will ever go inside the house and celebrate. The father has done his part, but it remains unclear whether the older son will do his. It remains unclear whether the strained familial relationships will ever be restored. It remains unclear whether the older brother will ever "come to himself," confess his sinfulness, and humbly reunite with his father and brother. At the conclusion of the parable, the older son still resembles a person who believes he does not need to repent (15:8).

Just as the younger son depicts the reaction of the sinners and tax collectors to Jesus' ministry, here the older son depicts the reaction of the Pharisees and scribes to Jesus' ministry (Fitzmyer, *Luke*, 2:1091; Parsons, *Luke*, 242). They are stuck in a cycle of anger and grumbling due to the mercy shown to the sinners and tax collectors (15:1-2). Even though Jesus hopes they, too, will join the celebration, their future course of action remains in doubt. It remains unclear whether they can "come to themselves," confess their sinfulness, and humbly reunite with God's household. Forgiveness of sin awaits, but repentance seems to be the hurdle.

As we have seen in other instances, Luke's first readers may have detected a second layer of application in Luke 15. In addition to the context and intended meaning in Jesus' day, some readers in Luke's day may have detected an additional commentary on the sometimes challenging Jew-Gentile relationships within the early Christian communities. For example, Luke alludes to strained relationships between some Jewish and Gentile Christians in Acts 11:1-3 and 15:5 (cf. Acts 6:1-6). In this train of thought, some Jewish Christians in the latter half of the first century CE may have resembled the Pharisees, scribes, and older brother who struggled to welcome and celebrate the inclusion of Gentile believers within the Christian fold. Evidence marshaled from Luke 15 to support this view includes the close association between tax collectors and their Gentile overlords (15:1); the fact that the younger son goes to a distant country (15:13), works with swine (15:15), allegedly visits prostitutes (15:30), and engages in "dissolute living" (15:13); and the general belief that the Pharisaic movement morphed into Rabbinic Judaism in the later part of the first century CE. If so, the father's impassioned invitation to the older son depicts an emotionally painful struggle that is similar Paul's in Rom 9–11 when he discusses the broader question of God's love for the Jewish people and the Gentile believers. The door remains wide open to the elder sons (and daughters) among the children of God, but it remains unclear how many will now join the celebration.

Parables about Wealth (16:1-31)

(1) Luke 16:1-13. The parable of the dishonest manager presents interpreters with numerous challenges. For example, the Greek word *kurios*, or "lord," refers to both the rich man in the parable (16:5, 8) and to God in the post-parable explanation (16:13), which raises the disturbing question of whether the rich man in the parable depicts an aspect of God's character. Even more challenging, at the end of the parable, both the rich man (16:8a) and Jesus (16:8b-9) appear to commend the dishonest manager for engaging

Jesus' Journey to Jerusalem

in crooked business transactions (Gk. *mamōnas*) (16:9). Moreover, Jesus goes on to describe a proper relationship between God and humans in light of this unsettling parable (16:10-13). As a result, one must rely heavily on the preceding material (the parable of the lost son in 15:11-24) and the subsequent material (the parable of the rich man and Lazarus in 16:19-31) in order to navigate this challenging story. We will consider the broader narrative context first.

The parable of the dishonest steward and its explanation (16:1-13) is embedded in a unified narrative context that runs from 15:1–17:10 (see e.g., Brobst-Renaud, "The Elder Son's Quandary," 169–252). While journeying to Jerusalem, the Pharisees and scribes criticize Jesus for welcoming and eating with tax collectors and sinners (15:1-2). Immediately after addressing the Pharisees and their complaints in 15:3-32, Jesus turns to address his disciples in 16:1-13 before directly addressing the Pharisees again in 16:14-31. The Pharisees and scribes as well as the disciples all appear to be present throughout Luke 15:1–17:10, but Jesus addresses his disciples as his focal audience in 16:1-13.

By placing the parable of the lost son (15:11-24), the parable of the dishonest manager (16:1-8), and the parable of the rich man and Lazarus (16:19-31) in a consecutive order, Luke helps his readers understand the character of both the manager and the rich man in the parable of the dishonest manager. For instance, both the younger son in the parable of the lost son and the manager in the parable of the dishonest manager irresponsibly "squander" (Gk. *diaskorpiz*) (15:13; 16:1) the wealth that has been entrusted to them. In both cases Jesus characterizes the squandering of possessions negatively. Most certainly, prior to "coming to himself" (15:11-16), the younger son provides a negative example of one who makes grave mistakes. So also the dishonest manager represents a negative character in 16:1-2 who does his own reflective soul searching in 16:3-4 (Scott, *Hear then the Parable*, 260–62).

Yet thereafter their paths diverge. Whereas the younger son relies on humility, confession, and a request for mercy (15:17-21), the dishonest manager becomes even more deceitful (16:4-7). In essence, rather than repenting and requesting mercy as we see with the prodigal son (15:11-24), the dishonest manager relies on himself and doubles down on his underhanded dealings. The dishonest manager establishes obligatory reciprocity among the rich man's debtors (16:4) by altering the rich man's business records and lowering the amount of money that the debtors owe the rich man (16:5-7). In essence, he gives away his master's money behind his master's back. Moreover, whereas the younger son in Luke 15 requests to work as one of his father's servants (15:19), this dishonest manager has no ability or desire to work as a typical servant. He is "not strong enough to dig" and he is "ashamed to beg" (16:3). As a servant, he is worthless. Rather than electing a different path after engaging in soul searching (15:17-19; 16:3-4), his true identity becomes even clearer as he engages in subterfuge. Unlike the positive example of the younger son's repentance, the dishonest manager provides a negative example throughout 16:1-8a.

We see a similar comparison between the father of the lost son (or the prodigal son) in the previous parable (15:11-24) and the rich man who fires his manager in the parable of the dishonest manager (16:1-8a). Even though Luke never describes the father of the two sons in Luke 15 as "rich" (Gk. *plousios*), the father in Luke 15 clearly possesses significant financial resources. Rather than being a subsistence-level farmer, the father is capable of giving substantial assets to the younger son (15:12-13). In addition, the redeeming father has servants or slaves, valuable clothes, a fatted calf, and presumably goats (15:22-23, 29). Despite these riches, Jesus clearly portrays the father in Luke 15 in a positive light.

That is not the case, however, with the "rich man" in Luke 16:1-8a. Though both the father of the prodigal son and the rich man in 16:1-8a have significant assets, Jesus' portrayal of the two men diverges greatly. When Jesus refers to the man in the parable of the dishonest manager as "rich" (16:1), Jesus has already placed the man in a negative light. For instance, at numerous points in Luke's Gospel, Luke employs the adjective "rich" (Gk. *plousios*) to paint a negative portrait of a wealthy person (1:53; 6:24; 12:16, 21; 14:12; 16:19, 21; 18:23, 25; 19:2; 21:1; Furfey, "PLOUSIOS," 243–63). Indeed, Luke never uses the word "rich" to place a person in a positive light. Perhaps the best example of the moral bankruptcy associated with "rich" people in Luke's Gospel can be found in the next parable, the parable of the rich man and Lazarus (16:19-31). Here also (16:1-8a) Jesus depicts the rich man in the parable of the dishonest manager negatively (Scott, *Hear then the Parable*, 260–62). Notice that the rich man simply hears a report of his servant's dishonesty. In Jesus' parable, the rich man never even verifies the accuracy of the report about his servant. The rich man simply elects to fire his servant on the spot.

Consequently, despite the fact that Luke characterizes both men as wealthy individuals, we see a stark contrast between the reaction of the redeeming father in Luke 15 and the rich man in 16:1-8a. Despite his son squandering his possessions, the redeeming father welcomes the prodigal son and restores him to his original status whenever his son asks for mercy. Conversely, the rich man in 16:1-8a demonstrates no mercy whatsoever. He merely hears a report that his manager is squandering his property, and he immediately elects to remove the manager from a position of authority. The manager's hope that the rich man's debtors will welcome him "into their homes" (16:4) suggests that the manager has been or will be expelled from the rich man's household altogether.

As a result, whereas Luke portrays the father in Luke 15 in an exceedingly positive light, he portrays the rich man in 16:1-8a in an equally negative light. In short, neither Jesus nor Luke wants his audiences to see images of God in the parable of the dishonest manager. Similarly, they do not want their audiences to emulate the character of the rich man or the manager in 16:1-8a. Both are negative characters that illustrate negative cultural realities in antiquity (Scott, *Hear Then the Parable*, 260–65). The manager fails to exhibit actions associated with repentance, and the rich man fails to exhibit actions associated with mercy.

If Luke's audience is to view both the rich man and his manager negatively, what then is the point of Jesus' parable? As we have seen at other points in this Gospel, Jesus frequently employs the logic of the lesser to the greater while teaching his disciples. Jesus does so again in Luke 16:1-8a. In short, Jesus first describes a common cultural reality of his day before using that lesser cultural reality as an illustration of a greater spiritual reality. Jesus sketches the former in 16:1-8a, and Jesus expounds on the latter in 16:8b-13.

The manager proves to be dishonest because he encourages his master's debtors to alter their bills so that they will now only pay the master between 50 and 80 percent of what they previously owed him (16:5-7). The manager's dishonesty accomplishes two objectives. First, he out-maneuvers his rich master. After notifying the manager of his impending termination, the rich master makes the mistake of allowing the manager to remain temporarily as the spokesperson for his business operations. The rich man unwisely affords his manager with time to undercut him. In the process, the dishonest manager legally and permanently alters the bills. He decreases the debts that the rich man's customers owe. Now, even if the rich man cries foul and attempts to increase the amounts his customers owe him, the rich man will forever lose the trust and goodwill of his customers. The rich man has been checkmated by the manager whom he deemed to be unworthy of the position.

Second, the manager establishes reciprocity with the rich man's debtors. Having aided each of the rich man's debtors, the terminated manager has positioned himself well for the future. He will now be able to request favors of his own from the rich man's debtors. In the process, the manager has now shown considerable initiative, and he has almost certainly secured a brighter future for himself. Due to his newly established alliances, the dismissed manager can likely avoid digging or begging as he hopes (16:3). At the conclusion of this parable, the rich man can do nothing except compliment the manager for his cunning strategy and shrewd decision-making (16:8a).

Jesus then makes a series of comments about the parable of the dishonest manager. He first makes a "lesser" cultural observation before he moves on to make a "greater" spiritual application that derives from the parable. For instance, in 16:8a Jesus provides commentary on the cultural context of his day by pointing out that "the children of this age" are shrewder than "the children of light." Presumably, Jesus' disciples are included among "the children of light." Jesus therefore comments on the broader culture of his day ("the children of this age") as he addresses his own disciples ("the children of light").

In some ways, the dishonest manager may well have reminded Luke's Greco-Roman readers of their own legendary heroes, like Odysseus. Ancient writers repeatedly praise Odysseus for out-maneuvering his adversaries. For example, Odysseus concocts the plan to build a large wooden horse, smuggle Greek soldiers inside Troy's city walls by hiding them in the belly of the horse, and subsequently overthrow Greece's enemies (Virgil, *Aen.*, 2.17–319; cf. Homer, *Il.* 23.68–91, 24.778–79). On another occasion, Odysseus wisely lies to the Cyclops and claims his name is "Noman" or "Nobody" (Homer, *Od.*, 9.360–68). Consequently, once Odysseus blinds the Cyclops by shoving a spear into the Cyclops's eye, Odysseus is able to escape the territory unhindered while the Cyclops shouts to his fellow barbarians asking for help and telling them that "Noman is killing me" (Homer, *Od.*, 9:407). Whereas the Cyclopes would have otherwise begun hunting the perpetrator, they instead conclude that their colleague injured himself since "no man" did this to him. Accordingly, Homer's primary epitaph for Odysseus in the *Odyssey* is "cunning Odysseus" (e.g., Homer, *Od.*, 13.299–310). Odysseus is revered for his cunning deceit and shrewd dishonesty, traits that the Greeks still valued in first-century CE contexts.

Thus, in Luke 16:8b Jesus states what would have been obvious to Luke's readers. The manager exemplifies the cultural reality that being shrewd with one's material possessions allows one to secure one's future just as the dishonest manager does. In Luke 16:9, however, Jesus pivots from "the lesser" to "the greater." Shockingly, Jesus directs his disciples to make friends using mammon (or material possessions) so that they, too, can set up future homes for themselves (16:9). If Jesus stopped teaching in 16:9, one might think that Jesus is exhorting his disciples to be like the dishonest manager. Yet by reading the material that directly follows Jesus' exhortation in 16:10-31, it becomes clear that Jesus is saying just the opposite.

As early as Luke 12:15, Jesus warned his disciples to avoid greed. Instead, he taught them to sell their possessions, give to the poor, and thereby store up treasure in heaven (12:32-34). Here in 16:9, the disciples should recall the lessons that Jesus has already taught them. In particular, Jesus has already taught "the children of light" to be shrewd with their money; being shrewd with money, however, looks different for "the children of light" than it does for "the children of this age." Jesus wants them to store up heavenly treasures and dwellings as opposed to material treasures and earthly dwellings (12:33; 16:9, 22-23). In essence, Jesus' comments in 16:8b are about the obvious dynamics of the world in which the disciples live, but his comments in 16:9 are about the distinctive manner in which disciples must live as "children of the light."

Jesus further illuminates this distinct manner of life for disciples in 16:10-13. He establishes two fundamental contrasts. First, in 16:11 Jesus contrasts mammon (Gk. *mamōnas*), or earthly riches, with true riches. Faithfulness with the former leads to the latter, but unfaithfulness with the former prevents one from experiencing the latter. Moreover, "faithfulness" is the proper terminology because it is a matter of stewardship. Jesus teaches his disciples that earthly riches belong "to another" (16:12). Children of the light properly view themselves as managers or caretakers of "another's" resources—presumably God's resources. This conviction segues into the second contrast, which is a contrast between God and mammon. In the fictive world of the parable, Jesus only referred to one master, but now he refers to two. Jesus contends that "no slave can serve two masters" (16:13). Rather, whereas the children of this age serve mammon as their master, the children of light must exclusively serve God.

(2) Luke 16:14-31. Despite the challenges that modern interpreters face when deciphering Jesus' points in 16:1-13, the Pharisees understood Jesus' message perfectly (16:14). The Pharisees, who have been present since 15:1-2 and who were Jesus' primary audience in 15:3-32, once again become his focal audience beginning in 16:14. Perhaps articulating the harshest critique of the Pharisees in Luke's Gospel, Luke tells us that the Pharisees are "lovers of money" and that when they hear Jesus' remarks about the parable of the dishonest manager (16:1-13), they scoff at Jesus (16:14). When Jesus tells the disciples that they cannot serve both material possessions, or mammon, and God as their masters (16:13), the Pharisees mock and ridicule Jesus. Luke implies that the Pharisees ultimately attempt to serve material possessions as their master alongside God (16:14-15).

This clash between Jesus and the Pharisees over the proper perspective on material possessions provides the backdrop for Jesus' remaining comments in

16:14-31. Furthermore, the remainder of Luke 16 falls into an aba'b' chiastic pattern. Jesus' comments in Luke 16:14-15 correspond to the first half of the parable of the rich man and Lazarus (16:19-24), and Jesus' comments in Luke 16:16-18 correspond to the last half of the parable (16:25-31) (Ellis, *Gospel of Luke*, 201).

Jesus' teaching in 16:14-15 is simple enough. Whereas Luke describes the Pharisees as lovers of money (or literally, "lovers of silver"), Jesus strongly critiques them for being out of step with God. Publicly, they proclaim or portray themselves as righteous, but God cares about the heart—and God deems those who prize silver over God to be detestable.

Jesus illustrates this teaching (16:14-15) in the first half of the parable of the rich man and Lazarus (16:19-24). The rich man is the embodiment of one who loves money. He dresses in the most extravagant clothes, and every day he eats large amounts of the finest foods (16:19). Jesus then illustrates his previous statement in 16:15 more fully: "God knows your hearts; for what is prized by human beings is an abomination in the sight of God." Counter to the prevailing notions of the day that frequently considered material possessions to be an indication of God's favor (Talbert, *Reading Luke*, 186), Jesus claims that God's judgment focuses on the human heart (or the seat of moral, ethical, and spiritual decision-making); the presence or the absence of possessions are not reliable indicators of God's judgment (Talbert, *Reading Luke*, 186). For example, Jesus discloses how God evaluates the rich man's heart whenever Jesus introduces "a poor man named Lazarus" into the story. Lazarus lays at the rich man's gate "covered with sores"—an implicit request for assistance from the rich man. He longs to satisfy his hunger with the scraps "from the rich man's table" (16:20-21). Yet no one, and in particular the rich man, aids him. Instead, wild dogs lick his sores while he is unable to fend them off. Notably, Jesus does not give his audience any reason to think that this poor, sick man is responsible for his own predicament. Rather, as far as we know, he is a helpless victim in need of mercy. The rich man, however, shows no sign whatsoever of being merciful.

At this point, Lazarus's miserable state may remind us of the lost (or prodigal) son's miserable state in 15:14-16 or the crisis that befell the dishonest manager in 16:1-2. As a result, comparing the reactions of the wealthy men to those facing a crisis in the three parables proves profitable. For the second time in Luke 16 we see a "rich man" who responds far differently than the merciful father in Luke 15 (16:19; cf. 16:1). Whereas the father of the lost or prodigal son in Luke 15:22-24 restores his needy son to full status, the first rich man in Luke 16 rejects mercy and definitively banishes his dishonest manager (16:1-2). Similarly, the second rich man in Luke 16 fails to extend any form of mercy to Lazarus (16:19). Unlike the first rich man (16:1-2) who responds with harsh action, this second rich man (16:19-21) is guilty of negligence. He commits a sin of omission by failing to assist the one in need. Moreover, unlike the lost son who willfully terminates a relationship with his father (15:12-13) and squanders his inheritance (15:13) or the manager who opts for dishonest actions (16:8a) and carelessly squanders his master's assets (15:13; 16:1), Jesus does not indicate that poor Lazarus (16:20-21) does anything to justify his miserable state. In essence, the "heart" of the rich man in this parable is especially calloused. Daily he indulges himself, while daily he neglects the needs of a blameless person.

Jesus then demonstrates how God judges based on the human heart rather than human esteem (16:15) when he narrates the eternal outcome of the two men in the parable of the rich man and Lazarus (16:22-24). Their fates may remind attentive readers of Mary's *Magnificat*. After hearing the news of Jesus' conception, Mary proclaimed that God has "filled the hungry with good things and sent the rich away empty" (1:53).

When poor Lazarus dies, the angels carry him to Abraham's bosom—an exceedingly positive destination. Jewish writers from the period between the testaments envision Abraham as the person whom God has selected to welcome and to host God's faithful followers into the afterlife (e.g., 4 Macc 13:17; see Marshall, *Luke*, 636). Likely God's choice of Abraham for this role was due to the magnanimous hospitality that Abraham extended to the three travelers (or angels) in Gen 18:1-16 (Arterbury, "Abraham's Hospitality," 359–76). Abraham not only eagerly welcomed the strangers but was also incredibly generous in his hospitality. For example, he ran out to greet passing strangers; he did not wait for them to request aid. Moreover, Abraham hurriedly prepared vast amounts of food—far more than his guests could have ever eaten in one sitting (Hamilton, *Genesis*, 11). In short, by seeing Lazarus at Abraham's side in the afterlife, Luke's first readers would know that though poor Lazarus suffered daily during his life, in death God rewards him with an unimaginably blissful existence.

Conversely, when the rich man dies, not even a proper burial aids him in the afterlife (16:22). Instead, he finds himself in Hades where he is tormented by the flames (16:24). Moreover, he is able to see Lazarus at Abraham's side, and both are far removed from him (16:23). Even worse, because he is now separated from Abraham, the ancestor of the Jewish people, it stands to reason that he is likewise separated from God's own presence. All the rich man can do is call out for mercy (16:24).

Perhaps the Pharisees to whom Jesus is speaking (as well as Luke's audience) may again recall the younger son in Luke 15 who likewise requests mercy (15:17-21). If the prodigal son can deny a relationship with his father, go to a far country, squander all his possessions, and still receive mercy from his welcoming father, perhaps "Father Abraham" will respond similarly (16:24). Perhaps "Father Abraham" will graciously rescue the rich man from Hades or at least mercifully reduce his agony (16:23-24). Yet when the rich man in 16:19-31 requests mercy, he provides a stark contrast to the prodigal son in Luke 15. The prodigal son combined actions of repentance with a request for mercy. The rich man, however, only asks for mercy. He exhibits no remorse over his prior neglect of Lazarus. Instead, he now hopes that Abraham will send the one whom he failed to assist on a daily basis to assist him. Abraham's stoic response, which falls in the second half of the parable (16:25-31), squelches this rich man's petition for mercy.

Jesus relies on the second half of the parable of the rich man and Lazarus (16:25-31) to illuminate the second portion of his teachings in 16:16-18. Akin to 16:14-15, Jesus' teachings in 16:16-18 are seemingly straightforward, but the implications of his comments are considerably more complicated than 16:14-15. Jesus addresses the topic of the OT law in 16:16-18. He points out that the Law and the Prophets guided God's people until the arrival of John the Baptist. As Mary (1:46-55) and Zechariah (1:67-79) foretold, John the Baptist announced that the "salvation" of God's people "by the forgiveness of their sins" was at hand (1:77; 3:3-6). He heralded good news of a new day; he proclaimed the arrival of "the kingdom of God" (16:16). In essence, John announced that God's promises to Abraham (1:54-55, 72-74) and David (1:68-71) as chronicled in the Law and the Prophets were most fully realized in Jesus' arrival (24:27, 44; Werline, *Pray Like This*, 115). A dramatic shift in God's salvific work has taken place (16:16). Jesus himself later describes it as the inauguration of a new covenant previously prophesied by Jeremiah (Luke 22:20; Jer 31:31-34; 32:38-40). In sum, Jesus' presence, as heralded by John, introduces a new form of God's rescue and redemption in the world.

Through the proclamation of both John and Jesus, Luke wants his readers to conclude that God has kept God's covenant promises (1:1). While God has been faithful to rescue God's people throughout the centuries, God's salvation has now been most fully enacted through the forgiveness of sins as inaugurated by and through Jesus (24:45-47). Consequently, Jesus claims that everyone desperately wants to participate in this long-awaited kingdom of God, so much so that they attempt to enter it by force (16:16). This urgency seemingly grows out of an awareness of this new development in God's longstanding salvific work. The rich man in 16:19-31 and the Pharisees to whom Jesus is speaking, however, appear to be examples of those who hope to enter the kingdom of God by some means other than God's mercy and forgiveness.

Yet John not only proclaims the fulfillment of God's covenant promises through the forgiveness of sins in Luke's Gospel but also insists that claiming Abraham as one's ancestor, or literally "father," is not enough. Instead, to be counted among Abraham's descendants—and therefore to be counted among God's people—one must "bear good fruit" or risk being like a tree that "is cut down and thrown into the fire" (3:7-14). The inauguration of this good news about the arrival of God's kingdom does not now render the Law and the Prophets useless or invalid. Rather, as Jesus says in 16:17, "it is easier for heaven and earth to pass away than for one stroke of a letter in the law to be dropped." In short, the word of the Lord that came through the Law and the Prophets remains a faithful guide according to both John and Jesus even after the dramatic shift of Jesus' arrival. God's past instruction continues to reveal God's character and God's desires for God's people. The same God who has been rescuing and redeeming God's people for centuries is at work both before and after Jesus' birth. "Forgiveness of sin" and "the kingdom of God" are now essential for "salvation," but the Law and the Prophets remain relevant.

Jesus then provides a specific example of this dynamic—the realization that Jesus' presence ushers in a new means of salvation even though the importance of the Law and the Prophets has not been diminished. To illustrate his point, Jesus refers to instructions about divorce in the OT (16:18). To divorce one's spouse in order to marry another as Herod Antipas does in Luke 3:19-20 is nothing short of adultery (Matt 19:9; Mark 10:11-12). Even if one attempts to issue a proper decree of divorce, God forbade adultery in the past and forbids it in the present. In that regard, the Law will not be dropped (16:17). When one goes against the Law and the Prophets as in the case of adultery, it reveals the state of one's heart (16:15).

Jesus then further illustrates the relevance of the Law and the Prophets in the latter half of the parable of the rich man and Lazarus (16:25-31). Throughout the Law and the Prophets, God repeatedly calls the Hebraic people to repentance, just as John does in Luke 3:1-14. That call to repentance frequently includes a call for the rich to remember God's covenant demands and to assist the poor (e.g., Lev 19:9-10; 23:22; Amos 4:1-3; 5:11-15). The rich man, however, ignored the teachings of the Law and the Prophets throughout his lifetime even though they remain in force (16:16-21). In the afterlife, the rich man asks "father Abraham" to commission Lazarus to minister to him in his burning agony. Even now the rich man's heart reveals that he sees himself as the one who should be served and Lazarus as the one who should serve (16:15). The rich man's request shows no sign of true repentance even as he endures tormenting flames. He requests mercy, but he does not embrace repentance. As a result, Abraham speaks of a cosmic reversal that is reminiscent of the reversal that Mary first proclaimed in the *Magnificat* (16:25; cf. 1:53). Abraham declares that God's judgment has been rendered; the rich man's cry for mercy is rejected (16:24-26).

The rich man then makes a second plea for mercy. He asks "father" Abraham to send Lazarus as a messenger to his family in the hope they that may repent before it is too late and thereby avoid his own mistakes. If his personal plea for mercy was rejected, perhaps a plea of mercy for others will be well received. (Again, Luke's audience would almost certainly recall the prodigal son's plea for mercy, which was granted in abundance in 15:18-21 but which was accompanied by repentance.) Abraham, however, sees no reason to send Lazarus to rescue the rich man's family. Instead, he indicates that "they have Moses and the prophets; they should listen to them" (16:29). In essence, they are already ignoring God's urgent calls to repentance found throughout the OT. Therefore, no additional voice is needed. In particular, if they will not listen to the Scriptures, "neither will they be convinced even if someone rises from the dead" (16:31).

Jesus' conclusion to the parable seems to address directly not only the rich man in the parable but also the rich Pharisees to whom Jesus is speaking (16:14). The conclusion narrates Abraham's critique of the rich man's family within the parable as well as Jesus' critique of the Pharisees in Luke's Gospel. Jesus' reference to someone rising from the dead alludes to his own impending death and resurrection, which functions as a far greater sign than a ghostly appearance from Lazarus. In other words, Jesus functions as the clearest revelation of God and God's work in the world, and he is standing right in front of the Pharisees calling them to repentance and forgiveness. Yet if neither the OT Scriptures, on which Luke relies to interpret Jesus and his ministry, nor Jesus himself are enough to persuade the Pharisees to request God's mercy for their transgressions and to repent, then their fate is forever sealed.

Exhorting his Disciples (17:1-10)

The final section of the narrative unit that runs from 15:1 to 17:10 begins in 17:1. Jesus began by addressing the Pharisees (15:1), turned to speak with the disciples (16:1), returned to chastise the Pharisees, and now concludes by providing some final exhortations to the disciples (17:1) all in one setting. When Jesus wraps up this lengthy dialogue, which includes five of his parables (the lost sheep, the lost coin, the lost son, the dishonest manager, and the rich man and Lazarus), he begins with a philosophical tone by saying "Occasions for stumbling are bound to come" (17:1). In other words, Jesus acknowledges that it is impossible to prevent all temptations or instances of tripping over sin. At this point, careful readers will likely recall the unrepentant and joyless elder brother, the dishonest manager, and the rich man who neglects to assist poor Lazarus as instances of "stumbling" or tripping over sin in this narrative unit (15:1–17:10). Furthermore, Luke's first readers almost certainly considered the Pharisees and scribes' judgmental questioning (15:1-2) and love of money (16:14-15) to be instances of stumbling as well. Jesus, however, warns his disciples against tripping over these types of sinful mistakes (17:1). Even more, Jesus cautions his disciples against leading others, specifically their fellow disciples, or literally "these little ones," down similar paths. The consequences for such mistakes will be dire (17:1-2). Jesus therefore commands them to pay attention to or to guard against these predictable temptations (17:3a), an exhortation that Jesus will use increasingly throughout the rest of Luke's Gospel (e.g., 21:34, 36; 22:40, 46).

Jesus then takes the conversation in a different direction. After prohibiting his disciples from being sources of temptation or guides who lead their fellow disciples toward sin, Jesus now talks about a situation in which a fellow disciple, literally "a brother," is the one who stumbles. How should the disciples who have not sinned respond? First, Jesus wants the disciples to rebuke their fellow disciple who has sinned. Second, if the offender repents, Jesus is quick to say that his disciples must forgive (17:3). Furthermore, forgiveness is the correct response to a repentant, fellow disciple regardless of how many times that disciple stumbles—as many as seven times a day (17:4).

These topics of repentance and forgiveness are notable in part because of the role they play in the preceding parables found in this narrative unit. In the last three parables, repentance and forgiveness, either one or both, are missing in each parable. The elder brother is unrepentant (15:25-32). The rich man is unforgiving of the manager who squanders his property (16:1-2). The dishonest manager does not change his ways after being confronted (16:3), and the second rich man remains unremorseful for his failure to care for Lazarus even when he is experiencing agony in the flames of Hades (16:23-31). Conversely, repentance and forgiveness are most clearly modeled for the disciples in the parable of the prodigal son and the loving father (15:11-24). The son repents, and the father forgives. Here in 17:3-4, Jesus simply reminds his disciples of the most important points he has just made while teaching them from 15:1 to 17:10. The two actions, repentance and forgiveness, go hand in hand.

In addition to the topics of forgiveness and repentance, the conclusion to this unit focuses on two other attributes that Jesus hopes will characterize his disciples. The disciples request that Jesus increase their faith. Jesus responds by saying that even the smallest amount of faith in God is sufficient. Its presence is far more important than its amount. In addition, Jesus reminds his disciples about the importance of humble obedience. He cautions them against obeying God out of a desire for personal reward or accolades. Rather, proper obedience grows out of a sense of gratitude.

More Healing and Teaching (17:11–18:8)

As Jesus inches closer to Jerusalem, he again announces to his disciples that he will be rejected and killed once he arrives (17:25; cf. 9:22; 18:31-34). Similarly, Jesus' words and deeds take on a more observable eschatological tone as he discusses authentic faith (17:19), the kingdom of God (17:20-21), and the arrival of the Son of Man (17:22-37; 18:8, 31; 19:10).

Cleansing Ten Lepers (17:11-19)

Luke continues to remind his readers that Jesus is traveling south toward Jerusalem, the place of his impending death (e.g., 9:51, 53; 13:22, 33-34). As he passes between Galilee and Samaria, a group of ten men with leprosy call out to Jesus for help. In particular, they ask Jesus, whom they address as master or commander, to extend mercy to them (Gk. *eleeō*) just as a blind man will do in 18:38 (cf. 16:24). Previously, while Jesus was still in Galilee, he healed a leper in Luke 5:12-16. Now as he approaches Samaria, he performs the same type of miracle in a new region. Consequently, Luke's readers can conclude that both Jesus' power and his mercy extend far beyond the boundaries of his home region.

In addition, as discussed in the unit on 5:12-16, modern interpreters of the Gospels must distinguish between contemporary and ancient understandings of leprosy. In a contemporary setting, leprosy narrowly refers to a bacterial infection known as Hansen's Disease. This disease frequently causes a person to lose the ability to feel pain in their extremities and therefore places them in acute danger of sustaining injuries to those extremities. In antiquity, however, the term "leper" (Gk. *lepros*) referred to a person who suffered from a skin malady, which could have been caused by any number of sources. Furthermore, it was commonly assumed that skin maladies were God's punishment upon lepers due to sin (Lev 14:18-20). As a result, there was no human cure to this disease. It was believed that only God could heal this sickness. Furthermore, leprosy resulted in the victim being declared ceremonially unclean, which meant the leper could not participate with his or her fellow Jews in their ceremonial worship practices (Lev 13:2-3). If, however, the leper experienced healing due to the mercy of God, then the leper would show himself or herself to a priest. In response, the priests, as witnesses to the work of God, would instruct the healed leper to make the proper sacrifices to God, and they would declare the leper to be "clean" (Lev 14:2-32). This declaration allowed the former leper to reintegrate into communal worship and life.

In 17:12-14, the ten leprous men who seek Jesus' mercy follow the typical protocols of their day. In particular, they separate themselves from the rest of the villagers, huddle together, and maintain a safe distance from Jesus. In contrast to the prevailing thought of the time, however, they somehow believe that Jesus possesses the power and authority of God to heal leprosy (cf. 5:12). As distinct from the priests, religious leaders, and physicians of their day, the lepers address Jesus as their master (Gk. *epistatēs*), and they express their confidence that he can heal them—a power that was assumed to belong to God alone. In response, Jesus says to the lepers, "Go and show yourselves to the priests" (17:14a). Notably, Jesus' instructions require the ten lepers to exhibit a significant degree of faith before acting on his instructions. Luke indicates, for example, that the ten lepers are cleansed or healed after they have departed. Their healing occurs in the midst of their trek to see the priests (17:14b). Luke implies that their skin was still leprous when they began seeking out the priests who would inspect them for signs of God's miraculous healing. Consequently, in this instance, Jesus' healing occurs as the leprous men take active steps of faith. Active faith precedes its benefit.

As compared with the healing of the leper in 5:12-16, Luke takes the conversation a step further in 17:11-17 when he discusses the response of the Samaritan leper. Beyond the question of Jesus' ability to heal and perform miracles, Luke uses this opportunity to illustrate how one should respond in light of Jesus' healing. When a healed leper made sacrifices to God, those sacrifices served as a thank offering to God for the mercy God had extended to him or her. In this passage, Luke narrates the actions of the Samaritan leper to illustrate an even better way to express one's gratitude to God.

Presumably Jesus heals nine Jews and one Samaritan in 17:12-14. All of them beg Jesus for mercy. All of them depart to see the priests, and all of them experience Jesus' healing power. Yet only the Samaritan, the one whom most Jews in the first century would have dismissed as a foreigner and a heretic, expresses his gratitude to Jesus in an appropriate manner. The others seem to think that the sacrificial system allows them to interact with God effectively—but not the Samaritan. Once he realizes that he has been healed and before he seeks out the priests or offers ritual sacrifices, he first turns back, praises God, and thanks Jesus (17:15-16). His actions reveal the close link between God and Jesus (17:18). Praising God and thanking Jesus for the healing he has experienced are synonymous. The ritual sacrifices alone will not do. The Samaritan leper takes the opportunity to prostrate himself before Jesus while praising God.

In response, Jesus asks probing questions that point out the flaws in the responses of the nine Jews whom Jesus also healed. They had enough faith to begin walking, but they lack a complete faith. A complete faith results in proper gratitude as the Samaritan demonstrates (17:19; Garland, *Luke*, 692). True discipleship pairs a faithful reception of Jesus' authority and power with the types of actions that grow out of gratitude for what God has done through Jesus.

Teaching about the Kingdom of God (17:20–18:8)

Luke 17:20–18:8 is composed of three smaller units: 17:20-21; 17:22-37; and 18:1-8. Collectively these three units constitute Jesus' broad answer to the Pharisees' question about the timing of the kingdom of God in 17:20. Jesus first seeks to redirect the Pharisees in 17:20-21 before instructing his disciples in 17:22–18:8.

(1) Luke 17:20-21. When the Pharisees ask Jesus about the timing of the kingdom of God's arrival (17:20), Jesus redirects their focus. Rather than address the time of the kingdom's arrival, Jesus elects to address the nature of the kingdom of God (17:20-21). Apparently, the Pharisees anticipate a tangible kingdom that resembles other kingdoms they have known or read about in the Scriptures (e.g., the kingdom of Israel under King David). In essence, the Pharisees assume they understand the nature of the kingdom of God. They simply want to know when it will arrive. Jesus, however, shifts the conversation in an unexpected direction. Jesus informs the Pharisees that "the kingdom of God is among you" (17:21), and he also indicates that the kingdom of God cannot be seen with human eyes in the way that the Pharisees expect (17:20-21).

Here, Jesus suggests that the kingdom of God is intimately linked with him and his ministry. For example, in 4:43 Jesus says that he proclaims "the good news of the kingdom of God," and here in 17:21 Jesus declares that it is already present in some fashion. Moreover, in 4:43 Jesus indicates that the act of proclaiming the kingdom of God constitutes his God's given purpose (cf. 6:20; 8:1; 9:2; 10:9-11; 16:16). In essence, Jesus can announce that the kingdom of God is already "among you" because he himself is ushering in the in-breaking of God's reign on earth in the present. Jesus and his ministry are inaugurating God's kingdom on earth. In short, the essence of the kingdom of God is intimately linked with Jesus' presence (Fitzmyer, *Luke*, 2:1159). The kingdom can be found where Jesus is. Of course, even though Jesus stands directly in front of them, the Pharisees are overlooking the in-breaking of God's kingdom through Jesus and his ministry. Jesus does not directly address the question about the timing of God's kingdom because the Pharisees do not yet understand its nature.

(2) Luke 17:22-37. Beginning in 17:22, after having addressed the nature of God's kingdom in 17:20-21, Jesus now addresses the timing of the kingdom's arrival—the subject of the Pharisees' question that prompted this larger discussion (17:20). Yet when Jesus speaks about matters of timing, he refers to the arrival of the Son of Man and addresses his comments to the disciples rather than to the Pharisees (17:20, 22). There are numerous debates about the meaning of the term "the Son of Man." That term may carry a variety of connotations even within Luke's Gospel. Here, however, Jesus alludes to the apocalyptic figure Dan 7:13-14 describes who will bring God's reign and judgment to the earth (cf. Dan 8:17). Notably, Luke includes other sayings from Jesus that likewise buttress this apocalyptic understanding of "the Son of Man" (Luke 9:26; 12:8, 10, 40; 18:8; 21:25-36).

Just as in the previous section where the kingdom of God is intimately linked with Jesus' presence and ministry, here Jesus addresses the question about the timing of the kingdom of God by discussing the arrival of the Son of Man (17:24). One cannot speak about the kingdom of God without speaking about Jesus, and Jesus focuses the disciples' attention on his future work as judge and king. Before the Son of Man returns to judge and to rule humanity, however, he must first suffer and "be rejected by this generation"—a clear allusion to Jesus' impending death (17:25; cf. 9:22).

In regard to the actual timing of the Son of Man's arrival, Jesus says little. He indicates that the kingdom of God will not be fully realized until the Son of Man arrives, but he does not say when the Son of Man will arrive. Instead, Jesus suggests that the Son of Man will arrive quickly whenever it happens (17:24, 31), and he focuses his attention in this literary subunit on those who are unprepared for God's decisive intervention into human history. Just as distinctively "human" activities distracted the people during the days of Noah and Lot—activities that recall the excuses provided by those who missed out on the great banquet in 14:18-20—"so too it will be in the days of the Son of Man" (17:26-30). Those consumed with "human" activities and foci like food, drink, marriage, and acquiring possessions will be unprepared for the presence and work of God via the arrival of the Son of Man.

Finally, the disciples ask "where" the kingdom of God will be set up or headquartered (17:37a). Jesus responds with an ominous answer. Contrary to the assumptions of the Pharisees (17:20), the Son of Man's arrival will bring divine judgment and punishment to many—to those focused on consumption and acquisition of possessions rather than yielding to the will of God. As a result, just as vultures provide a highly visible sign of where a corpse can be found, so also when the Son of Man first arrives, the kingdom of God will be found where divine punishment and death reside.

(3) Luke 18:1-8. This pericope is connected to the two previous pericopes. Jesus' comments in 17:20–18:8 provide Jesus' collective response to the Pharisees' question about the arrival of the kingdom of God (17:20). First, Jesus seeks to reshape the Pharisees' understanding of the nature of God's kingdom (17:20-21). Next, Jesus describes what is means to be unprepared for the arrival of the Son of Man, the kingdom of God, and divine judgment (17:22-37). Finally, in this pericope Jesus sketches what a proper anticipation of the Son of Man's arrival looks like (18:1-8). Jesus tells his disciples the parable of the unjust judge and the persistent widow. Notably, Luke summarizes Jesus' points by inserting a preface prior to the parable before he relays the parable itself. Apparently Luke, as author of this Gospel, feels the need to clarify the content and purpose of Jesus' exhortations to his disciples. The presence of Luke's preface suggests that poor readers of his Gospel might misinterpret this parable—they might misunderstand the nature of God or of prayer.

Regardless, Luke clarifies that the parable will first and foremost illustrate the disciples' "need to pray always and not to lose heart" while awaiting Jesus' return (18:1; cf. 21:34-36). In essence, vigilant prayer and sustained trust in God constitute proper actions for disciples who await the arrival of the Son of Man and divine judgment (18:8). These proper actions of ongoing prayer and trust in God provide a stark contrast to the distracted and irresponsible actions of those in the days of Noah and Lot (17:26-28)—human actions that were primarily focused on consumption and the acquisition of spouses and possessions.

The parable itself, the parable of the unjust judge and the persistent widow, runs from 18:2 to 18:8a. Within the parable, the widow illustrates the primary lesson that Jesus' disciples are to learn about praying always and not losing heart (18:1). In essence, the widow is a positive example of what Jesus' disciples should do while awaiting the arrival of the Son of Man (18:8; cf. 17:20). The widow illustrates persistence and constancy—traits that should characterize the prayers of the disciples. Furthermore, both her actions and her hope remain in sync with one another, and they remain steady throughout the timeframe of the parable. Jesus' disciples should likewise exhibit faith in God's justice while praying continuously, perhaps praying specifically for "the completion of the kingdom's coming" (Blomberg, *Interpreting the Parables*, 368; Nolland, *Luke*, 2:871). Their beliefs about God's justice and their faithfulness in prayer should sync with one another, and they should remain consistent until the end.

The judge in this parable, however, is a negative character. Twice Jesus says that the judge does not fear God or respect people (18:2, 4). Both traits are exceedingly undesirable for a Judean judge in the first century. The only reason the unjust judge grants justice to this widow is because he is tired of the widow bothering him (18:5). In the end the judge acts rightly, but not because he cares about the widow or justice. Instead, the unjust judge acts out of selfishness. Jesus then uses this negative judge as a contrast to God who cares for both people and justice (18:7-8; cf. 21:22). (Here justice refers to the avenging of an injured person; cf. Acts 7:24.) Moreover, God does not delay in caring for "his chosen ones" or granting justice. Rather, unlike the unjust judge, God responds quickly to the cries of God's chosen ones (18:8).

At the conclusion of the parable, Jesus then returns his disciples to the broader question about the arrival of the Son of Man (18:8). When God intervened in human history in the times of Noah and Lot (17:26-29), the people failed to exhibit faith in or faithfulness to God. Jesus now asks his disciples what the Son of Man, the apocalyptic judge and ruler of the earth who will usher in the kingdom of God (cf. Dan 7:13-14; 8:17), will find when he arrives. Will he find the type of faith and/or faithfulness (Gk. *pistis*) that the widow displays in 18:3? Will he find ongoing prayer and an unwavering trust in the justice of God (18:1)? Or will he find those who have dedicated their energies to consumption and the acquisition of possessions as was seen in the days of Noah and Lot (17:26-29; cf. 14:18-20)?

On Approaching God with Humility, Not Arrogance (18:9–19:27)

Luke 18:9–19:27 forms a literary unit that repeatedly contrasts two vastly different manners in which one might approach God. One, the path of arrogant confidence in one's own righteousness, is foolhardy. The other, the path of humble submission to and reliance on the mercy of God, is wise. This contrast plays out in the parable of a Pharisee and tax collector, Jesus' encounters with children and the rich ruler, Jesus' third passion prediction, the healing of the blind man, and the story of Zacchaeus's transformation.

Parable of a Pharisee and Tax Collector (18:9-14)

Of all the parables in Luke's Gospel, the parable of the Pharisee and the tax collector may be the easiest to interpret. Readers benefit both from Luke's explanatory preface (18:9) and Jesus' explanatory conclusion (18:14). Luke's explanatory preface in 18:9 helps us to make sense of all the material from 18:9 to 19:10.

Luke introduces the parable by telling his readers about Jesus' audience and their spiritual dispositions. The parable functions as an antidote to those who trust in their own righteousness while critically disregarding others (18:9). These people suffer from a double illness. They think too highly of their own stature before God, and they think too little of others' stature before God. When Jesus then narrates the parable, it functions like a mirror that Jesus holds up before their eyes, helping them to see themselves more accurately.

Jesus sets the scene in 19:10: "Two men went up to the temple to pray, one a Pharisee and the other a tax collector." In a first-century context, many Jews would have agreed with Josephus's assessment that the Pharisees were "known for surpassing others in the observances of piety and exact interpretation of the laws" (Josephus, *J.W.* 1.5.2; cf. Bock, *Luke*, 2:1461–62). Conversely, most first-century Jews would have held an equally negative view of tax collectors who essentially worked in concert with the Roman Empire. Up to this point in Luke's Gospel, however, Luke has ironically shown his readers a largely positive view of tax collectors (e.g., 3:12; 5:27-30; 7:29, 34; 15:1) and a largely negative image of the Pharisees (e.g., 5:21, 30; 6:7; 7:30, 39; 11:37-43, 53; 12:1; 15:2; 16:14). In 18:9-14, Luke now provides his readers with a straightforward explanation for this somewhat surprising contrast in his Gospel.

The Pharisee in Jesus' parable commits multiple missteps as he approaches God in prayer in 19:11-12. Whereas Jesus in 11:2-4 provides his disciples with a model for commendable prayer, this Pharisee in 19:11-12 provides Jesus' disciples with a negative counter example. First, Jesus says that the Pharisee literally "stands to himself," or perhaps he stands by himself (18:11). The vague phrase seems to suggest that the Pharisee's physical posture illustrates his singular confidence as he addresses God. Rather than collectively coming before God as one among many offering morning or afternoon prayers in the temple, he stands alone. Rather than adhering to the longstanding Jewish injunction to avoid haughtiness when approaching God in prayer (e.g., Sir 17.25-26), the Pharisee believes his merits have earned him a hearing before God. He sees himself as being set apart from others who are inferior to him.

Second, as the Pharisee offers his prayer, he does not begin by offering praise to God, seeking the arrival of God's kingdom, pleading for forgiveness, extending forgiveness to others, or beseeching God to help him avoid the times of trial or temptation as Jesus does in 11:2-4. Instead, the Pharisee voices to God his harsh judgment of "other" people, including the tax collector who is simultaneously praying to God in the temple. (The same word for "others" [Gk. *loipos*] is found in both 18:9 and 18:11.) Ultimately, he positions himself as their judge, and he declares that they have failed to be obedient to the law. Even worse, this Pharisee attempts to veil his contempt for others in the guise of thanksgiving that he offers to God. Finally, the Pharisee boasts to God about his own perceived righteousness. In particular, the Pharisee reminds God that he tithes off his income (cf. 16:14) and that he fasts twice a week rather than once per year on the Day of Atonement as the law prescribes (18:12) (Stern, *A Rabbi Looks at Jesus' Parables*, 199). In essence, the Pharisee's confidence in his own righteousness (18:9) and in his sense of spiritual superiority grows out of his perceived faithfulness to the law. He simply believes that he has been more faithful to God than his fellow Jews. Perhaps this Pharisee believes that God must be as impressed with him as he is of himself.

Jesus then contrasts the Pharisee with the tax collector in 18:13. Whereas public opinion would normally deem the tax collector to be a person of highly questionable character who merely adds to the hardships that God's people are already enduring under the Roman government, Jesus offers his audience a different image of this man. In particular, the tax collector provides Luke's readers with another positive model of commendable prayer (cf. 11:2-4; 18:1-8). The tax collector's actions provide a distinct contrast to the Pharisee's improper approach to prayer. First, whereas the Pharisee possesses a haughty or prideful posture, the tax collector approaches God with tremendous humility. Jesus tells his audience that this tax collector stood at a distance (18:13). It is difficult to know from what or whom the tax collector stands far off. Does he stand far off from the Pharisee, the holy of holies, or other people? Regardless, the other details that Jesus provides about the tax collector's physical demeanor while approaching God in prayer provide clarity. He positions himself as an unworthy beggar who beseeches God for mercy. He does not even desire to look in the direction where he perceives God's presence to be. Instead, he beats his chest, "a dramatic gesture usually reserved for women and used by men only in times of extreme emotion" (Blomberg, *Interpreting the Parables*, 344). Unlike the Pharisee, the tax collector's physical disposition demonstrates that he knows God is far greater than he is and that he regrets his shortcomings and failures (18:13).

In addition to deportment, the words that the tax collector utters to God also provide a distinct contrast to the Pharisee's improper prayer. Rather than judging others in the guise of thanksgiving or bragging on himself, the tax collector acknowledges God, pleads for mercy or pardon, and literally refers to himself as "the sinner." As a sinner, he articulates his proper standing before God (e.g., Sir 17.25-26). He sees God as powerful and himself as needy and helpless. He does not even petition God for daily provisions as Jesus taught his disciples to do (11:2-4). He merely requests that God be merciful to him or atone for his sinfulness (Gk. *hilaskomai*) (18:13) (Bock, *Luke*, 2:1464).

Jesus then sums up the parable in 18:14 by drawing a fundamental contrast. In the process, Jesus once again refers to righteousness or the state of having been justified by God. Beginning in 18:9, Luke refers to those who are convinced of their own righteousness (or good standing before God). They are confident in their own efforts. Now in 18:14, however, Jesus refers to the tax collector as the one who has been made righteous or pronounced righteous (i.e., justified; Gk. *dikaioō*) by God. Moreover, Jesus then makes a general declaration based on the dynamics that are present within the parable. Those who follow a prideful and judgmental path like this Pharisee will, at some point, be humbled, but those who follow a path of humility before God and others will one day be exalted. Both verbs—"be humbled" and "be exalted"—are voiced in the passive tense and point toward divine agency. Both the work of humbling and the work of exalting belong exclusively to God, not humans.

Finally, obvious connections exist between the parable of the unjust judge in 18:1-8 and the parable of a Pharisee and tax collector in 18:9-14. Even though Luke 18:9 marks a transition to a new thought unit in Luke's Gospel, Jesus' comments about prayer in Luke 18:1-14 provide a bridge that connects the literary unit of Luke 17:20–18:8, which discusses the arrival of the Son of Man, and the literary unit of Luke 18:9–19:10, which discusses humility before God.

For instance, the widow illustrates the nature of persistent and hopeful prayer as Jesus' disciples await the arrival of the Son of Man (18:1-8). She possesses determination, resolve, and boldness as she demands that the judge grant her justice. Yet when one makes the interpretive move from the lesser to the greater—when one moves from bold and persistent requests of an unjust judge to hopeful and persistent prayers to a just God who acts faithfully (18:7-8)—it would be incorrect to think that one approaches God with arrogance. Rather, despite the need to emulate the persistence and hopefulness of the widow in 18:1-8, Jesus' disciples should also approach God with the humility of the tax collector in 18:9-14. The two sets of traits must be paired together. Jesus' disciples should pray with both persistent hope and humble awareness of one's sinful nature in the presence of a holy God (18:13).

Receiving Children (18:15-17)

Jesus' interaction with some children then builds on the overriding theme that Luke is discussing in Luke 18:9–19:10. The fundamental conversation is about the proper way to approach God and therefore Jesus as Son of God. Luke 18:15-17 provides further clarification of Jesus' conclusion to the parable of a Pharisee and a tax collector. Jesus' words—"for all who exalt themselves will be humbled, but all who humble themselves will be exalted"—apply equally well to both the parable and Jesus' encounter with the children.

Frequently, first-century Mediterranean cultures held children in low regard. In societies that valued honor, power, and merit, "children were at the bottom of every societal hierarchical scale—physically, economically, and politically." Children possessed low status and no power. Consequently, vulnerability and dependence on others characterized their lives (Betsworth, *Children*, 124–25).

This modest status of children in antiquity is evident in 18:15. In many respects, Jesus' disciples respond to the people bringing their infants to Jesus much like his disciples would have responded to a tax collector who approached Jesus. The disciples observe what is happening, and they rebuke those bringing the babies (Gk. *epitimaō* or "rebuke" is also used in Luke 4:39; 8:24; 9:21, 42, 55; 17:3; 19:39; 23:40). The disciples appear to think they are protecting Jesus from an intrusion upon his time. Touching or caring for the babies is presumably beneath him. The implication is that Jesus has more important people to see and more important issues to address than investing in these children.

Jesus, however, surprises his disciples by expressing his desire to welcome the children, not turn them away. In particular, he uses the children as an object lesson about the kingdom of God and says "whoever does not receive the kingdom of God as a little child will never enter it" (18:17). Just as the tax collector is seen as moving from humility toward exaltation (18:13-14), so also the children are deemed to have little or no status, and yet Jesus welcomes them. Similarly, Jesus explains that anyone who belongs to the kingdom of God must depend solely on the mercy of God and move from a humble position to an exalted one.

The Rich Ruler (18:18-30)

The two previous literary units in Luke's Gospel (the parable of a Pharisee and tax collector in 18:9-14 and Jesus' encounter with the children in 18:15-17) explain how those who trust in their own righteousness come up short before God whereas those who depend humbly and wholly on God's mercy are embraced by God. The story of the rich ruler in Luke 18:18-30 provides further clarification about those in the first category—those who have trusted in themselves (18:9). For instance, Jesus just told his disciples about the Pharisee who thanks God that he is not like those who fail to keep the law. The Pharisee instead reminds God of how he not only observes the law but even fasts far more than the prescribed amount. Now, the rich ruler in 18:18-25 resembles the Pharisee from the parable (18:10-14). The rich ruler errs in much the same way as the Pharisee.

To begin, Luke merely identifies the man as "a certain ruler" (Gk. *archōn*) in 18:18. While Luke does not provide us with additional biographical details, we at least know that the man possesses an elevated social status beyond that of most adult males in a first-century Judean context. Next, Luke tells us that this man asks a question of Jesus. Notably, "a certain ruler" asks the exact same question in 18:18 that we heard "a certain lawyer" ask in 10:25 before Jesus narrated the parable of the good Samaritan. The question is "What must I do to inherit eternal life?" In and of itself, the question is appropriate. Yet when the lawyer asked that same question in Luke 10, Luke informed his readers that the lawyer was testing Jesus (10:25). As a result, Luke characterized the lawyer in Luke 10 negatively. Here in Luke 18, careful readers of Luke's Gospel must now wonder whether Luke is implicitly comparing the two men—the testing lawyer and the rich ruler. He identifies both with the indefinite Greek pronoun *tis*, which translates as "a certain one," and both ask the exact same question. While it appears that Luke implicitly raises questions about the character of the rich ruler from the outset, Luke's first readers likely had to read the entire pericope before definitively concluding that the rich ruler in Luke 18 provides a negative example for Luke's readers rather than a positive one.

So what is it about the rich ruler in Luke 18 that makes it difficult for Luke's first readers to evaluate his character? Almost certainly, most of Luke's readers would have been predisposed to esteem the rich ruler at the beginning of the passage. Both his social status and his words might initially lead Luke's first readers toward a positive estimation of the rich ruler.

First, as a ruler (Gk. *archōn*) (18:18), the man would have enjoyed a social rank beyond that of other adult males. Similarly, in antiquity many thought that wealth was a byproduct of, and therefore an indicator of, God's favor upon a person (e.g., Deut 28; cf. Luke 16:14). Consequently, when Luke describes this man as "very rich" (18:23), some would have equated his wealth with being "very blessed." Second, when the rich ruler initially presents himself to Jesus, he does so in a seemingly respectable manner. Unlike the lawyer who tests Jesus in 10:25, the rich ruler addresses Jesus not only as "Teacher" but as "Good Teacher" (18:18).

Third, the man asks Jesus about what he must do to inherit eternal life. If he is legitimately asking the question, it suggests that the subject matter is on his mind and that he wants to hear Jesus' opinion. Apparently, the rich ruler is not yet convinced that he knows the answer to his own question. Fourth, Jesus engages the query, which suggests that Jesus perceives the man to be asking a legitimate question regardless of the man's motives. Finally, when Jesus responds to the rich ruler, Jesus acknowledges that the man knows the Scriptures well (18:20). The rich ruler has been both knowledgeable about and obedient to the law since he was young (18:21). Luke therefore depicts the man as being a deeply religious and devoutly faithful Jew throughout most, if not all, of his life.

Essentially, the rich ruler has the appearance of a righteous person—the topic that Luke first introduced in 18:9 for the literary unit that runs from 18:9 to 19:10. Some of Luke's readers may have initially reasoned to themselves that if anyone can receive eternal life based on righteousness, faithfulness to the law, and a blessed life, this man has the best chance. He is wealthy, influential in society, and observant of the law.

By the end of the pericope, however, it becomes exceedingly clear that Luke intends for the rich ruler to provide a negative example for his readers rather than a positive one. (We see a similar transition in regard to the Pharisee in 18:10-14. Luke moves his readers from an initially positive presumption about the Pharisee in 18:10 to a sharply negative portrait of him by 18:14.) For instance, Luke provides a variety of clues about the rich ruler's questionable character even before we get explicit confirmation of his flaws.

First, as mentioned above, when the rich ruler initially approaches Jesus, we hear literary echoes that remind us of the lawyer who tests Jesus in Luke 10:25. Even if the rich ruler appears different from the testing lawyer at first glance, we learn that the rich ruler is no better off.

Second, every person whom Luke has described as "rich" (Gk. *plousios*) up to this point in his Gospel has turned out to provide a negative example for Luke's readers (e.g., Luke 12:16; 16:1, 19) (Furfey, "PLOUSIOS," 243-63). When Luke then identifies the "certain ruler" as not only rich (*plousios*) but extremely rich in 18:23, observant readers of Luke's Gospel should take notice.

Third, beyond the literary clues, Luke helps his readers adopt a negative opinion of the rich ruler by means of the dialogue that takes place between Jesus and the man in 18:18-23. After the man asks Jesus what he must do to inherit eternal life, Jesus first responds by asking the rich ruler to articulate his own answer to his question (18:21). Much like the self-confident Pharisee in 18:11-12, the rich ruler is sure he has fulfilled God's commands throughout his life. Jesus points out, however, that the rich ruler's answer is not sufficient; he is still lacking. As a result, Jesus instructs the man to sell all his possessions, give them to the poor, come, and follow him. In essence, Jesus points out that the rich ruler's current religious practices and commitments will not result in eternal life. The inadequacy of the rich man's standing before God is clear enough. Yet a conundrum remains. Having heard Jesus' response to the rich ruler, what conclusions should Luke's readers draw from this conversation? Does Jesus provide an answer to the question about eternal life? If so, what is that answer?

Interestingly, when Jesus begins to name God's covenant instructions from the Decalogue for the rich ruler, he only quotes the portions of Exod 20:1-17 that govern human-to-human interactions (18:20). For instance, Jesus names four prohibitions—those forbidding adultery, murder, theft, and false witness—and one command regarding honoring father and mother (Exod 20:12-16). The rich ruler not only knows these scriptural guidelines but is also able to claim with confidence that he has guarded or kept all of these directives since his boyhood. Jesus, in response, does not question the validity of the rich ruler's claims. As far as we know, the rich ruler has indeed carefully avoided adultery, murder, theft, and bearing false witness, and as far as we know, he has continuously honored his parents in ways that the Scriptures suggest.

We must, however, also pay attention to the portions of the Decalogue that Jesus does not quote. These omissions may tell us more than the instructions Jesus names. For instance, Jesus does not mention the prohibition against coveting (Exod 20:17), and he does not quote God's decrees about how humans are to remain in a proper, covenant relationship with God (Exod 20:1-11). For example, Jesus does not name the prohibitions against other gods, graven images, or misusing the Lord's name, and he does not mention the instruction to remember the Sabbath.

The rich ruler was able to respond with confidence in regard to the commandments that Jesus quoted, but perhaps the rich ruler should have also reflected on the other teachings from the Decalogue before answering Jesus so quickly. Perhaps he should have realized that Jesus had not yet introduced daunting topics like avoiding covetousness and properly loving God. Almost certainly, he would not have been able to assert so confidently that he has kept all of these instructions since his childhood.

When Jesus tells the rich ruler that he still lacks one thing, Jesus appears to infuse elements of the unnamed portions of the Decalogue into the conversation. Previously, Jesus told Martha that only one thing was needed (10:42). In particular, she needed to recognize that God's Son was in her midst, but her hospitable preparations prevented her either from that realization or from responding properly to that realization. Here, despite the fact that the rich ruler has been faithful to carry out many of God's commandments throughout his entire life, Jesus proclaims that he still lacks one thing. Using four different imperatives, Jesus commands the rich ruler to "sell all that you own and distribute the money to the poor" with the result that "you will have treasure in heaven." Thereafter "come, follow me" (18:22). Luke then tells us that the rich ruler becomes sad or grieved because he is extremely rich. He cannot or will not carry out Jesus' commands.

Given that Jesus orders the man to sell, give, come, and follow, it would be difficult to draw a one-to-one correspondence between a singular human action and "eternal life." It does not appear that either Jesus or Luke are establishing a simple equation for a salvific transaction—one specific human action that will lead to divine favor for eternity. Regardless, Jesus says that the rich ruler is missing one thing, and Luke informs his readers that the rich ruler's tremendous wealth is the cause of his sadness in light of Jesus' instructions. As a result, while it is clear that the man's extensive wealth is related to the one missing element, it is not clear whether his hesitancy to give away his possessions is the core problem or whether it is a symptom of a bigger problem.

In retrospect, perhaps we should give greater thought to Jesus' initial comments to the rich ruler. When the rich ruler initially greets Jesus, he refers to him as "Good Teacher" (18:18). Jesus responds by saying, "Why do you call me good? No one is good but God alone" (18:19). In essence, before all else, Jesus comments on the rich ruler's perception of Jesus' identity. If the rich ruler refers to Jesus as "good" and if Jesus declares that only God is good, Jesus is essentially forcing the rich ruler to make up his mind about Jesus' identity. Does Jesus, his ministry, and even his answer to the question about eternal life represent God or not? Is Jesus God's anointed one (4:18)? Is he the Son of God (3:22)? Does Jesus' arrival function as a "visitation from God" (19:44)?

Jesus forces the rich ruler to weigh Jesus' identity in relation to God (18:19) before Jesus ever introduces the topic of proper human reactions to other humans (18:20-22). In essence, the "one thing lacking" is that the rich ruler does not recognize Jesus as God's Son. Otherwise, the man would immediately give up his costly possessions and follow Jesus. The rich ruler's exorbitant wealth functions as the thermometer-like gauge that reveals to the audience that the rich ruler is not yet convinced that God's Son stands before him and asks him to relinquish his possessions. He does not perceive that God's Son is the one who directs him to "follow." He does not yet have the type of faith that Abraham and Sarah exhibited in Gen 12.

Regardless, it remains difficult to interpret the story of the rich ruler without the material that comes before it and after it in the broader literary unit of Luke 18:9–19:10. In Luke 18:9, Luke explains that Jesus is addressing those who trust in their own righteousness. Thereafter, Jesus describes a Pharisee who approaches God in prayer. The Pharisee thanks God that he is not like the thieves, unrighteous people, adulterers, and tax collectors. The rich ruler in 18:18-25 also claims that he has avoided the behavior of thieves, adulterers, and other unrighteous people (18:20-21). In essence, Luke further illustrates the spiritual problem first heard in the Pharisee's prayer by narrating Jesus' encounter with the rich ruler. Rather than approaching God like the tax collector who prays, "God, be merciful to me, a sinner!" (18:13) or like the little children who come to Jesus with no real status or authority (18:15-17), the rich ruler's primary problem is that he is not desperate enough. He wants to honor God, and he wants the eternal life that God intends. Yet he approaches God with confidence in himself and his actions rather than desperation. He does not deem following Jesus, God's beloved Son (3:22), to be worth the cost. He wants to learn from Jesus, but in the end, he does not want to release his fiscal assets, give them to the poor, and follow Jesus. Like the "would-be disciples" in Luke 9:57-62, the rich ruler cannot make the sacrifices it takes to follow Jesus. His love for his possessions outweighs his love for God (cf. 16:14).

Luke then most clearly reveals the inadequacies of the rich ruler's religious commitments by means of Jesus' general statements at the end of the pericope. In particular, Jesus comments in 18:24-25 on the way wealth functions as a deterrent to loving God. He claims that "it is easier for a camel to go through the eye of a needle than for someone who is rich to enter the kingdom of God" (18:25). Jesus' comments devastate those who are listening to him. Their astonishment can be heard when they ask, "Then who can be saved?" (18:26). If a man of high social status, enormous wealth, and exceptional devotion to the law only has as much chance of entering the kingdom of God as a camel attempting to go through the eye of a pin or needle, then the situation is hopeless. Eternal life appears to be beyond the reach of all humans.

In response to his audience's lament about whether anyone can be saved, Jesus provides a two-part reply (18:27). First, Jesus affirms their conclusion. The audience appears to conclude that there is nothing humans can do to inherit eternal life (18:18, 26). Jesus likewise refers to the situation as "impossible for mortals" (18:27). Humans cannot do anything to inherit eternal life. It is impossible. The second part of Jesus' answer provides the fulcrum on which the conversation turns. Jesus declares that "what is impossible for mortals is possible with God" (18:27). A camel cannot go through the eye of a needle, but God can. A human cannot do enough to inherit eternal life, but God can.

Interestingly, when Jesus makes that statement in 18:27, he is quoting the Jewish Scriptures. When Sarah failed to believe the word of the three strangers that she and Abraham would have a baby long after her childbearing years, the angelic strangers proclaimed that what is impossible for mortals is possible for God (Gen 18:14 LXX) (Arterbury, "Zacchaeus," 20–21). Thereafter, Hebraic writers (and eventually Christians) have commonly quoted that passage of Scripture (see e.g., Job 42:2; Jer 32:17).

Strikingly, Jesus' citation of Gen 18:14 in Luke 18:27 is now the second time that quotation has been cited in Luke's Gospel. When Mary questions how she, too, could have a baby given that she has never had sexual relations with a man in Luke 1, the angel Gabriel quotes Gen 18:14. He reminds her of the words first spoken to Abraham and Sarah prior to their miraculous conception that what is impossible for humans is possible for God. Here in Luke 18, Jesus cites the passage again. After his listeners wonder aloud how anyone can ever be saved if it is more difficult for a rich man to enter the kingdom of God than for a camel to pass through the eye of a needle, Jesus basically says, "Just watch. God can do the impossible." Jesus' words then set up a powerful expectation for readers of Luke's Gospel. Readers should expect to see God's miraculous intervention in the near future, even within the current literary unit that runs from Luke 18:9–19:10.

Unlike the Pharisee in 18:10-12 and unlike the rich ruler in 18:21 who seem to trust in themselves, Jesus links eternal life to the miraculous work of God. The tax collector in 18:13 and the little children in 18:15-17 are positive examples because they are helpless and therefore completely dependent on God for mercy and reception into the kingdom of God. Unfortunately, complete dependency on God's work in the world through Jesus is still lacking in the rich ruler.

The comments of Jesus' disciples then distinguish them from the rich ruler. Upon hearing the larger conversation, Peter claims that the disciples have left everything that was important to them in order to follow Jesus (18:28). Unlike the rich ruler, they understand enough about Jesus to know that allegiance to him is more valuable than all else. They understand that the call to follow Jesus surpasses all other priorities. Jesus then assures his disciples that those who recognize Jesus and prioritize following him, even if it comes at great cost, will experience the mercy of God both in this present life and in the eternal life to come (18:29-30). Jesus' followers are already experiencing what the rich ruler is seeking.

Foretelling His Death (18:31-34)
In the center of the literary unit that runs from 18:9 to 19:27, we hear the foreboding words of Jesus the prophet as he provides his disciples with the third prediction about his suffering and death (Cf. 9:22, 44-45; 17:25). Jesus relays these teachings only to his disciples. He wants them to realize that the events that will take place in the near future will not catch Jesus off guard. The rejection and suffering that Jesus will experience, and that Luke 22–23 will chronicle, will not surprise Jesus. Rather, unlike the rich ruler who refuses to make personal sacrifices in order to line up with God's will, Jesus knowingly chooses to travel to Jerusalem and portrays the events that will take place in Jerusalem as the fulfillment of the various prophecies about the Son of Man (18:31; cf. 24:25-27, 44-46; Ps 22; Isa 53; and Zech 13:7; see e.g., Tiede, *Luke*, 315).

Even though the disciples, in contrast to the rich ruler, have already grasped enough of Jesus' identity to follow him at great personal cost (18:28), Luke informs his readers that the disciples do not understand the meaning of Jesus' passion predictions (18:34). They seem to listen to his authoritative teaching, possess an awareness of his miraculous powers, and know that he is God's anointed one. They do not, however, realize that "going up to Jerusalem" (18:31) will result in Jesus' death, and they seem to have no inkling of the resurrection in the way that Jesus describes it (18:33).

"Seeing" Jesus Properly (18:35–19:10)
As stated above, the material found in Luke 18:9–19:27 forms a complete literary unit that focuses on the contrast between those who trust in their own righteousness versus those who trust in the mercy of God (18:9). The Pharisee in 18:10-14 and the rich ruler in 18:18-25 illustrate the first perspective, while the tax collector in 18:10-14 and the little children in 18:15-17 illustrate the second perspective. Next, in the middle of the literary unit Luke reminds his readers about the extreme sacrifices that Jesus' disciples (and Jesus) have made for the sake of the kingdom of God (18:28-35). Willingness to make extreme sacrifices for the sake of the kingdom of God is a byproduct of the decision to lean wholly upon the mercy of God. Now, we arrive at the final pair of Jesus' encounters in this literary unit: the healing of the blind man in 18:35-43 and the transformation of Zacchaeus in 19:1-10. These two stories further illustrate what it means to depend wholly upon the

mercy of God, much like the humble tax collector at the beginning of this literary unit (18:10-14).

Notably, these two stories parallel one another in numerous respects and therefore must be discussed as a pair. They share generic qualities and narrative details. In addition, their literary subject matter and theological themes complement one another. For instance, both the healing of the blind man and the transformation of Zacchaeus can be categorized generically as miracle stories. That designation is more readily apparent in the healing of the blind man (18:35-43). Yet Alan Culpepper, among others, has demonstrated that the Zacchaeus story is also best described as a miracle story ("Luke," 9:357). While focusing on Zacchaeus's actions within the pericope is tempting, Jesus' concluding statements force Luke's readers to interpret the entire story of Zacchaeus's transformation in light of Jesus' miraculous, behind-the-scenes work. In hindsight, Luke shows his readers that Jesus is the primary actor in the scene as he seeks and saves the lost (19:9-10).

Additionally, the two passages share many narrative details. First, both events take place near Jericho (18:35; 19:1). Second, Jesus' movements are portrayed as "passing by" (Gk. *parerchomai*) in 18:37 and "passing through" (Gk. *dierchomai*) in 19:1 and 19:4. Third, sight, or the ability "to see," has a prominent role in both pericopes. The blind man asks for sight (18:41-42), and Zacchaeus wants "to see" Jesus (19:3, 4). Fourth, the "crowd" (Gk. *ochlos*) is named in both passages (18:36; 19:3). Finally, Luke utilizes Greek imperatives in both pericopes. Jesus orders the blind man to be brought to him (18:40), and he orders Zacchaeus to "hurry and come down" (19:5). In short, the shared narrative details alone guide readers to interpret these two stories as a thematically linked pair.

Functionally, both stories also illustrate the miraculous power of God at work through Jesus, to which 18:26-27 alluded. In 18:26-27, the question was, "Then who can be saved?" (Gk. *sōzō*; 18:26), and Jesus' answer revolved around God's capacity to do "impossible" things (18:27). Rhetorically, Luke's first readers likely asked the same question that Jesus' disciples asked in 18:26. Not only Jesus' listeners but also Luke's readers likely asked, "If the rich ruler cannot be saved, then who can?" Jesus' optimistic answer about the power of God to accomplish deeds that are impossible for humans likewise creates an expectation on the part of Luke's readers. They, too, eagerly awaited a miraculous manifestation of God's salvific work within the storyline of Luke's Gospel. They, too, almost certainly wanted to see God do the impossible.

In this pair of stories that conclusively illustrate the lessons from 18:9–19:10, Luke provides his readers with two vivid depictions of God's miraculous and salvific intervention into the lives of humans. Both stories show Jesus, as the Son of God, miraculously performing the "impossible," and both stories' subject matter focuses on God's rescue or salvation (Gk. *sōzō*; 18:42; 19:9-10). The pair of stories together provides a two-part answer to the question of "Who can be saved?" In essence, they serve as a two-part demonstration of God's ability to perform a miracle in the face of human impossibilities.

Notably, when Mark narrates the same story of Jesus healing the blind beggar, Mark informs his readers that the man's name is Bartimaeus (Mark 10:46-52). In Mark, Jesus' trip from Galilee to Judea culminates in the Bartimaeus story. The healing of Bartimaeus provides the climactic bookend conclusion to the unit that began with the blind man whom Jesus heals in two stages in Mark 8:22-26 (Black, *Mark*, 234). The two blind men pericopes in Mark 8 and 10 establish the boundaries and the themes of the Markan travel narrative.

Luke, however, leaves out the blind man's name and adds the story of a repentant tax collector named Zacchaeus. If Luke had a copy of Mark as is commonly assumed, then Luke's edits and additions are intentional. In essence, Luke illustrates the power of God at work through Jesus with two miracle stories rather than one. Yet, as he does so, Luke places even greater emphasis on the second story of the tandem—the one with the named character. In other words, Luke wants the Zacchaeus story to serve as the final and climactic story in this literary unit. Providing physical and spiritual rescue and healing to a blind man is miraculous (18:42-43). Yet the odds of a highly questionable tax collector experiencing the salvation of God (19:9-10), especially when a religiously devout rich ruler comes up short (18:18-25), is as unlikely as a camel going through the eye of a needle (18:25). Only God can accomplish something so grand, and the story of Zacchaeus provides the clearest example of God's grandiose work.

(1) Luke 18:35-43. In 18:35, Jesus has arrived in Judea and is entering the city of Jericho. As he does so, he encounters a blind beggar (18:35). The disabled beggar is in need and apparently has no family or friends to help him. When he hears a commotion beginning to build on the road, he asks members of the crowd to explain what is happening (18:36). Their response is that "Jesus of Nazareth is passing by" (18:37).

Up to this point, the blind beggar would likely have elicited a negative response from Luke's audience. Unlike the rich ruler (18:18-25) whom many would assume God has blessed, many in a first-century Judean context would see this blind man as doubly cursed. On the surface, it appears that he enjoys neither the favor of God nor humans. Yet we quickly learn that this "certain (Gk. *tis*) blind man" in 18:35 is a counterexample to the "certain (Gk. *tis*) ruler" in 18:18. Whereas Luke's readers likely changed their initially positive opinion of the rich ruler to a negative opinion based on his dialogue with Jesus, here Luke's readers likely changed their initially negative opinion of the blind beggar to a positive one based on his dialogue with Jesus (18:38-42). In particular, numerous components of the dialogue portray the blind beggar as being keenly aware of God's redemptive work in the world.

First, the blind beggar cries out to get Jesus' attention in both 18:38 and 18:39. After the first instance, the crowd rebukes the blind beggar hoping to silence him, but he shouts even louder. In the process, Luke characterizes the blind beggar as a person who is desperate for Jesus' help. Unlike the rich ruler who must weigh following Jesus versus his many possessions (18:23), the blind beggar does not need to weigh anything. He confidently defies the crowd in order to interact with Jesus. Here, the blind beggar foreshadows those in the book of Acts who will likewise refuse to be silent when it comes to speaking about Jesus (e.g., Acts 4:17-20).

Second, whereas the rich ruler addresses Jesus as a "good teacher" (18:18), the blind beggar twice refers to Jesus as "Son of David" (18:38, 39). Notably, at the beginning of Luke's Gospel it was the angels and those who possess great spiritual insight who connected David's lineage with Jesus. For instance, in addition to Luke as narrator (1:27; 2:4; 3:31), the angel Gabriel (1:32), Zechariah (1:69), and "an angel of the Lord" (2:11) all point out that Jesus is a descendant of David, in part to accentuate Jesus' role as Savior and Messiah (e.g., 2:11). In Acts 13:22-23, Paul does the same thing. Here, in Luke 18:37 and 39, the blind beggar twice identifies Jesus as "Son of David." As a result, Luke groups the blind beggar among those who best understand Jesus' identity. The blind beggar's use of that title places him in an exceedingly positive light.

Third, the blind beggar twice asks Jesus to "have mercy" or pity (Gk. *eleeō*) on him (18:38-39). Notably, this is the same petition that the tax collector, who identifies himself as a sinner, prays in 18:13. (The rich man in Hades and the ten lepers also previously requested "mercy" in 16:24 and 17:13, respectively.) Whereas the humble tax collector asks God for mercy, however, the blind beggar now makes the same request of Jesus. The blind beggar's request—"Jesus, Son of David, have mercy upon me!"—simultaneously reveals that he considers himself to be in a position of need (cf. 18:13) and that he considers Jesus to be capable of helping him. By requesting "mercy" from Jesus rather than God as the tax collector did in 18:13, the blind beggar (and perhaps more important, Luke as narrator) exhibits a high Christology.

At that point, Jesus stops moving (18:40). He is no longer "passing by" the man (18:37). Rather, Jesus engages the blind beggar by asking how he would like Jesus to help him, and the blind man singularly requests sight (18:41). When Jesus heals the man, he simply speaks the words, "Receive your sight; your faith has saved you." As we see in other instances in Luke's Gospel, the Greek word for "rescue" or "save" (Gk. *sōzō*) carries a multidimensional quality in antiquity (cf., Foerster, "*sōzō, sōtēria, sōtēr, sōtērios*," *TDNT* 7:965–1024). Jesus clearly gives physical sight to the blind man, but the vocabulary suggests that Jesus does more than simply improve the man's physical health. The use of the word *sōzō* suggests that Jesus rescues or saves the man in a comprehensive fashion. Jesus provides the man with wholeness—physically, socially, and spiritually.

Similarly, Jesus connects the blind beggar's healing with his faith (Gk. *pistis*) (18:42). The Greek word *pistis* also carries multifaceted meanings. At the beginning, the blind man has faith that Jesus can help him, but immediately thereafter the healed man faithfully follows Jesus and glorifies God (18:43). He trusts Jesus before the healing, and he exhibits the marks of true discipleship afterward. Jesus provides the rescue (Gk. *sōzō*), and the man responds with faith and faithfulness (Gk. *pistis*) before and after the healing.

By the end of the pericope, we should notice a stark contrast between the rich ruler in 18:18-25 and the blind beggar in 18:35-43. Interpreting the rich ruler passage presents exegetes with many complications, but Jesus' interaction with the blind beggar is straightforward and easy to explain. For instance, even though the rich ruler has the appearance of a righteous man in 18:18-21, we soon learn that it is virtually impossible for a person like him "to enter the kingdom of God" (18:24-25). Jesus basically claims that it takes an incomprehensible miracle of God for a camel to go through the eye of a needle or for a rich man to enter the kingdom of God (18:26-27). In the passage about the blind beggar, however, we see a straightforward miracle of Jesus. While many in antiquity would have assumed that the blind beggar is far from a righteous man, Jesus' power to transform his life physically and spiritually is self-evident. For Luke's readers, who have already seen Jesus heal a hemorrhaging woman, a dying girl, a bent-over woman, and ten lepers (8:40-56; 13:10-17; 17:11-19), this miracle almost looks easy for Jesus by this point in Luke's Gospel. Luke merely reminds his readers that the power of God is at work in Jesus to counter disease, death, and the devil. Yet given the miracles that Jesus has already performed in Luke's Gospel, this event hardly fits the "impossible" label that we see in 18:27. The next pericope, however, does.

(2) Luke 19:1-10. As noted above, the healing of the blind beggar and the transformation of Zacchaeus function as twin miracle stories that together serve as counterparts to the story of the rich ruler in 18:18-25. In addition, Jesus' redemptive interaction with Zacchaeus most clearly fulfills Jesus' prophetic claim that "What is impossible for mortals is possible for God" (18:27). Furthermore, Jesus' declaration that Zacchaeus is a "son of Abraham" closely links this pericope with the Lukan birth narrative and the preaching of John the Baptist. As a result, these twin miracle stories—and in particular the Zacchaeus story—mark the climax of Jesus' ministry as he journeys to Jerusalem, which begins in 9:51 and ends in 19:28.

In contrast to the rich ruler in 18:18-25, Luke's readers would have been predisposed to despise Zacchaeus from the beginning. Luke provides at least three details that portray Zacchaeus as a negative figure. First, up to this point, every time Luke has employed the Greek term *plousios* (or "rich"), it has referred to a highly undesirable person or group of people (see e.g., Luke 6:24; 12:16; 14:12; 16:1, 19, 21, 22; 18:23, 25) (Furfey, "PLOUSIOS," 243–63). Now Luke uses the same negative terminology to refer to Zacchaeus (19:2).

Second, Zacchaeus is not only a tax collector (Gk. *telōnēs*) but a chief tax collector (Gk. *architelōnēs*). Notice that Luke creates a verbal comparison between the rich "ruler" (Gk. *archōn*) in 18:18 and a "ruling" tax collector (Gk. *architelōnēs*) in 19:2. In essence, whereas most first-century Jews would have despised tax collectors as traitors who confiscated significant portions of their income in the service of Rome (Parsons, *Luke*, 277–78), Zacchaeus is an arch-traitor as a supervisor of other tax collectors. The crowd has no difficulty labeling Zacchaeus as "a sinner" (19:7).

Finally, Mikeal Parsons has shown that Zacchaeus's stature would have provided another clue to Luke's first readers that Zacchaeus was a religiously bankrupt person (Parsons, *Luke*, 278; cf. Cyril of Alexandria, *Comm. Luke*, homily 127). In antiquity, one's physical condition was generally thought to mirror one's moral condition. Accordingly, by informing his readers of Zacchaeus's height deficiency, Luke has simultaneously indicated that Zacchaeus does not measure up morally or ethically to the covenant standards found in the OT.

As a result, Luke has painted a composite portrait of Zacchaeus in 19:1-3 that is as initially negative as the rich ruler's portrait was initially positive in 18:18-21. If many initially considered the rich ruler to be a righteous man whom God would almost certainly embrace in the coming kingdom, almost no one would have viewed Zacchaeus that way. He was about the last person a faithful Jew in the first century might have expected God to embrace.

Beginning with 19:3, however, Luke alters the perception of Zacchaeus. Akin to the blind man in 18:35-43, Zacchaeus wants "to see" Jesus (19:3). He goes to great lengths, even engaging in activities like climbing a tree that would have been rare for adult males in a first-century Mediterranean context (Parsons, *Luke*, 279). In response, Jesus singles out Zacchaeus in order to speak with him, just as Jesus did with the blind beggar (18:40-42; 19:5-10). Shockingly, Jesus informs this chief tax collector that he intends to be Zacchaeus's guest; Jesus intends for Zacchaeus to extend hospitality to him, which Zacchaeus readily does (19:5-6) (Arterbury, *Entertaining Angels*, 145–46). Notably, the bystanders respond much like the Pharisees and scribes in Luke 15:1-2. They grumble about Jesus' kind embrace of tax collectors and sinners (19:7). The crowd attempts to hinder Jesus' relationship with Zacchaeus just as they attempted to prevent the blind beggar from speaking with Jesus in 18:39.

In response to Jesus' magnanimous embrace of this despised man, Zacchaeus is transformed. He repents of past transgressions by dramatically altering his actions. He vows to give half of his possessions to the poor (19:8). Jesus told the rich ruler to give his possessions to the poor and then come and follow (18:22), but the previous rich ruler was not able to do so. Yet wealthy Zacchaeus, without even being asked by Jesus to do so, voluntarily loosens his grip on his possessions and promises to give them to the poor.

For Luke, both parts are equally important. Zacchaeus is able to recognize that an intimate relationship with Jesus, like a hospitality relationship, requires him to show more loyalty to Jesus than to his possessions. At the same time, Zacchaeus is able to recognize that following Jesus requires proper stewardship. Zacchaeus does not vow to build impressive structures or make civic donations that will enhance his honor within his community. Instead, Zacchaeus selects the poor as the object of his generosity. His wise stewardship is as pivotal as the act of giving away half of his possessions. In addition, Zacchaeus promises to make restitution to anyone whom he has defrauded or falsely accused. Beyond living up to the requirements of the law (e.g., Lev 6:5; Num 5:6-7), Zacchaeus pledges to pay the victims back far beyond the extra 20 percent the law prescribes. Encountering Jesus has changed Zacchaeus. His attitude toward his possessions provides an outward sign of an inward transformation.

As noted above, Culpepper and others refer to the story of Zacchaeus as a miracle story ("Luke," 9:357). Admittedly, at first glance this appears to be a story about human repentance rather than divine intervention. For instance, Luke tells us that Zacchaeus runs, climbs, and hopes to see Jesus (19:4). Luke also narrates Zacchaeus's decision to release half of his possessions, give them to the poor, and pay back those whom he has defrauded "four times as much" (19:8). Yet Jesus' final comments do not place the emphasis on Zacchaeus or his actions. Rather, Jesus focuses on God's redemptive work in the world and Jesus' own purposes. For example, despite hearing that Zacchaeus wanted "to see" Jesus (19:3), Jesus informs his audience that he himself was the one seeking and saving "the lost," who in this case was Zacchaeus (19:10). In retrospect, we learn that Jesus wanted "to see" Zacchaeus. Luke informs his readers that Jesus is the one propelling the action forward, even though Jesus' work mostly takes place beyond the vision of the readers. Jesus is the primary actor rather than Zacchaeus. Similarly, Jesus refers to "salvation" (Gk. *sōtēria*) as the subject of the sentence in 19:9. Salvation has arrived at Zacchaeus's house. God's redemptive presence has arrived. No wonder Zacchaeus is transformed.

Finally, Jesus declares Zacchaeus to be "a child of Abraham" in conjunction with the arrival of God's salvation (19:9). That title previously played a major role in John the Baptist's ministry. While quoting Isa 40:3-5, John announces that "all flesh shall see the salvation of God" (3:6). John therefore "proclaims a baptism of repentance for the forgiveness of sins" (3:3), yet he warns the crowds that they must "bear fruits worthy of repentance" rather than merely claiming Abraham as their ancestor (3:8). John essentially tells the crowds that claiming Abraham as one's ancestor is useless if one's actions do not match up with those of Abraham's. Notably, John explains that God "is able from these stones to raise up children to Abraham" (3:8). John argues that God's loyalty to the people of the covenant does not extend to those who identify with the covenant in name only rather than in active faithfulness. Finally, when some tax collectors respond to John's exhortation and wish to be baptized, John instructs them to "collect no more than the amount prescribed for you" (3:12).

Zacchaeus's encounter with Jesus matches up with John the Baptist's preaching in Luke 3. Zacchaeus has encountered God's salvation. He responds by repenting. He renounces greed, and he provides restitution to those whom he has defrauded. Seemingly, even without hearing John's preaching, Zacchaeus instinctively knows what it means for a tax collector to repent.

In addition, Jesus informs Zacchaeus that he must be a guest in Zacchaeus's house, and Zacchaeus responds by welcoming the traveler (Jesus). Notably, Abraham provided the quintessential example of hospitality for Jewish and Christian adherents in antiquity. In Gen 18:1-16, Abraham eagerly and extravagantly hosts three travelers, whom he thought were merely strangers passing by. In the process, Abraham essentially defines hospitality for those who worship the God of Abraham (Arterbury, "Abraham's Hospitality," 362–65). Philo describes Abraham's faithfulness as "living law" (Philo, *Abr.* 5). Consequently, by welcoming Jesus and by being generous, Zacchaeus now resembles Abraham—perhaps for the first time in his life. Finally, his actions reveal that he is indeed a descendant of Abraham (19:9).

Importantly, while Abraham extends magnanimous hospitality to the three travelers in Gen 18:1-16, the incognito angels announce that Sarah will have a baby. When she scoffs, we hear the proclamation for the first time that "What is impossible for mortals is possible with God" (Gen 18:14). The angel, Gabriel, quotes that same phrase when announcing the miraculous birth of Jesus to Mary in Luke 2:37. Finally, we see the same quotation in Luke 18:27 when Jesus foreshadows the miraculous arrival of God's salvation in a humanly impossible situation. The fulfillment of that prediction appears to take place precisely when Jesus is referring to another type of birth and another type of "son of Abraham." Rather than the physical birth of a son to a barren woman or a virgin, Jesus is describing the spiritual birth of a grown man (19:9).

In short, from 19:3 to 19:10 we see a seemingly impossible miracle unfold (18:27). Even though the healing of the blind man and the restoration of Zacchaeus function as twin miracle stories, Luke places the emphasis on this second story. The offer of God's mercy to a rich, unethical tax collector in Luke's Gospel is startling. Neither the rich man in the parable of the rich man and Lazarus (16:19-30) nor the rich ruler (18:18-25) were granted mercy. The restoration of Zacchaeus, however, serves as an object lesson for Jesus' comment in 18:27 when Jesus says, "What is impossible for mortals is possible with God." Zacchaeus represents an impossible situation. Rich people cannot enter the kingdom of God. Yet Zacchaeus is the exception. Readers watch the camel pass through the eye of a needle (18:25) when Jesus announces Zacchaeus's salvation (19:9). The redemption of Zacchaeus demonstrates the extent of Jesus' power at a level that has not been seen up to this point in Luke's Gospel.

The Parable of the Pounds (19:11-27)
Before Jesus tells the parable of the pounds, Luke again prefaces Jesus' teaching with some explanatory comments (cf. 18:1). First, Luke explains that Jesus has just departed from Jericho (19:1) and is nearing Jerusalem (19:11), which Jesus has repeatedly identified with his impending death (cf. 13:33-34; 18:31). As a result, Luke wants his readers to realize that Jesus tells this parable as a way of helping his disciples prepare for the events of the

passion narrative. Second, Jesus utilizes this parable to address the disciples' expectation that "the kingdom of God was to appear immediately" (19:11). The opening context of Jesus' parable provides a familiar scenario for those traveling with Jesus. Jesus begins by saying that "a nobleman went to a distant country to get royal powers for himself and then return" (19:12). This scenario resembles events in Jesus' own day. For example, Josephus reports that in 4 BCE Archelaus traveled to Rome upon Herod the Great's death hoping to secure his father's kingdom before returning to Jerusalem as a client ruler of Rome; the people of Judea likewise sent emissaries to Rome seeking to block Archelaus's appointment. Eventually, though, Archelaus exacted revenge on his opponents (Josephus, *Ant.* 17.9.4; 17.10; *J.W.* 2.80–100). Notably, Archelaus later renovated a large complex for himself in Jericho, which Jesus just departed (19:1) and which was "still standing in Jesus' day" (Blomberg, *Interpreting the Parables*, 276). Jesus' hearers could therefore easily imagine the type of scenario that Jesus describes in 19:12 and 14. Yet as Luke points out in 19:11, within the parable itself Jesus does not directly address matters related to Herod's former kingdom. Rather, Jesus addresses the disciples' own suppositions about the kingdom of God. Luke uses the same word for kingdom (Gk. *basileia*) in both 19:11 and 19:12 to establish this contrast.

Within the narrative world of the parable, before the nobleman departs to secure his kingdom, he first entrusts ten servants with ten pounds (or gold coins) each (19:13). A *mina*, or a pound, equated to approximately three months of wages for a common laborer. The nobleman therefore supplies each servant with approximately two and a half years of wages with which to trade and do business during his absence. In short, he supplies them with ample resources, though not extravagant resources as we see in Matt 25:15, to enable their work while he is gone.

Upon the nobleman's return, the newly crowned king then examines his servants to see what type of profit they have garnered with the use of his resources while he was away (19:15). In particular, Jesus describes the conversation between the newly crowned king and three of his ten servants. He portrays the first two servants as positive servants who make good use of the king's resources. The differences between their levels of profit are of no consequence (Blomberg, *Interpreting the Parables*, 270). The king commends and rewards both of them (19:16-19). They function as two examples of responsible behavior in the nobleman's absence.

Jesus, however, portrays the third servant negatively. This servant not only fails to engage in trading or business as the nobleman previously instructed but also fails to earn interest on the king's resources. He simply hides the ten pounds in a piece of cloth (19:20). Because this third servant fundamentally misunderstands the character of his master and newly crowned king, he squanders the resources that are entrusted to him (19:20-24). Consequently, the king denounces and punishes this irresponsible servant by confiscating all his resources.

Finally, the king's reprimand of this irresponsible servant pales in comparison to the king's treatment of his enemies (19:26-27). The newly crowned king chastises and punishes his irresponsible servant, but he puts the enemies who outright opposed his dominion to death (19:14). In essence, both the irresponsible servant and the enemies function as negative responses to the nobleman who goes away to secure his kingdom. Yet the servants of the king's household, even foolish servants, fare far better than those who outright reject the nobleman as their king.

There is little doubt that the nobleman who departs to secure his kingdom alludes to Jesus' impending death and future exaltation as "both Lord and Messiah" (Acts 2:32-36). Luke's preface to the parable clearly justifies this interpretation. Luke points out that Jesus tells this parable in response to the disciples' expectations about the kingdom of God (19:11). Given that Jesus and his disciples are already on the outskirts of Jerusalem (19:11) and that the triumphal entry will be the next event in the Gospel of Luke (19:28-40), Luke portrays the disciples as possessing heightened expectations of what is about to take place in Jerusalem upon Jesus' arrival. They are prepared for immediate regime change in their homeland. They likely expect their newly crowned king to oust the Romans just as King David ousted the Philistines.

Jesus, however, prepares his disciples for his absence (18:31). The ultimate inauguration of God's kingdom will not take place immediately. The nobleman in the parable secures his kingdom, but he does so by means of his absence. His reign is enacted after his return. Similarly, Luke 19:15 and 21:25-28 allude to the second coming of Jesus as the Son of Man (cf. Dan 7:13-14; Luke 17:22-37). Jesus will indeed serve as the apocalyptic king and judge in the kingdom of God, but that kingdom will be most fully realized at Jesus' second coming. In the meantime, Jesus leaves his disciples with sufficient resources to carry on his work. Then, when he arrives as the Son of Man, all will experience judgment. Faithful servants will be commended and rewarded. Negligent servants will be reprimanded, and those who outright oppose Jesus' kingship will be destroyed.

Entry into Jerusalem (19:28-44)

Having featured the blind man (18:35-43) and Zacchaeus (19:1-10) as examples of both salvation and transformation that spring forth from Jesus' ministry and having just narrated Jesus' parable about a newly appointed king who begins to reign (19:11-27), Luke now completes his narration of Jesus' journey (9:51–19:28) as Jesus arrives in Jerusalem. This transitional bridge in the narrative of Luke's Gospel—from Jesus' journey to Jesus' ministry in Jerusalem—is matched by a transition of topics. Throughout the journey, Luke especially focuses his readers' attention on the demands of authentic discipleship. Beginning with the parable of the pounds (19:11-27), however, Luke returns his readers' focus back to the overarching question of Jesus' identity. In particular, Luke begins this conversation by portraying Jesus as both a faithful prophet and a king whose royalty and dominion are being announced (19:12, 14-15, 27, 38).

As we have seen, Luke, far more than the others Gospel writers, greatly accentuates Jesus' sixty-mile journey to Jerusalem by dedicating ten out of the twenty-four chapters in his Gospel to this relatively short journey. In some ways, time feels as if it moves in slow motion while Jesus travels from Galilee through Samaria to Judea and now into Jerusalem. For instance, Jesus began this journey to Jerusalem in 9:51. Ten chapters later Jesus finally arrives. Along the way, Jesus notes that Jerusalem is the city that kills God's prophets—a theme that occurs primarily in Luke (13:31-35; cf. 9:51, 53; 18:31). Luke has therefore heightened not only the length of the journey for his readers but also its ominous nature. Luke has amplified within his readers the anticipation of Jesus' arrival in Jerusalem. Jesus' arrival in Jerusalem carries a pronounced climactic tone to it in Luke. Luke 19:28-44 (Jesus' arrival in Jerusalem) functions as the culmination of Luke 9:51–19:27 (Jesus' journey to Jerusalem).

(1) Luke's portrait of Jesus. First, even as Jesus completes his journey, Luke continues to portray Jesus as a faithful prophet of God. From here to the end of Luke's Gospel, readers should notice a prophecy-fulfillment rhythm to this part of Luke's narrative. Jesus repeatedly predicts an event, and then that event comes to fruition as he described it. The most obvious example of this dynamic is 18:31-33. Jesus predicts that as the Son of Man, he will be arrested, mocked, insulted, spat upon, flogged, and killed (cf. 9:22, 44; 17:25). Jesus likewise predicts his resurrection from the dead. Of course, all of these events manifest themselves between Luke 22:47 and 24:12.

On a smaller scale, we see other prophecies of Jesus fulfilled as well. For example, he predicts that two of his disciples will find a colt that has never been ridden tied up in the village on the outskirts of Jerusalem (19:30). The disciples then find the colt "as he had told them" (19:32). Jesus prophesies about the destruction of Jerusalem (21:20-23), the guest room where they will eat the Passover (22:10-13), his suffering (22:15-16), Judas's betrayal (22:21), and Peter's denial (22:31-34). Furthermore, the angels at the empty tomb (24:6-8) instruct the women to recall Jesus' passion predictions that he voiced while he was still in Galilee (9:22; 13:32-33). Finally, the book of Acts will unfold in a similar prophecy-fulfillment schema (e.g., Acts 1:8).

In short, even as Jesus enters the city of Jerusalem, Luke further enhances the portrait of Jesus as a faithful prophet of God. The events that unfold in Jerusalem will not catch Jesus by surprise. Jesus will not die simply because a rogue disciple double-crosses him or because an anemic Roman governor caves to the demands of an irrational crowd. Rather, as a faithful prophet of God, Jesus knows what will happen in Jerusalem, but he enters the city anyway. He does so because it is "necessary" according to the divinely ordained plan of God to redeem humanity (24:26; cf. Cosgrove, "Divine DEI," 168–90). He faithfully speaks the word of the Lord. Yet he will die as an innocent martyr nonetheless.

Second, and perhaps even more straightforwardly, Luke continues to enhance the portrait of Jesus as Israel's king in this Gospel—a theme that Gabriel in 1:32 and Zechariah in 1:69 (cf. 2:11) first introduced and that Jesus reintroduced in the previous passage, the parable of the pounds (19:11-27). Now as Jesus and his disciples prepare to enter Jerusalem from the Mount of Olives, the disciples place Jesus on a colt (19:35), spread "their cloaks on the road" (19:35-36), form a large processional with Jesus as the leader, and loudly proclaim to all who will listen that Jesus is Israel's king (19:37-40). All of these actions buttress Jesus' role as a newly appointed king of Israel. For example, in antiquity, spreading cloaks on the ground before an appointed leader helped either to mark regime changes (e.g., 2 Kgs 9:11-13) or to celebrate the victories of a conquering king (e.g., Aeschylus, *Agamemnon*, 916–922). Processionals evoked images of military parades that accompanied the arrival of a ruler or general (Dowd, *Reading Mark*, 118), and paraphrasing Ps 118:26 makes the disciples' implicit message explicit for the bystanders who are present (19:38).

Furthermore, by informing his readers that Jesus enters Jerusalem in a processional while riding on a young donkey, Luke not only depicts Jesus as a king but also characterizes the nature of Jesus' kingship. At least two elements are worth noting. First, Luke alone informs his readers that the disciples hoisted Jesus onto the colt (19:35). Jesus does not elevate himself. Rather, the disciples proclaim Jesus' kingship by means of their actions and their words when they set him on the donkey and announce the king's arrival. As a result, in keeping with the humble imagery of Jesus' birth (2:7), naming (2:24), baptism (3:21), and teaching (6:17), here Luke portrays Jesus as a powerful though humble king. He does not need to exalt or announce himself; the disciples do that for him.

Second, Luke mentions the animal that Jesus rides as he enters the city. Here, Luke employs the Greek word *pōlos*, which in antiquity generally referred to a young animal (19:30, 33, 35) (Michel, "*pōlos*," *TDNT* 6:959–61). Most often, though, it referred to a young horse or donkey, the latter of which appears to be Luke's intention. Zechariah prophesied about a king who would enter Jerusalem riding on the colt of a donkey. Rather than riding a warhorse (Zech 9:10), Israel's king would ride in on a donkey—a humble gesture that illustrates the king's peaceful rather than militaristic intentions (Zech 9:9-10; Meyers and Meyers, *Zechariah 9–14*, 129–30). All four Gospel writers appear to have this text in mind when they describe Jesus' royal procession into Jerusalem on a colt. John cites it explicitly in John 12:15.

In short, when Jesus rides into Jerusalem on a donkey, it not only characterizes him as the messianic king but also suggests that first and foremost Jesus is a king who seeks to establish a peaceful rule rather than war (19:38; cf. 1 Kgs 1:33-35)—a theme that was also established early on in Luke's Gospel and then carried on throughout the narrative (1:79; 2:14; 7:50; 8:48; 10:5; 14:32; 19:42; 24:36). Strikingly, however, here the disciples praise Jesus for ushering in "peace in heaven" in 19:38 (cf. Ps 118:26) rather than peace on earth (cf. 2:14).

(2) *Luke's portrait of the disciples.* While narrating Jesus' triumphal entry into Jerusalem, Luke also uses this opportunity to characterize Jesus' disciples in an exceedingly positive manner. In Luke, the disciples grow in number throughout the Gospel. Jesus selects twelve apostles in 6:12-16. He appoints seventy-two others in 10:1-16. By the time Jesus arrives in Jerusalem, a multitude (Gk. *plēthos*) of disciples now proclaims Jesus' kingship. As a result, Luke portrays the disciples as an ever-widening movement of Jesus followers (cf. Acts 1:15; 2:41).

Yet matching this numerical expansion of the disciples is an expansion and maturation of their ability to understand the significance of Jesus. The disciples grow not only numerically but also spiritually in Luke's Gospel. For example, from the moment that Peter first follows Jesus, he is able to recognize his own sin as well as Jesus' superiority (5:1-11). Later, while carrying out Jesus' instructions, the seventy-two disciples discover on their own that they can cast out demons in Jesus' name (10:17). Near the end of Jesus' journey to Jerusalem, Zacchaeus comprehends that an encounter with Jesus must alter the way he conducts his business as a tax collector (19:8-10). The pinnacle of the disciples' understanding of Jesus' identity prior to the resurrection in Luke's Gospel takes place here at the triumphal entry. The disciples not only set Jesus on the donkey (19:35) and spread their cloaks on the road (19:35-36) but also "praise God joyfully with a loud voice for all the deeds of power that they had seen" while proclaiming Jesus as king (19:37-38). The disciples in Luke's Gospel mature as they spend time with Jesus, and they understand a great deal about Jesus' importance as they enter Jerusalem.

Precisely at this point, numerous parallels can be detected between Jesus' birth in 2:1-20 and Jesus' arrival in Jerusalem in 19:28-44. Both passages narrate an arrival of Jesus. Strikingly, in 2:13-14 a multitude (Gk. *plēthos*) of angels—a heavenly army of angels—praise God upon Jesus' birth. Here in 19:37-38 at Jesus' arrival into Jerusalem, Luke no longer refers to the multitude of angels. Rather, Luke now speaks about the multitude of disciples who praise God as Jesus enters the city. Because their number and their comprehension have grown, the disciples in 19:37-38 now function in the same role that God's angels previously carried out in 2:13-14.

Furthermore, the words that the angels proclaimed in Luke 2 and the words that the disciples proclaim in Luke 19 share obvious similarities and important differences. The angels in 2:13-14 proclaim, "Glory to God in the highest heaven, and on earth peace among those whom he favors." The disciples in 19:37-38 proclaim, "Blessed is the king who comes in the names of the Lord! Peace in heaven and glory in the highest heaven." Both groups praise the God of the highest heaven. Yet the heavenly angels announce peace on earth whereas the earthly disciples announce peace in heaven (cf. 10:18). The entire cosmos is affected by the all-encompassing event of Jesus' birth, life, and ministry. Jesus' arrival introduces peace in both realms. This peace, though, is directly connected to Jesus' dominion as king (2:13; 19:38). Peace is announced as King Jesus arrives.

Notably, many in the first century praised Caesar Augustus as the "savior" who brought peace to the Roman empire when he seized control, defeated his rivals, and put an end to Roman civil wars. In addition, for about two hundred and fifty years—a period that ran from the first century BCE to the third century CE—the Roman military maintained unshakable control over the Roman territories. Romans, like Seneca the younger, referred to this peaceful period as the "*Pax Romana*" or the peace of Rome. Strikingly, both the angels in 2:13-14 and Jesus' disciples in 19:37-38 refer to the peace that Jesus, the new king, brings. Jesus' peace, however, impacts the entire cosmos rather than merely the Roman Empire. As a result, Luke's first readers likely heard an implicit comparison in this passage between the inferior Roman ruler and the superior King Jesus by means of both the proclamation of the angels in chapter 2 and the proclamation of Jesus' disciples in chapter 19.

(3) Luke's portrait of Jesus' critics. As distinct from Matthew and Mark, Luke shows that some who witnessed Jesus' triumphal entry were critical of the processional into Jerusalem. In particular, in 19:39 some Pharisees ask Jesus to silence his disciples, who are proclaiming him to be the newly appointed king. Here, the Pharisees appear to be grumbling just as they have done many times before (cf. 5:21-22, 29-30, 33; 6:1-2, 6-7; 7:39; 11:37-54; 14:1-6; 15:1-2; 16:14; 19:7). In essence, Luke informs his readers that Jesus' detractors and opponents are present from the beginning. These critics do not participate when the disciples proclaim Jesus' kingship (19:37-38). Rather, the initial reaction of the Pharisees foreshadows the crowd's desire to crucify Jesus at the end of the week (23:21). The Pharisees and the religious leaders will not welcome or praise Jesus at any point during Luke's passion narrative.

(4) Jesus' reaction to the city and the temple. When Jesus first sees the city of Jerusalem in 19:41, he weeps for it. In particular, he laments the fact that the residents of Jerusalem do not recognize "the things that make for peace" (19:42), and they do not recognize the time of God's visitation in the person of Jesus (19:44). The Christology espoused in 19:44 is especially lofty. When the Pharisees, religious leaders, and Roman officials misunderstand Jesus' identity, they also misunderstand God's identity. God visits them in the person of Jesus, but they do not perceive God's presence.

Furthermore, the multitude of Jesus' disciples just announced the "peace in heaven" that comes with the arrival of Jesus' kingship (19:37-38; cf. 24:36). Unfortunately, the residents of Jerusalem do not and will not affirm Jesus' kingship. As a result, neither will they experience the peace that comes with the kingdom of God. Even though they dislike the Roman rulers of their day, the residents of Jerusalem appear to cast their lots with the *Pax Romana* (the peace of Rome) rather than the peace of God's Messiah.

In Virgil's *Aeneid*, when Aeneas and the Trojans first arrive in Italy, Aeneas sends a delegation to offer peace and friendship to the inhabitants of Latium. When the residents of Italy reject that peace, however, Aeneas and the Trojans must take possession of the land that they are destined to possess through warfare. Aeneas and the Trojans desired to found Rome through peace, but the reaction of the previous inhabitants forces them to found it through a hard-fought battle (Virgil, *Aen.*, 7–12).

Jesus in Luke 19:41-44 seems to lament a similar tragedy. Had the residents of Jerusalem recognized their visitation of God when Jesus rode into the city, they would have recognized "the things that make for peace." Had they acknowledged Jesus' kingship and authority, the story would have ended differently. Yet "the things that make for peace" were hidden from their eyes (cf. 24:31). Consequently, because the residents of Jerusalem reject Jesus' kingship, they will likewise experience hardship rather than peace in the days ahead (cf. 19:15-27). Jesus prophesies about the downfall that awaits Jerusalem in 19:43-44 (cf. 21:6, 20-24). Ironically, even though the residents of Jerusalem trust in Pontius Pilate and the peace of Rome rather than the peace of God, they will experience destruction at the hands of the Roman Empire during the Jewish War with Rome from 66–73 CE. In a devastating attack responding to a Jewish revolt against the state, the Romans sacked the city of Jerusalem and destroyed its temple in 70 CE. Luke 19:43-44 and 21:5-24 describe this disheartening event. Furthermore, even though Jesus prophesies about the future destruction of Jerusalem in 19:43-44 and 21:5-24, Luke's readers are likely already living in a post-temple context. Almost certainly in 19:43-44 and 21:20-24, Luke invites his readers to recall the Roman siege of Jerusalem as a past reality rather than a future prophecy.

Jesus in Jerusalem

Luke 19:45–24:53

Introduction

Luke narrates Jesus' prophetic ministry in Judea as well as his arrest, trials, death, resurrection, and post-resurrection appearances in Luke 19:45–24:53. First, in 19:45–21:38, Jesus teaches in the temple on numerous occasions. As a faithful prophet, he proclaims the word of the Lord, prepares people for future events, and points out the inadequacies of their present beliefs and actions. Second, in 22:1–24:53, Luke narrates the death and resurrection of Jesus. Here, Luke highlights Jesus' role as an innocent martyr. For instance, Pontius Pilate (23:4, 14, 22), Herod Antipas (23:15), a criminal on the cross next to Jesus (23:41), and a Roman centurion (23:47) all proclaim Jesus "innocent" of any crimes against the state. Furthermore, despite possessing foreknowledge of his impending death (e.g., 22:15), Jesus remains faithful to the Father until the end (23:46); Jesus himself indicates that his suffering and death are "necessary" in the larger scope of God's salvation history (24:26). Finally, after the resurrection, Jesus explains how God's promises are fulfilled in his life, death, and resurrection. In particular, Jesus explains the meaning of the Scriptures to his disciples (24:25-32, 44-46) and commissions them (24:47-49) prior to his ascension (24:50-53).

Jesus' Ministry in Jerusalem (19:45–21:38)

Unlike Matthew and Mark who depict Jesus as visiting the temple only briefly, Luke indicates that Jesus spent many days in the temple (19:45–21:38). In Luke's Gospel, all of Jesus' teachings in Jerusalem prior to the Last Supper (22:14-23) occur within the temple setting. Furthermore, Luke continues to portray Jesus as a faithful prophet (see previous unit on 19:28-44). Jesus in Luke therefore provides an extended prophetic critique of the temple. Rather than a brief description of Jesus "cleansing" the temple, Luke provides his readers with Jesus' comprehensive appraisal of the temple and those who oversee it. For example, while in the temple, Jesus critiques the temple as an institution (19:45-46), counters the chief priests, scribes, Sadducees, and other leaders of the people who desire to kill him (19:47–20:19), and foretells the destruction of the temple and the arrival of the Son of Man (21:5-33). Thus, compared to Matthew and Mark, Luke not only portrays Jesus as investing more time and energy into the temple by teaching there on numerous occasions (19:45, 47; 20:1; 21:37) but also portrays Jesus, as a faithful prophet, providing a much more exhaustive critique of the temple along with those who frequent its precincts.

Disrupting the Temple (19:45-48)
Akin to Mark, Matthew, and John, Luke briefly narrates the event often known as Jesus' "cleansing of the temple" in 19:45-46 (cf. Matt 21:12-13; Mark 11:15-27; John 2:13-17). Upon entering Jerusalem, Jesus goes directly to the temple. While there, he casts out (Gk. *ekballō*) those who sell the animals that worshipers will offer as sacrifices, and he criticizes the overall operation of the temple. As a result, both Jesus' words and his actions contribute to his prophetic critique of the temple.

In particular, Jesus' actions appear to correlate with the words of Malachi, the fifth-century BCE prophet. Malachi warned the postexilic residents of Judea about the arrival of the day of the Lord. He not only cautioned the people in general about their unfaithfulness, but he especially lamented the corruption of the priests (Mal 1:6–2:9). Malachi forewarned his readers that when the Lord arrives, the Lord will go directly to the temple and seek to refine and to purify Israel's offerings and worship until they are pleasing to the Lord (Mal 3:1-4). Luke portrays Jesus in a similar light. Jesus arrives in Jerusalem, goes straightaway to the temple, and seeks to refine the processes and the people that oversee worship and sacrifices in the temple.

While citing Jer 7:11, Jesus then claims that the temple currently functions as a den for robbers. Rather than exposing wrongdoing and seeking to correct it, the temple has become a refuge where those who do improper things go to hide, elude capture, or receive absolution for their improper deeds (Dowd, *Reading Mark*, 119). Instead, Jesus clarifies, while citing Isa 56:7, that the temple should be "a house of prayer." Throughout this Gospel, Luke has repeatedly emphasized Jesus' teachings about and emphasis on prayer—far more than the authors of the other Gospels. In particular, as we have already seen, a correlation between prayer and revelation or divine enlightenment exists in Luke's Gospel (e.g., Luke 3:21-22; 9:28-36; 22:41-44; Acts 12:6-17). Rather than a temple system that provides camouflage for "robbers," Jesus reminds his listeners that God intends for the temple to be a place where those who pray earnestly might experience true insight about the character, ways, and purposes of God. Jesus contends that the temple is far from fulfilling its God-intended purpose.

Finally, in 19:47-48, in case Jesus' initial interaction with the temple authorities failed to provide enough clarity for his readers (19:45-46), Luke provides a summary statement or overview about Jesus' presence in the temple. This summary statement in 19:47-48 establishes the essential lens through which Luke's readers will read the rest of Jesus' comments and teachings (20:1–21:38)—teachings that Luke alone indicates Jesus voiced entirely within the temple grounds. As a result, Luke portrays Jesus' efforts to reform and purify the temple as a daily activity during his stay in Jerusalem rather than a one-time event.

Perhaps even more important is that Luke goes on to describe two different reactions to Jesus. First, the Jewish religious authorities continually look for a way to kill Jesus. They not only want to discredit or silence him; they want to end his life. Moreover, Luke bolsters this depiction of the Jewish religious leaders by mentioning their desire to kill Jesus both at the beginning and end of Jesus' visits to the temple (19:47; 22:2).

Second, the Jewish people (Gk. *laos*) who are present in temple listen to Jesus and are in awe of his teaching. Luke claims that this favorable reaction of "the people" prevents the religious leaders from acting on their death wish for Jesus. These two groups, the religious leaders and the people, then drive the action throughout the following pericopes.

Challenges to Jesus' Authority (20:1-44)

In a lengthy section that runs from Luke 20:1–21:4 and falls within the overarching unit of 19:45–21:38, the Jewish religious leaders repeatedly challenge Jesus' authority to teach on at least three occasions (20:2, 20-23, 27-33). Jesus in turn counters their various displays of aggression and disapproval. The first instance of this antagonistic dynamic occurs in 20:1-8 and sets the tone and pattern for the rest of the larger unit. In essence, "Luke presents it as an archetype of expected activity in the temple" (Green, *Luke*, 699).

(1) Luke 20:1-8. While Jesus proclaims "good news" about the in-breaking of God's kingdom (4:18; 8:1; 16:16; cf. 2:10) and while "the people" listen to Jesus' teaching, the chief priests, scribes, and elders question Jesus' authority to teach in the temple (20:1-2; cf. 19:47; 20:27-33). Ultimately, this debate, which takes place entirely within the temple compound, revolves around who is authorized to speak for God—Jesus or the religious authorities associated with the temple. Previously, Luke established for his readers that Jesus

has the authority to act and to speak for God (e.g., 4:32, 36; 5:24). Now Luke repeatedly and convincingly demonstrates that the religious leaders associated with the temple do not have the authority to speak for God:

> Jesus has reclaimed the temple for its legitimate use as a center of revelatory instruction concerned with the salvific purpose of God now materializing. The people, representing Israel, are the recipients of that teaching. Standing in opposition are the chief priests, legal experts, and elders, representative of the Jerusalem Sanhedrin, whose collective authority originates in the purity of their birthright (in the case of the priests), in their education (in the case of the scribes), in their good fortune in having been born into Jerusalem families of high status, and above all in their proximity and relationship to the Jerusalem temple. (Green, *Luke*, 700)

Jesus' authority, however, does not derive from the temple or other measures of human social status. Instead, Jesus' authority derives directly from God (e.g., 9:34-35).

Jesus outwits the religious leaders who question his authority. He responds to their question by asking a question of his own (20:3). Jesus essentially asks the religious leaders whether or not John the Baptist functioned as God's messenger (20:4). Luke further points out that "the people," as opposed to the religious leaders, fully believe that John was indeed a prophet of God (20:6). Due to the people's strong convictions, the religious leaders are therefore conscious of the political ramifications of a negative response. If they agree that John spoke for God, however, then the religious leaders will need to admit that Jesus does as well.

Notice that Jesus' question about John the Baptist refers to events that Luke first narrated at the beginning of his Gospel. From the outset, Luke linked John and his ministry to both Jesus and the religious leaders. On the one hand, Luke chronicles numerous similarities between John and Jesus in Luke 1–2. The angel Gabriel announces the births of both John and Jesus (1:8-20, 26-38). Both John and Jesus are born as a result of divine intervention. Prophecies foretell the way that God will utilize both of them (1:46-55, 67-79; 2:29-32), and Luke even informs his readers that they are related to one another through kinship (1:36). Finally, John's baptizing ministry in 3:1-20 serves as a precursor to Jesus' ministry (7:24-30). As a result, the criteria on which one would rely when vouching for John's authority to teach and to speak on God's behalf confirm that Jesus has even more authority to speak for God than John had.

On the other hand, Luke notes that while the crowds, tax collectors, and soldiers responded positively to John's call for repentance in Luke 3:10-14 (cf. 7:29), from the outset "the Pharisees and the lawyers rejected God's purpose for themselves" when they refused to be baptized by John (7:30). As a result, Jesus reminds the religious leaders that nothing has changed. Even though the people recognized John as a prophet of God and responded favorably to his exhortations in the past, the religious leaders never did. Now, the same dynamic manifests itself again. The people believe that Jesus is God's prophet, but the religious leaders remain unrepentant and opposed to the work of God that is taking place through Jesus. Jesus' question simply highlights an ongoing pattern among the Jewish religious leaders that has taken place since John first appeared. They have not and do not perceive the in-breaking of God's kingdom.

Even worse, throughout the literary unit that runs from 19:45 to 21:38, Luke depicts the religious leaders as having taken control of the temple or God's "house" (19:46), a place that Jesus referred to as "my Father's house" in 2:49. At numerous points within this unit, Luke's first readers may have recalled Homer's *Odyssey*. They may have pictured the suitors who spend their days in Odysseus's house, consuming his resources and hoping to marry his wife while he journeys homeward in great peril and amid great hardships. Even then, when Odysseus finally arrives at his home, the suitors fail to recognize him or to treat him with the respect he deserves (Homer, *Od.*, 17–21). Similarly, Luke portrays these religious leaders as interlopers. Jesus has already reminded the crowds that the temple is God's "house" (19:46), yet these religious leaders do not recognize the time of their "visitation from God" (19:44).

Furthermore, as noted in the preceding sections (19:41-48), throughout 19:45–21:38 Luke sets up a broad contrast between his portrait of the temple at the beginning of Luke's Gospel and his portrait of the temple toward the end of it. Whereas Luke portrays the temple with mostly positive images in Luke 2, in Luke 19:45–21:38 he portrays the temple as highly negative. Numerous echoes of Luke 2 appear in Luke 19–21 and help Luke's readers to make these comparisons.

For example, Jesus' family takes him to the temple for his naming and circumcision in 2:21-40. While there, Simeon and Anna both recognize at least some aspects of Jesus' identity. Luke describes Simeon as "righteous and devout, looking forward to the consolation of Israel"; Luke also says "the Holy Spirit rested on him" (2:25). Finally, "guided by the Spirit," Simeon praises God and identifies Jesus as God's salvation who will be "a light for revelation to the Gentiles" (2:27-32). Anna, a prophet and widow, also praises God and speaks about Jesus as Israel's redemption (2:36-38). Yet whereas Simeon and Anna were upright children of God who recognized God's redemptive work in and through Jesus, Luke characterizes those who now populate Jerusalem and the temple approximately thirty years later as unrighteous hypocrites who do not recognize their "visitation from God" in and through Jesus (19:44). Simeon and Anna recognized Jesus' divine purpose at this birth, but the chief priests, scribes, and religious elders cannot recognize Jesus' divine purpose at the time of his death.

Similarly, when Jesus is twelve years old, his family travels to Jerusalem for the Passover in 2:41-52. After accidentally leaving Jesus behind for three days, his parents eventually find Jesus "in the temple, sitting among the teachers, listening to them and asking them questions. And all who heard him were amazed at his understanding and his answers" (2:46-47). Thus, as a twelve-year-old, Jesus experiences a hospitable welcome in the temple. He sits in the middle of the teachers. He engages in fruitful dialogue with the rabbis who populate the temple. All are able to recognize the wisdom that Jesus possesses (2:40, 47, 52). Approximately twenty years later, however, the chief priests, scribes, and religious elders in 20:2 no longer receive Jesus hospitably. Instead, they now question his authority to teach within the temple precincts throughout 19:45–21:38. The temple's positive reception of Jesus in Luke 2 has morphed into a negative inquisition of Jesus in Luke 19–21.

(2) Luke 20:9-19. While still in the temple Jesus tells the parable of the wicked tenants (20:9-16a) to "the people" (cf. 19:48; 20:1). The subsequent dialogue in 20:16b-19 makes it clear, however, that the scribes and chief priests are also listening to Jesus as he teaches. In particular, Luke informs his readers that "the scribes and chief priests realized that he had told this parable against them" (20:19). As a result, we can rest assured that the most negative images in this parable correlate to the actions of the Jewish religious leaders of Jesus' day. It should also be noted that this parable contributes to Jesus' lengthy, prophetic critique in 19:45–21:38 of those who provide leadership for the temple.

As Jesus sets the scene within this parable, he describes a scenario that would have been commonplace in his day. A landowner leases land to tenant farmers with the stipulation that the tenant farmers must give a significant portion of the produce to the landowner as payment for their use of the land. In this case, the landowner plants a vineyard and then leases it to those who will work it.

The shocking twist in Jesus' parable occurs when the tenants elect not to honor their contractual agreement with the owner of the vineyard. Perhaps the fact that the landowner travels to another country and/or the fact that he remains abroad for "a long time" contributes to their defiant and risky decision (20:9). Regardless, the tenant farmers essentially become interlopers or trespassers on the land that rightfully belongs to the landowner. They become thieves and robbers when they pretend that they themselves own the vineyard and its produce. They attempt to control that which does not belong to them.

These tenant farmers then add insult to injury when they not only refuse to give the landowner his percentage of the vineyard's produce but also mistreat the landowner's servants and emissaries. For example, the tenants beat the first slave in 20:10. They beat and insult the second slave in 20:11, and they throw out and injure a third servant in 20:12. With these actions, they both refuse to honor the contractual obligations that they entered into willingly and respond with hostility and violence against the landowner's messengers.

The greatest tragedy, however, unfolds when the landowner elects to send his own son to reason with the tenant farmers. Perhaps he wonders whether the lack of respect shown towards his servants may have been linked to their status as slaves. Consequently, the landowner sends his son while anticipating that the tenants will receive his son in the same manner that they would receive the landowner himself (20:13). Perhaps dialoguing with the rightful heir of the one who graciously leased the vineyard to them from the beginning will now awaken their memories and their sense of propriety. Instead, the tenants tragically continue their rebellion against the owner of the vineyard. In an act of premeditated murder motivated by the hope of stealing the legal rights to the land (20:14), they kill the son of the one who owns and planted the vineyard (20:15).

The outcome of the scenario that Jesus describes in this parable would have been predictable for those listening to him (as well as for the first readers of Luke's Gospel). The landowner, who has far more resources at his disposal than the tenant farmers, will come and take that which rightfully belongs to him. He will "destroy those tenants," and he will lease the vineyard to other tenants who will honor their agreement (20:16). In essence, the selfish and violent actions of the tenant farmers are profoundly foolish and short-sighted. Their rebellion against the owner of the vineyard was doomed before it began. They would never be able to match the strength of the landowner. The reaction of Jesus' audience further confirms this verdict. They respond to Jesus' story by saying, "Heaven forbid!" or "May it never be!" (Gk. *mē genoito*; cf. Rom 6:2) (20:16).

Jesus' parable does not amount to an allegory, but it does possess great symbolism. Luke simplifies this symbolism for his readers when he notes that "the scribes and high priests realized that he told this parable against them" (20:19). In essence, Jesus compares the actions of the scribes and the high priests to those of the tenant farmers. They attempt to control and to possess that which does not belong to them while pretending that the one who planted and owns the vineyard does not exist. They have become interlopers and trespassers who violently defend that which they falsely claim to be their own. Notably, Jesus just leveled the same critique against the leaders of the temple in 19:46. Even though Jesus identifies the temple as God's "house," the temple leaders consider it their own. The temple now functions as their den or hideout (see 19:45-48 above) rather than God's domain.

Once Luke clarifies the correlation between the tenant farmers in the parable and the scribes and chief priests in Jesus' day, it allows his readers to decode even more symbolism in the parable. In particular, this parable helps Luke's readers to interpret the remaining portions of this Gospel, and it helps them to identify a consistent pattern that has already been manifest throughout salvation history. Consequently, the symbolism found in the parable of the wicked tenants appears to extend in at least three additional directions beyond that of the identity of the tenant farmers.

First, Jesus' reference to a vineyard likely carried significant meaning for Jesus' audience and Luke's first readers given that Jewish tradition often depicted Israel as God's vineyard. For example, Isa 5:1-7 is a love song about Israel as God's vineyard. In particular, the prophet says, "For the vineyard of the LORD of hosts is the house of Israel, and the people of Judah are his pleasant plantings" (Isa 5:7a). Notice that in Isa 5 God, or the "beloved," plants and owns the vineyard (Isa 5:1-2). Similarly, in the parable of the wicked tenants, Jesus claims that the landowner "planted a vineyard" before he entrusted it to others (20:9a). As a result, there seems to be a limited correlation between God and the landowner in Jesus' parable as well as the Jewish people and the vineyard in Jesus' parable.

Notably though, in Isa 5:1-7 the vineyard itself is the problem. The vineyard produces "wild grapes" rather than grapes that are good to eat (Isa 5:2-4). The vineyard fails to fulfill its purpose. As a result, God vows to destroy the vineyard (Isa 5:5-6). In Luke 20:9-19, however, when Jesus narrates the parable of the wicked tenants, he does not speak about an unfruitful vineyard. Rather he speaks about a fruitful vineyard that corrupt and selfish tenants control. Jesus' vineyard imagery likely evokes an association with Israel, but by portraying Israel positively it further accentuates Jesus' negative portrait of the scribes and chief priests as tenants of the vineyard. Israel's caretakers, and in particular their religious leaders, are the problem. They have attempted to confiscate that which rightfully belongs to God.

Second, throughout Luke's Gospel, Jesus repeatedly describes how generations of Jewish leaders have rejected God's prophets or God's messengers.

For example, in the synagogue at Nazareth, Jesus says, "no prophet is accepted in the prophet's hometown" (4:24). In the sermon on the plain, Jesus says, "Blessed are you when people hate you, and when they exclude you, revile you, and defame you on account of the Son of Man. Rejoice in that day and leap for joy, for surely your reward is great in heaven; for that is what their ancestors did to the prophets" (6:22-23). In 11:47, Jesus counters the Pharisees and lawyers when he says, "Woe to you! For you build the tombs of the prophets whom your ancestors killed" (cf. 11:42-52; Acts 7:52). Furthermore, earlier in this same chapter (20:3-8), Jesus describes John as a prophet while alluding to the fact that the chief priests, the scribes, and the elders of the people have failed to listen to the word of the Lord that John proclaimed. As a result, the tenant farmers' rejection of the landowner's servants in Jesus' parable further illustrates how the religious leaders in Jerusalem have repeatedly rejected God's prophets throughout salvation history.

Finally, this parable helps Jesus' listeners and Luke's readers to frame the tragic nature of Jesus' martyrdom in Jerusalem that Luke will narrate in the subsequent chapters. In other words, Jesus' parable of the wicked tenants in 20:9-19 predicts and interprets Jesus' crucifixion for those who hear it. It provides a lens through which to see the rest of the book. After the religious leaders in Jerusalem have rejected God's servants or prophets for centuries, God, akin to the landowner, has now sent "the Son of God" to set things right. Yet the religious leaders, like the tenant farmers, reject a right relationship with God. Even worse, they respond by killing "the Son of God" (1:35; 3:22; 4:3, 9, 41; 22:70). Jesus predicted this result even before he arrived in Jerusalem. In 13:33-34a, Jesus responds to the Pharisees and says, "I must be on my way, because it is impossible for a prophet to be killed outside of Jerusalem. Jerusalem, Jerusalem the city that kills the prophets and stones those who are sent to it!"

Despite the religious leaders' rejection of Jesus' prophetic message and ministry and despite their role in Jesus' death, Jesus cites Ps 118:22 to claim that he is the fulcrum, or cornerstone, for God's salvation (20:17-18). Later, in the book of Acts, when Peter addresses the Jewish "rulers, elders, and scribes assembled in Jerusalem" in addition to the high priest and his family (Acts 4:5), Peter also cites Ps 118:22 to explain Jesus' importance in God's salvation history. Filled with the Holy Spirit, Peter claims that "Jesus of Nazareth, whom you crucified, whom God raised from the dead. This Jesus is 'the stone that was rejected by you, the builders; it has become the cornerstone.' There is salvation in no one else, for there is no other name under heaven given among mortals by which we must be saved" (Acts 4:10b-12).

(3) Luke 20:20-26. After the Jewish religious leaders failed in their first attempt to discredit Jesus in 20:2, they devise a new strategy in 20:20-22. Continuing in the temple (20:1), the scribes and chief priests (20:19; cf. 19:47; 20:1) watch Jesus carefully while hoping to observe some type of wrongdoing or impropriety that will result in his arrest by the Roman authorities (20:20). In order to coax Jesus into speaking freely and thereby falling into their trap, the scribes and chief priests send spies who pretend to listen to Jesus' teachings with interest and support (20:20). Literally, these spies "feigned righteousness." Here, Luke describes their misdirection with the Greek verb *upokrinomai*, which can be translated as "to be a hypocrite." In essence, Luke depicts these representatives of the scribes and chief priests as knowingly hypocritical. They are not absentmindedly contradicting themselves. Instead, they intentionally act and speak one way while thinking, plotting, and scheming in another. Consequently, Luke's readers know from the outset that the emissaries of the scribes and chief priests lie when they say that Jesus teaches truthfully in the way of God (20:21). Rather, their hypocritical words simply lay the groundwork for a more effective trap in 20:22.

Next, the spies sent from the chief priests and scribes ask Jesus a particularly thorny question (20:22). Should faithful Jews pay tribute taxes (or poll taxes) to the Roman emperor or not? Refusal to pay taxes to the Roman emperor was a serious offense in the first century CE. If Jesus instructs his followers not to pay these taxes, the chief priests and scribes will have legitimate grounds to accuse him of breaking Roman laws and leading an insurrection against the Roman emperor. In fact, Jewish anti-taxation protests helped to sow the seeds of rebellion that led to first Jewish War with Rome in 66–73 CE (C. F. Evans, *Saint Luke*, 706–707). On the other hand, if he advocates for paying taxes to Caesar, some Jews may accuse him of disregarding the law, which demands loyalty to God alone (Exod 20:2-3). The spies therefore seek to trap Jesus by asking him an either/or question. As is often the case, however, Jesus perceives their trap, declines to answer their myopic question, and instead asks his own, more important question (20:23-24).

Essentially, the Jewish spies seek to discover where Jesus' ultimate allegiances lie. Should the Jewish people recognize, respect, and abide by the rule of Caesar and the Roman Empire or not? When he responds, Jesus does not forbid paying taxes to the Romans. Instead, he instructs the representatives of the scribes and chief priests to "give to the emperor the things that are the emperor's" (20:25). He encourages compliance with the demands of the government. At that point, however, Jesus takes the conversation a step further when he also instructs them to give "to God the things that are God's" (20:25).

Previously, Jesus affirmed in 10:27-28 that the key to inheriting eternal life is to "love the Lord your God with all of your heart, and with all of your soul, and with all of your strength, and with all of your mind; and your neighbor as yourself" (10:27-28). Jesus has no difficulty in saying that he and his fellow Jews should pay their Roman taxes. Yet when Jesus exhorts his fellow Jews to give to God what belongs to God, he alludes to things that are far more valuable and more wide-ranging than monetary assets. Jesus has already clarified that God demands and deserves one's heart, soul, strength, and mind. Caesar is simply a fellow human who happens to oversee the Roman Empire. He is an earthly authority figure who possesses limited power. Caesar, like all rulers, will ultimately answer to God for his decisions (cf. Acts 12:20-23; Talbert, *Reading Luke*, 224). God, on the other hand, is the Creator who breathes life into humanity (Gen 2:7). God is the almighty, who possesses ultimate authority. In short, Jesus answers their trap question by reframing their question. Jesus highlights the far greater debt that humans owe God as compared to the minuscule amount that those in the Roman Empire owe Caesar. In response, the Jewish spies who seek to trap Jesus can do nothing but stand in silent amazement (20:26).

Finally, Jesus' words in this unit help to clarify the actions of Jesus' disciples in the book of Acts. Rather than advocating for unquestioned obedience to the state as we see in Paul's Epistle to the Romans (Rom 13:1-7; cf. 1 Tim 2:1-2; Titus 3:1-2; 1 Pet 2:13) and rather than unilateral resistance to the Roman government as an instrument of Satan as we see in the book of Revelation (e.g., Rev 12–13), Jesus in Luke 20:20-26 charts somewhat of a middle ground (Talbert, *Reading Luke*, 225–26). Jesus encourages his listeners to cooperate with the governing authorities unless the demands of those authorities impinge upon their ultimate devotion to God.

Consequently, in the Acts of the Apostles, the Christians do not engage in rebellion against the state. They are not insurrectionists. Notice that in Acts 25:8 Paul defends himself by saying, "I have in no way committed an offense against the law of the Jews, or against the temple, or against the emperor." He claims to be a law-abiding Roman citizen. On the other hand, the apostles repeatedly testify before and resist the demands of disapproving authorities who demand their silence. For example, the rulers of the Jewish people and elders command Peter and John to speak no more to anyone about Jesus (Acts 4:18), but Peter and John reply, "Whether it is right in God's sight to listen to you rather than to God, you must judge; for we cannot keep from speaking about what we have seen and heard" (Acts 4:19-20). Jesus' words in Luke 20:25 provide the overriding logic that guides the decision-making of his disciples in Acts. They cooperate with the governing authorities when possible, but their devotion and ultimate allegiance unquestionably lies with God alone.

(4) Luke 20:27-44. After failing to discredit Jesus' authority to teach in 20:2 and 20:20-23, the Jewish religious leaders make a third attempt to derail Jesus' teaching in the temple in 20:27-33. This third time some of the Sadducees, an aristocratic sect of Jews who frequently provided leadership for the temple (cf. Acts 4:1-3; 5:17; 23:6-8), take aim at Jesus. They seek to diminish Jesus' authority by enticing him to wade into the deep end of an ongoing theological debate about whether or not there would be a future resurrection of the dead. Whereas the Pharisees passionately defended the concept, the Sadducees did not believe in a resurrection after death (20:27; cf. Acts 23:6-8; Josephus, *Ant.* 18.14; *J.W.* 2.8.14). Jesus has already proclaimed "the resurrection of the righteous" in 14:14 and told a parable that depicts life after death for both the rich man and Lazarus in 16:19-31. This group of Sadducees now hopes to expose Jesus by making him look foolish in the eyes of the crowd. They attempt to stump him with a riddle about the resurrection.

In 20:29, the Sadducees begin to sketch a realistic scenario that they then elevate to an absurd level. In Deut 25:5-10, Moses instructs the Hebrews to forge a levirate marriage when a married man dies and his widow has no surviving sons (cf. Gen 38:8; Ruth 3–4). For example, in a levirate marriage, the brother of the deceased man marries the widow and seeks to bear a son with her. This practice of levirate marriage had a dual function. First, in a context where one did not anticipate any type of resurrection of the dead, male descendants represented a form of ongoing legacy for a deceased man. A male heir would receive and carry forth the deceased man's name and ancestry into the future. In addition, if a male heir was born, he would retain his deceased father's land and assets. Consequently, these assets would remain within their original tribe rather than falling into the hands of other tribes or people groups. Second, between the retention of assets and the provisions that a male son would one day acquire for himself, the widow would likewise receive adequate care. Otherwise, the widow might become destitute if her own father was not able to provide for her.

In the Sadducees' hypothetical scenario found in 20:29-32, seven brothers all marry the same woman, and yet none of these marriages produce a male descendant. In this situation, far fewer complications arise if there is no resurrection of the dead. Without a resurrection of the dead, the situation would indeed be tragic, but it would not create any additional dilemmas. The Sadducees hope they can trip Jesus up precisely because he has already affirmed his belief in the resurrection. The Sadducees believe they have identified a complication that will dissuade the crowd from believing in the resurrection of the dead while simultaneously discrediting Jesus as an authoritative teacher.

Jesus, however, responds to their trick question about levirate marriage in a manner that resembles his response to the scribes and chief priests' trick question about paying taxes (20:22). He takes an earth-bound and time-bound question about human experiences and converts it into a conversation about a proper human relationship with the almighty God of the universe. Jesus shows that the primary relationship that defines ultimate reality for God's people is the God and human relationship. In addition, disciples as "children of God" and "children of the resurrection" are and will be related to one another first and foremost as siblings, not spouses, parents, friends, or strangers (20:34-36). Moreover, those who are raised in the resurrection to eternal life with God are not bound by temporal categories of the past, present, and future. Rather, when the age of the resurrection arrives, Abraham, Isaac, Jacob, and those associated with God will all simultaneously be in the "present" with God (20:37-38; cf. 16:19-31). They will not be bound by their earthly relationships or their earthly life spans. At that point, the Sadducees yield to Jesus' authoritative teaching just as those who previously tested him had done (20:19, 26, 40).

In 20:41-44, after successfully circumnavigating the Sadducees' trick question, Jesus now asks the Sadducees a question. The Sadducees first attempted to show Jesus' theological inadequacies; now after Jesus has proven to be an authoritative teacher, he asks the Sadducees a question that highlights their own insufficient understanding of the holy Scriptures and God's ways. In particular, in 20:42-43 Jesus begins with the commonplace teaching that the Messiah (or the Christ) would be a descendant of David whom God would "anoint" to reign perpetually as King of the Jews (cf. 1:32-33; Acts 13:22-23). Jesus then quotes Ps 110:1 and asks the Sadducees to explain it. Psalm 110 is a royal oracle that was generally thought to express David's own words. In addition, if it originated in a preexilic setting, this royal psalm may have been read at the coronation of the later Davidic kings (Tucker and Grant, *Psalms*, 589). Regardless, when Jesus quotes the passage to the Sadducees, whose view of God's work is too narrow from a temporal perspective due to their lack of belief in the resurrection as Jesus just demonstrated in 20:37-38, it sounds as if David calls his son or descendant his "Lord" (20:41-44). Jesus essentially asks how the Messiah can simultaneously be David's son and his Lord.

The Sadducees never answer Jesus' question, but the question and the Scripture passage play an important role in Luke's writings nonetheless. In particular, when Peter seeks to explain the importance of Jesus in God's salvation history, he cites Ps 110:1 in his Spirit-inspired sermon at Pentecost to sum up the fullness of Jesus' identity (Acts 2:29-36). Having already established Jesus' ancestry from David (Luke 1:27, 32, 69; 2:4; 3:31; 18:38), Luke firmly demonstrates throughout his writings that Jesus is indeed the long-expected Messiah (e.g., Luke 2:11, 26; 4:41; 24:26, 46; Acts 2:31, 36, 38; 3:6, 18, 20). Yet Jesus' divine lordship will not be fully realized until after his resurrection, ascension, and exaltation when Jesus ascends to the right hand of God (Luke 24:50-53; Acts 1:9-11; 2:32). In essence, God's exaltation of Jesus demonstrates that "God has made him both Lord and Messiah" (Acts 2:36).

Thus, when Jesus asks the Sadducees his own riddle in Luke 20:41-44, they are unable to answer it. Especially since they do not believe in the resurrection of the dead, they have no way of knowing how anyone could be both the Messiah who has descended from David and the Lord who sits at the right hand of God (Ps 110:1; Luke 20:42; Acts 2:34). Instead, only God, who works outside the bounds of human time and human limitations, can simultaneously declare Jesus to be both the Davidic Messiah and the resurrected and exalted Lord in the heavenly realm who sits at the right hand of God. Notably, not even Jesus' disciples will be able to understand Jesus' questions in 20:41-44 until the Spirit provides clarification through Peter's words at Pentecost.

The Temple's Fate (20:45–21:38)

(1) Luke 20:45-47. After three failed attempts by the Jewish religious leaders to discredit Jesus' teaching authority in 20:1-19, 20-26, and 27-44, Jesus now turns to his disciples in 20:45-47 and warns them about the hypocrisy of the Jewish religious leaders. In particular, Jesus describes how the scribes relish the honor and social status that come with their role as religious leaders (20:46), yet they fail to care for widows in the community, and they perform religious actions for show rather than as an act of devotion to God (20:47).

Here, Jesus' critique of the scribes is reminiscent of the eighth-century prophets' critiques of Israel and Judah as well as Jesus' previous critique of the Pharisees and lawyers in Luke 11. Recall, for example, how Amos chastised the Israelites for oppressing the poor and crushing the needy while also making sacrifices and bringing their offerings regularly to their houses of worship (Amos 4:1-5). As a result, the Lord says, "I hate, I despise your festivals and I take no delight in your solemn assemblies. Even though you offer me your burnt offerings and grain offerings, I will not accept them

. . . . But let justice roll down like waters, and righteousness like an ever-flowing stream" (Amos 5:21-24).

Likewise, Jesus rebukes the Pharisees, who are closely affiliated with the scribes (e.g., 5:21, 30; 6:7; 11:53; 15:2), in a similar manner in Luke 11:37-52. As with the scribes in 20:46, Jesus notes that the Pharisees love "the seat of honor in the synagogues," and they, too, relish respectful marketplace greetings (11:43). Yet Jesus goes on to critique their hypocrisy. He claims that the Pharisees simultaneously focus on worship practices like ceremonial washings and tithing while being "full of greed and wickedness" (11:39, 42). Even as they engage in their worship rituals, they neglect "justice and the love of God" (11:42). As a result, Jesus instructs the Pharisees in 11:41 to draw upon their own resources and give alms or donations to the poor.

Here in 20:45-47, Jesus similarly criticizes the hypocrisy of the scribes. The scribes participate in empty worship practices like long, showy prayers. At the same time, however, they "devour widows' houses" (20:47). At the very least, these scribes sit idly by while watching widows descend so far into debt that they lose their homes. Yet regardless of whether the scribes are performing acts of commission or omission, Jesus criticizes them for focusing exclusively on religious rituals while neglecting the care of widows in their community.

(2) Luke 21:1-4. At that point, Jesus sees and comments on a scenario that plays out in the temple precincts in front of him and his disciples. In particular, people are in the process of giving their offerings to the temple treasury. In other words, Luke does not separate his narration of Jesus' critique of the scribes in 20:45-47 from the gift giving of the "rich people" and "a poor widow" in 21:1-4. Despite the chapter break that later interpreters inserted, Jesus' critique of the scribes and the passage frequently known as "the widow's mite" should be read together as one continuous unit. Furthermore, it should be noted that when Mark narrates the story of the widow's gift in his Gospel, he refers to three distinct participants—the crowd, many rich people, and a poor widow (Mark 12:41-42). Luke, however, while almost certainly relying on Mark's Gospel as a source text, elects to narrow the focus of his readers to only two participants. He leaves the crowd out of the discussion. By not mentioning the crowd, Luke intensifies the contrast between the actions of the "rich people" and "a poor widow" in 21:1-2.

Additionally, given the context of Jesus' critique of the scribes who "devour widows' houses" in the verses that immediately precede the widow's gift (20:47), it would have been difficult for Luke's first readers to idealize the poor widow in the way that many modern readers have done. Rather than lifting her up as a model to emulate, Jesus appears to portray the widow as a victim of the scribes and their religious hypocrisy. They have taught her to sacrifice more than they do, to give until she has nothing left, and to give her money to the temple treasury. Jesus says that she gives "all she had to live on" (21:4). Quite literally, she gives "all her life (Gk. *bios*)." Despite the fact that Jesus draws attention to these inequitable dynamics, he never praises the widow for her actions. Rather her actions are illustrative of a larger, systemic problem. She is a victim of the scribes' hypocrisy.

Earlier in Luke, when Jesus' parents offer the sacrifice of a poor family (2:24; cf. Lev 5:7), they encounter Anna, a widow who lives out her entire existence in the temple (2:36-37). At the beginning of Luke's Gospel, the temple provides Anna, a widow, with a place of refuge and service. Now, however, at the end of the Luke's Gospel, the temple has become a place where widows are devoured rather than sustained (cf. 19:45–20:8 and our earlier discussion about Luke's portrait of the temple at the beginning versus the end of this Gospel).

Perhaps most relevant for this discussion are Jesus' previous teachings about money and the poor in Luke's Gospel. For example, as cited above, when Jesus criticizes the hypocrisy of the Pharisees in 11:37-44 (which is similar to his critique of the scribes in 20:45-47), he instructs them to give alms (or charity to the poor). In contrast to his Pharisaic host who only invites honored guests capable of extending reciprocity to him, Jesus instead instructs him to "invite the poor, the crippled, the lame, and the blind" whenever he hosts a banquet in the future (14:1-14). The wealthy man in Jesus' parable of the rich man and Lazarus experiences post-mortem torment in part because he neglected to assist poor Lazarus who laid at his gate (16:19-31). When a rich ruler asks what he must do to inherit eternal life, Jesus tells him to "Sell all that you own and distribute the money to the poor" (18:22). Finally, when Zacchaeus is transformed by his interaction with Jesus, he gives half of his possessions "to the poor" (19:8). In essence, in Luke's Gospel, faithful disciples give alms. They give sacrificially *to the poor*. Yet in 21:1-4, both the rich people and the poor widow are giving their financial resources *to the temple treasury*, a repository of funds that was used in part to care for widows and orphans (cf. 2 Macc 3.10). Thus, in light of Luke's Gospel, the offerings in Luke 21:1-4 appear to be given to the wrong recipient.

Buttressing the idea that this widow is a victim of a corrupt temple system and its leadership are the comments that precede this story (20:45-47; cf. 19:45-46) and also those that immediately follow it (21:5-6). Unlike Mark 13:1-2 where Jesus physically leaves the temple after he comments on the widow's gift, Luke does not separate the widow's gift from Jesus' comments in 21:5-6. Rather, Jesus remains in the same location presumably dialoguing with the same people.

Luke 20:45–21:36 therefore functions as a single literary scene. Furthermore, Luke alone locates Jesus' teachings about the destruction of the temple within the temple (21:5-36; cf. Matt 24:1-44; Mark 13:1-37). Consequently, in Luke's Gospel, Jesus' comments in 21:5-36 contribute to Jesus' lengthy prophetic critique of the temple and his poor appraisal of the religious leaders who guide it (19:45–21:38). They also contribute to the story of the widow and her mite (21:1-4) because the pericope about the widow's mite falls in the midst of Jesus' lengthy critique of the temple.

(3) Luke 21:5-24. In 21:5, following directly on the heels of the poor widow who gives all of her financial resources to the temple treasury (21:1-4), some who are present comment on the grandeur of the temple. They admire the temple's beautiful appearance as well as the offerings that have been set aside for God within its precincts (cf. Josephus, *J.W.* 5.207–208, 222–224). The votive offerings, which had been dedicated to God, were likely ornamental objects or structures (Fitzmyer, *Luke*, 2:1331). Regardless, on a much smaller scale, the widow's two copper coins are akin to these dedicated offerings that are being praised in Jesus' hearing.

Jesus, however, does not marvel at the temple's beauty or celebrate its votive offerings. Instead, in 21:6 Jesus informs his disciples and the people standing nearby (20:45) that the temple will be torn down and destroyed (cf. 19:41-44). Here, Jesus' prophecy "echoes the prophecy of the destruction of the temple by Micah (3:12) and Jeremiah (7; 22:5) in earlier times" (Talbert, *Reading Luke*, 229). Tragically, the poor widow just gave everything she had to live on to an institution Jesus says will not last much longer. By the time Luke's first readers encounter Luke's Gospel in perhaps the mid-80s CE, the temple has already laid in ruins for at least a decade after the Roman armies destroyed the temple and large portions of Jerusalem in 70 CE.

Once Jesus predicts the destruction of the temple in 21:5-6, those standing nearby predictably and urgently ask follow-up questions. In particular, they ask when the destruction of the temple will take place and what the signs of its impending destruction will be (21:7). As a faithful prophet, Jesus takes the opportunity not only to address the upcoming destruction of the temple but also to comment on a broader and much more important subject as well—the eschaton or the climactic arrival of the Son of Man and the kingdom of God (21:27, 31). In essence, when Jesus answers their questions about the temple, he does so within "an apocalyptic discourse (vv. 8-36) that sets the fate of the temple in a much larger context" (Talbert, *Reading Luke*,

229). The fate of the temple pales in comparison to the much grander work of God in the world that will be manifest when the Son of Man arrives.

Jesus' prophetic oracle in Luke 21:8-36 then unfolds in a logical order. First, in 21:8-19 Jesus describes for his disciples and others who are listening the type of circumstances they can expect to encounter in the period prior to the destruction of the temple. False messiahs and false prophets will arise who deceptively claim to speak for God while saying that "the time is near" (21:8). Political upheaval and even natural disasters will manifest themselves while portending things to come (21:9-11). Finally, armies will surround Jerusalem. This latter event will then function as the sign that the destruction of the temple is imminent (21:20). As a result, by 21:20 Jesus has answered the two questions that were posed to him in 21:7. He has described the sign—armies surrounding Jerusalem—that denotes the timing of the temple's destruction, which Jesus prophesied in 21:6.

Interspersed within Jesus' comments about the temple's destruction, Jesus instructs his disciples (20:45) about how they are to navigate these events: the arrival of false messiahs, political upheaval, and natural disasters. For instance, he instructs them to ignore the false messiahs who proclaim a message different than his own (20:8; cf. 17:20; Acts 5:34-39). When events like "the battles of A.D. 69, when four claimants contended for the imperial throne vacated by the suicide of Nero, and the eruption of Vesuvius in A.D. 79" take place, the false prophets will wrongly confuse them with the final climax of history (Caird, *Saint Luke*, 230). Jesus, however, separates the former from the latter.

Notably, Jesus also warns his audience to expect persecution prior to the temple's destruction (21:12-19). Even before the false messiahs, political upheaval, and natural disasters, Jesus' disciples should anticipate religious oppression by both Jewish religious leaders and Roman governors (21:12). Perhaps most important, Jesus points out that this maltreatment at the hands of the unbelievers will provide his followers with an opportunity to testify to the hope they have in God's redemptive plan as enacted through Jesus (21:13). Jesus even promises to provide his disciples with the words and the wisdom they will need to withstand their trials and tribulations. Strikingly, this dynamic—the persecution of Jesus' followers at the hands of the civil and religious authorities—manifests itself on numerous occasions in the book of Acts (e.g., Acts 4:1-22; 5:17-42; 6:8–8:1; 12:1-17; 13:50; 16:19-34; 18:12-15; 21:27–26:32). Stephen even sees "Jesus standing at the right hand of God," presumably strengthening him as the Jewish religious authorities martyr him in Acts 7:55.

Second, Jesus refers to the temple's destruction in 21:20. As stated above, this event occurred in 70 CE when Titus led Roman forces to destroy and burn the temple and large portions of Jerusalem. Here again, Jesus coaches his disciples in 21:21-24 about how to respond to this traumatic event. Jesus does not instruct them to stay in the city and fight to protect the temple. Rather, Jesus has already chronicled numerous problems with the temple's leadership and current operations. He indicates that the temple's fate has already been determined in an act of divine judgment (21:22; Caird, *Saint Luke*, 228; Fitzmyer, *Luke*, 2:1329). The Gentiles (or the Romans) will trample Jerusalem and its temple under foot. Yet Jesus goes on to point out that even the time of the Gentiles (or the Romans) will come to an end. Their era will also arrive at its completion one day (21:24). The reign of the Roman Empire will not outlast God's salvation history.

In short, by means of a prophetic oracle, Jesus predicts the destruction of the temple in 21:8-24. The event should not catch his followers off guard; in Luke alone Jesus predicts the destruction of the temple on two separate occasions in both 19:41-44 and in 21:6, 20-24. Instead of being surprised, Jesus' disciples should anticipate the downfall of the temple and be prepared to flee quickly from Jerusalem when these events begin to take place (21:21). More important though, the disciples must realize that their most pressing concern revolves around their response to persecution and trials. They should endure unavoidable trials while seeing them as opportunities for a testimony. These venues will afford Jesus' followers with occasions to provide a witness to God's salvation through Jesus (21:13, 19).

(4) Luke 21:25-33. Jesus then broadens the conversation from the local to the universal. Despite the fact that his questioners ask exclusively about the destruction of the temple in Jerusalem (21:7), Jesus reframes the discussion. He now places the conversation about the destruction of the temple within a far grander conversation about the arrival of the Son of Man (21:27). By this point, the tragic destruction of the temple in Jerusalem merely functions as one of several signs that point toward a pivotal moment in God's salvation history. Other signs now include developments "in the sun, the moon, the stars, and on the earth" (21:25; cf. Acts 2:19-21; Joel 2:30-32).

While there are debates about the meaning of the phrase "the Son of Man" in other places, here Jesus refers to himself in his exalted state as the apocalyptic judge and king as Dan 7:13-14 describes (cf. 22:69; Acts 2:32-36; 7:56). In contrast to the signs that portend the destruction of the temple (21:8-20), the signs that point to the Son of Man's arrival are even more cosmic and universal (21:25-26; cf. Acts 2:19-21). As was the case with the temple's destruction, the arrival of the Son of Man will function as a manifestation of God's judgment on the earth (Fitzmyer, *Luke*, 2:1329). This time, however, the Son of Man will reign and the kingdom of God will be firmly and permanently established.

Here again, Jesus instructs his disciples regarding the proper response to this climactic event. Unlike the temple's destruction, which will result in distress and possibly death for those in Jerusalem and is an event from which they should flee (21:21-24), the Son of Man's arrival represents both judgment and redemption—judgment for those who oppress God's people and redemption for those who are devoted to God (21:28). Accordingly, this development requires a different response from and provides a far different outcome for Jesus' disciples. When the Son of Man arrives, Jesus' followers will simply stand up, raise their heads, and realize that their redemption is near (21:25-28). They should realize that God's kingdom will be finally and permanently established on earth (21:31; cf. 11:2).

(5) Luke 21:34-36. Finally, Jesus insists that his disciples must live by an apocalyptic ethic during the interim period (cf. 12:35-48). In essence, Jesus ends his critique of the temple (19:45–21:38) and his prophetic oracle about things to come (21:8-36)—referencing both the destruction of the temple and the arrival of the Son of Man—by providing his disciples with instructions about how to live in the period before the arrival of the Son of Man. In contradistinction to the religious leaders who have made God's temple "a den of robbers" rather than "a house of prayer" (19:46) and regardless of whether it is a time of political upheaval, natural disaster, destruction, or persecution, Jesus provides overarching instructions for his followers about how to live as they await the future arrival of the Son of Man in 21:34-36 (cf. 12:35-48).

In particular Jesus warns his disciples against drunkenness and the worries of this life (21:34-35). These two activities run in opposite directions. The first prohibition refers to acts of carelessness and irresponsibility whereas the second prohibition refers to anxious impulses that seek to control one's fortunes in life. Either approach will leave one "weighed down" and unprepared for the arrival of the Son of Man. Instead, Jesus instructs his disciples to "be alert." Jesus calls for spiritual vigilance, and prayer, in part, enables his disciples to remain wide awake. As we have seen repeatedly, prayer often serves a revelatory function in Luke's Gospel. For instance, by means of prayer, Jesus' disciples can request the words and wisdom that only Jesus can provide to those who are enduring persecution (21:15; cf. Acts 7:59). By means of prayer, God provides believers with "the strength to escape all these things that will take place, and to stand before the Son of Man" (21:36; cf. 21:8-28). In short, the proper disposition for Jesus' disciples as they await the Son of Man revolves around spiritual alertness and the activity of prayer.

(6) Luke 21:37-38. Luke's summary statement in 21:37-38 concludes Jesus' ministry in the Jerusalem temple. Jesus first enters the temple in 19:45. Luke alone repeatedly shows Jesus entering the temple, teaching in its precincts, and navigating the theological traps the religious leaders set throughout 19:45–21:38. In the process, Jesus provides a prophetic critique of the temple as an institution. Its leaders have transformed the temple into something other than what God intended (19:45-46). In the end, however, Jesus casts a far grander vision than that of the temple. Instead, Jesus lifts up the image of the apocalyptic arrival of the Son of Man as the culminating event in salvation history. When the Son of Man arrives to serve as judge and king, he will finally and definitively usher in the reign of God on earth (21:27, 31).

The Death of the Messiah (22:1–23:56a)

As one would expect, Luke's passion narrative shares many commonalities with the passion narratives found in Matthew and Mark. Yet Luke also accentuates some themes in his own distinctive manner. For instance, Luke first and foremost portrays Jesus as an obedient martyr who dies according to the will of God, thereby allowing "a new covenant" to be forged between God and humans (22:20). In addition, Luke demonstrates for his readers that Jesus is engaged in a cosmic conflict in Luke 22–23. Jesus does not merely withstand an unwarranted arrest, false accusations, and a brutal death at the hands of the Jewish and Roman leaders. Rather, he and his disciples weather attacks by Satan and the forces of "darkness" (e.g., 22:3, 53), and he expresses his trust in the Father by means of his last words from the cross. Finally, Luke alone narrates Jesus' post-resurrection appearances in Judea, which will help his readers to understand better the overarching role of Jesus within God's salvation history.

Conspiring against Jesus (22:1-6)
(1) Luke 22:1-2. After Jesus completes his prophetic critique of the temple in 19:45–21:38, Luke sets the scene for the last week of Jesus' life. His last week coincides with the seven-day Festival of Unleavened Bread, which many in Jesus' day simply referred to as Passover (22:1-2) (Nolland, *Luke*, 3:1027). The Festival of Unleavened Bread provides an opportunity for the Jewish people to recall God's salvific work in the past, namely their escape from Egyptian slavery (Exod 12:14-20). In particular, when Pharaoh relented and God, by means of Moses's leadership, brought the Hebrew people out of Egypt, the Hebrews were required to act quickly. The unleavened bread reminds them of the speed with which their ancestors fled; there was no time

for the bread to rise (Exod 12:33-39). Accordingly, during the weeklong Feast of Unleavened Bread, the Jewish people removed all leaven from their homes and only ate unleavened bread (Nolland, *Luke*, 3:1027). Furthermore, the name "Passover" recalls the death angel's act of passing over the household doorposts marked with lamb's blood (Exod 12:21-27). As a result, "Passover is properly the feast prepared for by the slaughter of the lamb in the late afternoon of 14 Nisan and celebrated in family or wider groupings . . . after sunset . . . with an elaborate meal built around the lamb" (Nolland, *Luke*, 3:1027). Consequently, the Feast of Unleavened Bread (and/or Passover) was a time of celebration for God's redemptive work in the past that rescued them from their enemies.

(2) Luke 22:3-6. Luke further sets the scene for the last week of Jesus' life in 22:3-6. At this point, however, Luke no longer focuses exclusively on the human conflict that surrounds Jesus. Instead, he reintroduces the cosmic conflict between Jesus and satanic forces (cf. 4:1-13; 13:16; Acts 10:38; 26:18). For example, unlike Matthew and Mark, Luke associates Judas and his acts of betrayal with the work of Satan. Notice, for example, that Satan takes possession of Judas in 22:3 (cf. John 13:2). The last time Luke narrated the words and actions of Satan, or the devil (the two terms functioned synonymously by the time of Jesus), occurred at the conclusion of Jesus' temptation in 4:13. Jesus resisted Satan's temptations over a forty-day period while relying on Scripture to clarify God's will (4:1-12). Finally, when Jesus had withstood every test that Satan could throw at him (all of them; Gk. *panta*), the devil "departed from him until an opportune time" (4:13).

In 22:3, Satan now identifies that opportune time and seizes it. Having failed to influence Jesus' decision-making, Satan elects to attack Jesus' followers. Even though Jesus demonstrates in 4:1-13 that resisting the devil's allure is now possible (in contrast to Adam in the garden and Israel in the wilderness; cf. 3:38; 4:1), Judas tragically fails to resist Satan. Judas allows Satan to take over his reasoning and his actions while apostatizing. In 22:1-4, Luke even accentuates Judas's culpability by making Judas the subject of five active verbs (cf. 6:16). Judas is not Satan's victim as much as he is Satan's cohort. Consequently, Judas now functions as the embodiment of Satan for the remainder of the Lukan passion narrative. Whenever Luke's readers see Judas speak or act, they should realize that none other than Satan himself inspired and guided those words and actions. Previously, Satan waited for an opportune time to thwart Jesus' ministry (4:13). Now, Judas is the one, as an agent of Satan, who looks "for an opportunity to betray" Jesus (22:6).

Furthermore, from the outset of the passion narrative, Luke also links the words and actions of "the chief priests and officers of the temple police" with

Satan (22:4). The chief priests and officers of the temple police confer with Judas, the possessed one, about how to betray Jesus. As a result, they make a deal with the devil. Judas's suggestions please them, and they agree to reward him with money if he will guide them to Jesus when the crowds are absent (22:5-6). These same people who are conferring with the Satan-possessed Judas will also be the ones who arrest Jesus and try him before their Sanhedrin (22:52, 54, 66). Notably, Luke alone indicates that the chief priests are present at Jesus' arrest (22:52), and the chief priests and scribes are particularly active in Luke's Gospel during Jesus' trials (22:66; 23:4, 10, 13; 24:20).

In essence, from the beginning of his passion narrative, Luke draws attention to both the seen and unseen forces at work in the arrest, trials, and death of Jesus. Unlike Matthew and Mark, Luke seeks to lay bare Satan's work for his readers. In particular, Luke wants his readers to realize that Jesus will be opposed by human adversaries—a rogue disciple, Jewish religious leaders, a Roman governor, the crowd in Jerusalem, and Roman soldiers—as well as by Satan and "the power of darkness" (22:3, 53; cf. Eph 6:12). Luke wants his readers to realize that Jesus will not die simply because one greedy disciple dupes Jesus. Jesus will not die because Judas pulled off a superbly-planned, strategic operation. Instead, Luke raises the curtain and reveals what is happening behind the scenes. The primary conflict is a cosmic one. The forces of evil are attempting to thwart the will of God. Yet they do not realize that the death of Jesus is a necessary component of God's larger salvific plan (22:42; 24:26). Even though the events of Jesus' passion will be instigated by Satan and precipitated by Judas's betrayal, "Jesus remains supremely in charge even as he goes to his death" (Nolland, *Luke*, 3:1016).

The Last Supper (22:7-38)

(1) Luke 22:7-13. In Luke 22:7-13 Luke narrates Jesus and his disciples' preparation for the Passover meal (see 22:1-2), which they will eat in 22:14-20. In the process, Luke further enhances his portrait of Jesus as a faithful prophet. Jesus first informs Peter and John that they will see a man carrying a jar when they enter a city. If they follow him and request hospitality from the owner of the house, he will grant them use of the guest room on the upper floor of his house for their Passover meal (22:10-12). Next, Peter and John find "everything as he had told them" (22:13). Jesus' accurate foreknowledge about these lesser matters will then help Jesus' disciples (and Luke's readers) to trust Jesus' predictions about far weightier events that will soon take place. For instance, Jesus has already alluded to his impending suffering, death, and resurrection (9:22; 13:32-34; 17:25; cf. 22:15).

(2) Luke 22:14-20. In Luke 22:14-20, Jesus and the apostles then partake of their Passover meal, a meal that commemorates God's salvific work in the past (22:14). In the midst of their meal (22:15), however, Jesus seizes an opportunity to discuss the future with his disciples. He refers to imminent events, an interim period, and the culmination of God's salvific work in the world. The times to which Jesus alludes include his impending betrayal, suffering, and death (22:15, 21-22); the period between his death and the arrival of the kingdom of God (22:16, 18; cf. 21:31); and God's "ultimate future" (22:16, 18) (Bovon, *Luke*, 3:153, 157).

The betrayal and Jesus' arrest will take place shortly after the meal concludes (22:47–23:56). Marking the interim period will be Jesus' absence (22:16, 18) and the disciples' vigilance, which will include sharing this meal with one another (22:17), remembering Jesus' martyrdom (22:19), and anticipating the future (22:16, 18). The ultimate future, however, will be realized when God establishes God's unhindered reign throughout the earth (22:16, 18). As a result,

> What Jesus now is doing, the disciples will have to do (by implication from now until the in-breaking of the kingdom of God): Take a cup and share it. Why? To experience solidarity . . . , to make up for Jesus' absence . . . , and to wait for the future, encouraged by the symbolic, strengthening, and festive force of the wine . . . . Verses 16-18 . . . attest that the Eucharist of the first Christians was not only a memorial of the death of Jesus but also a joyful anticipation of the end. (Bovon, *Luke*, 3:157)

Furthermore, as Luke narrates the Last Supper, he incorporates three elements into his account that stand out as distinct from the other Gospels. As a result, all three likely caught the attention of Luke's first readers.

(a) First, Luke alone depicts Jesus as referencing the cup on two occasions during the Last Supper. He refers to a cup both before and after he refers to the bread. For instance, he first mentions a cup in 22:17-18. Then, he mentions a cup again in 22:20-22.

Jesus' two references to the cup metaphorically correspond to two distinct referents. Jesus does not specifically link either cup at the Last Supper to any of the four cups present at a traditional Passover meal. Regardless, Jesus' first reference to the cup undoubtedly focuses on the Passover meal that Jesus and the apostles are sharing (22:17-18). The cup along with the entire meal recall God's redemptive work in the past when God liberated the Hebrews from slavery in Egypt. Jesus claims that he will not partake of this Passover meal again (22:15-18).

Then, after he and the apostles complete their Passover meal, Jesus takes up a cup again (22:20). This second cup points to the rescuing work of God in the present. The "cup that is poured out for you" refers to Jesus' suffering and death. The cup, which symbolizes Jesus' blood, will now correspond to the blood of a covenant sacrifice that forges a new relationship between God and the people (e.g., Gen 15:7-21; Jer 34:18). Consequently, whereas the first cup is a part of the Passover meal that recalls God's work in the past, the second cup is part of a memorial meal that Jesus institutes in 22:19-20. This second cup points to the new work that God is doing through Jesus to liberate God's people in the present (Brown, *Introduction*, 256).

Here, it may be helpful to recall that Luke began his Gospel with a similar two-step movement. For instance, Luke begins Jesus' biography by narrating the ministry and message of John the Baptist, who recalls and resembles the work of God's prophets in ages past. Yet Luke then goes on to show the even grander way that God is at work through Jesus' ministry to bring salvation to God's people in the present (see Luke 1–2). Similarly, the first cup of the Last Supper appears to celebrate a powerful manifestation of God's work in the past, but the second cup appears to commemorate an even grander work of God through Jesus the Christ.

Notably, even though Jesus only refers to the bread of the Passover meal once (22:19), Jesus nevertheless places great emphasis on the bread in Luke's Gospel. In particular, Jesus' call for remembrance occurs in conjunction with his comments about the bread. Notice that after he distributes the bread, Jesus says, "This is my body, which is given for you. Do this in remembrance of me" (22:19).

From that point, the bread not only recalls God's salvific work in the past but also it will now elicit memories of Jesus' ministry and death. In essence, the unleavened bread will now remind Jesus' disciples about multiple aspects of God's redemptive work throughout time but especially those associated with Jesus. For instance, the bread should remind Jesus' disciples (and Luke's readers) of the life-giving nature of Jesus' ministry and message. When Jesus fed the five thousand, he took the loaves (and fish), blessed them, broke them, and gave them to the disciples for distribution (9:16). So also, here in 22:19 Luke employs the same set of verbs in the same sequence. Jesus takes the bread, gives thanks, breaks it, and gives it to them. Similarly, when the resurrected Jesus dines with two disciples in Emmaus, he takes the bread, blesses it, breaks it, and gives it to them (24:30). The repetition of verbs in a mealtime setting conjoins these passages for Luke's readers. As a result, when Jesus' disciples (and Luke's readers) eat bread in remembrance of Jesus (cf. Acts 2:42, 46; 20:7, 11; 27:35), they should recall events from Jesus' ministry and not merely his death. This memorial meal, which takes place on the last night of Jesus' life, should cause its participants to consider the whole of Jesus' time on earth.

The Lukan Jesus also associates the broken bread of the Passover meal with his own body and in particular his suffering and death (22:15, 19). Those who partake of the memorial meal in the future will not be able to escape the similarities between the broken bread and Jesus' obedient martyrdom.

Finally, in part because Jesus mentions the kingdom of God twice in the midst of the Last Supper (22:16, 18; cf. 22:30), during the interim period of Christ's absence the meal will henceforth foreshadow God's ultimate end for those who participate in it. At numerous points in this Gospel, Jesus has highlighted the motif of the messianic banquet. Jewish writers who wrote about the eschatological banquet repeatedly visualized God's future salvation as an extravagant meal of great abundance for those who worship God (e.g., Isa 25:6-10a; *1 En.* 60.24; Luke 13:29; 14:15-24; 22:30). Those who remain faithful to God until the judgment and the shift of the ages will participate in this great feast. Consequently, this new memorial meal, built on the foundation of the Passover meal, now carries overtones of the messianic banquet. When Jesus' disciples (and Luke's readers) partake of the Lord's Supper, this interim meal will not only point backward to Jesus' life and death but will also point forward to the arrival of the kingdom of God. It will point forward to a time when the Lord's Supper, the interim meal, will be replaced with a grander meal—the messianic banquet.

(b) The second distinct element in the Lukan Last Supper relates to 1 Cor 11:23-26. Luke's description of the Last Supper shares a great deal in common with Paul's description of the Last Supper; the similarities are so strong that it suggests that Luke was either familiar with Paul's teaching on the Last Supper or familiar with an oral tradition that both Paul and Luke drew upon when writing. Notice, for example, that Paul and Luke, as distinct from Matthew and Mark, share similar statements by Jesus about the bread and the cup.

In regard to the bread, Paul quotes Jesus as saying, "This is my body that is for you. Do this in remembrance of me" (1 Cor 11:23-24). Luke likewise quotes Jesus as saying "This is my body, which is given for you. Do this in remembrance of me" (Luke 22:19). Jesus' injunction to "Do this in remembrance of me" is only found in 1 Cor 11 and Luke 22, not Matt 26 or Mark 14. Similarly, both Paul and Luke indicate that Jesus referred specifically to "a *new* covenant in my blood" (1 Cor 11:25; Luke 22:20). Matthew and Mark simply refer to "my blood of the covenant" (Matt 26:28; Mark 14:24).

(c) Third, Jesus' words about the cup and its relationship with God's covenant are distinct from Matthew and Mark. When Luke refers to a "*new* covenant" that is connected to the blood of Jesus, he makes a significant contribution to the discussion about the implications of Jesus' death. Jeremiah first spoke about a "new covenant" that God would forge with the people early in the sixth century BCE in an eschatological section of the book of Jeremiah. For instance, Jeremiah prophesies,

> The days are surely coming, says the LORD, when I will make a new covenant with the house of Israel and the house of Judah. It will not be like the covenant that I made with their ancestors, when I took them by the hand to bring them out of Egypt—a covenant that they broke, though I was their husband, says the LORD. But this is the covenant that I will make with the house of Israel after those days, says the LORD: I will put my law within them, and I will write it on their hearts; and I will be their God, and they shall be my people. No longer shall they teach one another, or say to each other, "Know the LORD," for they shall all know me, from the least of them to the greatest, says the LORD; for I will forgive their iniquity, and remember their sin no more. (Jer 31:31-34; cf. 32:38-41)

With the Babylonian exile as his backdrop, Jeremiah contrasts the covenant that God previously made with those whom God led out of Egypt—an event the Passover meal like the one Jesus and his apostles just finished celebrates—with a new and grander covenant. Rather than writing instructions on stone tablets, God will now write on the hearts of God's people. Rather than an intermediary like Moses who teaches the people, now they will all have an intimate relationship with God. In addition, in conjunction with this new covenant, God promises to forgive the sins of the people.

Unlike Matthew and Mark, in Luke's Gospel Jesus appears to link the "new covenant" Jeremiah prophesied with his own blood and the new memorial meal that he institutes (22:20). In essence, Jesus is linking his life, death, and resurrection with the realization of the new covenant that Jeremiah spoke about long ago. Consequently, Jesus' blood takes on the connotations of a covenant sacrifice in which the blood of the sacrificial animals seals the agreed-upon arrangement. Even more, in the course of a Passover meal that celebrated God's past deliverance and covenant with the people as introduced through Moses, Jesus proclaims that a new era has begun. God has inaugurated a "new covenant" through Jesus' blood (22:20). Through Jesus, God introduces a new, everlasting covenant that the people cannot break and that leads to the forgiveness of their sins (24:46-47; Acts 5:31; 10:43; 13:38; 26:18).

(3) Luke 22:21-38. In Luke 22:21-38 Jesus seeks to prepare the apostles for the events that will take place in the coming hours. Altogether, Jesus addresses five different topics in this after-dinner setting: Judas's betrayal, greatness, the eschatological banquet, Satan's attack, and modified travel instructions. In essence, just as Jesus discussed his suffering (22:15) and the new memorial meal in the context of the Last Supper (22:19-20), so also Jesus takes the time to comment on these topics while still in the upper room. His attention to these conversations given the limited time that remains prior to his arrest points to their importance. As a result, Jesus' comments can be considered a miniature farewell speech that takes place in an intimate yet solemn context of worship, fellowship, and hopefulness about the ultimate end of God's work.

(a) First, in 22:21-23, rather than discuss it before the meal as we see in Matthew (26:21-25) and Mark (14:18-21), in Luke's Gospel Jesus predicts Judas's betrayal after they have already shared the bread and wine but before the group has left the upper room. As a result, the Lukan Jesus asks his disciples to digest the importance of their meal before he moves on to predict Judas's betrayal. On the one hand, Luke's arrangement gives priority to the memorial meal that Jesus institutes over Judas's act of betrayal. On the other hand, given the intimacy of the Last Supper context, Judas's actions of betrayal are cast in an even more destructive light. Judas fully participates in the Last Supper with his cohorts before Jesus enlightens them about the plot that is afoot. Luke has already informed his readers that Satan has taken possession of Judas (22:3-6), so his readers should anticipate Judas's public betrayal of Jesus (22:47-48).

(b) Second, in 22:24-27, the apostles debate among themselves which of them is the greatest (22:24). Notably, some of Jesus' disciples (and likely some of the same apostles who are present with Jesus in the upper room) have already debated this topic in 9:46 (cf. 9:43), and in 9:47-48 Jesus has already sought to redirect their aspirations. Here in chapter 22, however, Luke shows his first readers that the human desire to achieve societal greatness can be a particularly stubborn fixation. Luke illustrates for his readers that even after journeying with Jesus over an extended period of time, the disciples are still vulnerable to the lure of societal esteem and influence. They have not yet fully understood or fully adopted Jesus' teachings on this matter. Given that Jesus has previously addressed this topic, Jesus' comments in 22:25-27 appear to be teeming with added weight and great seriousness. Because his previous comments have not yet sunk in, Jesus takes what little time he has left with his disciples to define greatness once again.

When Jesus does weigh in on the debate, he makes his point by means of a contrast. He differentiates the ways of the Gentile kings and their benefactors from those of children and servants. Generally speaking, Gentile rulers (or "rulers of the nations") relied on military might and power as leverage when imposing their will upon others. They dominated others with strength. The Romans were particularly characterized in this fashion (e.g., Virgil, *Aen.*, 7–12). Similarly, ancient benefactors sought to influence political and social outcomes using their wealth, status, and influence (22:25). These Gentile patrons assisted others, but their generosity was housed within a reciprocity-based paradigm. Recipients of benefaction knew they were obligated to praise their benefactors in all circumstances and to carry out their wishes enthusiastically (Parsons, *Luke*, 312–13).

Jesus, however, charts an alternative path for his followers. He does not seek to equate greatness with military might, wealth, or societal influence. Instead, as he has done before, Jesus lifts up children and servants as models for his disciples (22:26). Jesus points to those without social standing or influence, those without financial strength, and those without military might when he seeks to define greatness. Moreover, Jesus personally self-identifies as "one who serves" (22:27). As a result, hours before his arrest, Jesus once again beseeches his disciples to follow the pathway of humble servanthood in a society that operates with different aims. Jesus will embrace this definition of greatness as he dies, but his disciples will need to embrace this definition of greatness as they live.

(c) Third, in 22:28-30 Jesus follows up his exhortation for humble servitude with further encouragement. Earlier, Jesus informed the disciples of the hardships they will face as they serve as his disciples and messengers (e.g., 9:5; 10:3, 10-11, 16). Now Jesus' warnings about the future mistreatment of his humble servants become increasingly pertinent as he and his disciples prepare to leave the upper room (22:28; cf. 21:12-17; 22:35-38). As a result, he once again assures his disciples that those who endure to the end while remaining faithful to Jesus will be rewarded (22:29-30; cf. 21:19).

In particular, just as Jesus referenced the kingdom of God twice during the meal (22:16, 18), Jesus once again lifts up God's coming kingdom as the ultimate fulfillment of God's redemptive plan and as a powerful motivator of their fidelity. Those who remain faithful to Jesus amid trials will be rewarded in the coming kingdom. The arrival of the Son of Man will mean that their "redemption is drawing near" (21:27-28).

Jesus then relies on two images in 22:30 to illustrate the future bliss of kingdom life for his disciples: the messianic banquet and the coming judgment. As mentioned above (see 22:16, 18), existence in the kingdom of God after God's Messiah begins to reign was often portrayed in antiquity as a grand banquet (e.g., Isa 25:6-10a; *1 En.* 60.24; Luke 13:29; 14:15-24; cf. 16:19-31). Disciples who endure to the end can look forward to a banquet that has enough room and enough food for all.

In addition, rather than being judged, examined, and tried by those who fail to follow Jesus (e.g., 21:12-19; Acts 4:1-22; 5:17-42; 6:8–8:1; 12:1-17; 13:50; 16:19-34; 18:12-15; 21:27–26:32), the arrival of the Son of Man represents good news for Jesus' disciples (21:27-28). When the Son of Man begins to reign and to judge the world (cf. Dan 7:13-14), the wrongs that Jesus' disciples have endured amid their trials will be righted. Justice will prevail. Those who have lived as Jesus' humble servants will now judge others in the kingdom of God.

(d) Fourth, in 22:31-34 Luke once again redirects his readers' attention to the cosmic battle that is taking place behind the scenes. Just as Luke spoke about the nefarious intentions of the chief priests and scribes in 22:1-2 before exposing the unseen work of Satan in 22:3-6 (cf. 22:53), so also after alluding to trials and tribulations presumably conducted by human agents in 22:28, Luke alone of the canonical Gospel writers now discloses the hidden work of Satan in 22:31-34.

Here, within the context of the Last Supper and Jesus' final instructions to the disciples, Jesus directly addresses Peter's impending denial of him (22:54-62). After failing to sidetrack Jesus from his mission and purpose during the temptation (4:1-13), Satan has waited for his opportune moment and has elected to attack Jesus' disciples first (4:13; 22:3). With echoes of the heavenly council that meets in the presence of God to which Job 1:6-12 alludes (cf. 1 Kgs 22:19-22; Job 15:8; Ps 82:1; 89:7; Jer 23:18), Satan "has demanded permission to sift all" of the disciples "like wheat" (22:31). Here, the Greek verb meaning "to sift" (*siniazō*) "implies violent shaking" designed "to separate them from Jesus and to eliminate them from salvation" (Garland, *Luke*, 869). Perhaps like the overzealous prosecuting attorney image that we see in Job 1:6-12, Satan (literally, "the accuser" or "the adversary" in Hebrew) seeks to expose the disciples' weak and duplicitous nature. As a result, in 22:31-34 Jesus depicts Peter as a temporary victim of Satan's schemes. Peter's upcoming denial (22:54-62) will not unfold as an act of willful disobedience. Rather, it will unfold as the by-product of Satan's onslaught against the disciples.

Jesus, however, informs Peter in 22:32 that he has countered Satan's attacks. Whereas Satan functions as the accuser of the disciples who hopes to shake them loose, Jesus functions as their advocate who keeps them tethered to him (Crump, *Jesus the Intercessor*, 154–75; Arterbury, "I Have Prayed for You," 165–71). Unlike Judas, Jesus claims that Peter's faith will not fail. Peter will not become an apostate. Yet the only explanation Jesus supplies for the survival of Peter's faith revolves around Jesus' own prayer of petition for Peter (cf. 21:15) (Arterbury, "I Have Prayed for You," 165). Peter will not survive Satan's attacks due to his own strength, resolve, or character. His faith will survive because Jesus prays for him—because Jesus advocates before God for him. Jesus' prayer prevents Peter from being shaken loose by Satan.

Then, Jesus shares his plan for how the faith of the remaining apostles will survive as well. Jesus' prayer will sustain Peter. Thereafter, Jesus will work in conjunction with or perhaps through Peter. Jesus asks Peter to strengthen the others when he has "turned back" (22:32). Obviously, Jesus' plan appears somewhat risky. Jesus knows that Peter will deny him before the evening is over despite Peter's own vows of loyalty (22:33-34). Jesus is so confident in his effectual prayers for Peter, however, that Jesus simply focuses on the time when Peter will turn back. Jesus does not take this opportunity to articulate his profound disappointment in Peter's upcoming denial. He does not focus on Peter's misstep. Rather, Jesus elects to focus on the time of Peter's repentance (Garland, *Luke*, 868–69) and already commissions Peter regarding what he should do after he denies Jesus and after he repents. Jesus will then use Peter to strengthen the other disciples who are similarly weakened by Satan's sifting. Jesus will be the ultimate reason that all of the disciples survive Satan's attack, but Jesus plans to accomplish much of this work through a repentant Peter (24:12, 34; Acts 1:15–2:47).

(e) Finally, in 22:35-38 Jesus revises the travel instructions that he previously gave to his disciples. In 9:1-6, Jesus commissioned the twelve. In 10:1-16, he commissioned seventy-two more. As he did so, he prepared his disciples for the rejection of his ministry and message (see 22:28 above; 9:5; 10:3-16). Despite their challenging contexts, Jesus nevertheless sent them out without provisions or protection (9:3; 10:4-8). His messengers were to be dependent on hospitable hosts whom they encountered along the way. By requiring his disciples to depend on the hospitality of others, Jesus ensured a more equitable relationship between those who announced the good news and those who received it.

Now, however, as we saw in 22:31-34, Jesus further prepares his disciples for a spiritual battle. Jesus just informed his disciples that Satan wants to sift all of them like wheat (22:31). To communicate the gravity of this cosmic battle with Satan and "the power of darkness" (22:53; cf. Eph 6:12), Jesus now instructs his disciples to carry their own provisions (22:36). In a post-Last Supper context, they should no longer anticipate hospitable contexts. They will need to care for themselves.

Similarly, Jesus now instructs his disciples to buy a sword—to prepare for battle (22:36). The disciples here envision a physical battle rather than a spiritual one. (This fact becomes even clearer in 22:49-51 when one of the disciples uses his sword to attack the slave of the high priest during Jesus' arrest.) As a result, they quickly announce that they have "two swords." Jesus simply responds by saying, "It is enough" (22:38). Whereas the disciples are envisioning a physical defense against those who might harm Jesus, Jesus says it is necessary for him to be "counted among the lawless" (22:37; Isa 53:12). Rather, Jesus is asking them to prepare themselves for Satan's onslaught (22:31–34), which will begin almost immediately after the disciples arrive on the Mount of Olives (22:39-53).

The Mount of Olives (22:39-53)
The spiritual battle about which Jesus just warned his disciples moves to the forefront of Luke's narration as Jesus and his disciples leave the upper room and go to the Mount of Olives. Notably, when Luke narrates Jesus' time on the Mount of Olives in 22:39-53, he does so in his own distinct manner. For instance, unlike Mark's Gospel, Luke does not separate Jesus' time of prayer from his arrest (Mark 14:32-42, 43-50). Jesus does not move about from place to place within the Garden of Gethsemane (e.g., Mark 14:33, 35, 37, 39) or officially conclude their time of prayer (Mark 14:41-42). Rather, Luke takes these two scenes that Mark separated by location and activity and weaves them together (Arterbury, "Battle on the Mount of Olives," 37–51). In Luke, the place of Jesus' prayer and the place of his arrest are one in the same. Both happen on the Mount of Olives in the exact same location. Furthermore, Jesus never concludes the time of prayer in Luke's Gospel; he exhorts his disciples to pray even as his arrest is beginning (22:46-47). In essence, Luke crafts 22:39-53 into one continuous unit. Both halves of this scene then help to illuminate each other.

In addition, Luke places Jesus' disciples in a much more favorable light than Mark does. In Mark, Jesus finds the disciples sleeping on three occasions (Mark 14:37-41). Furthermore, Mark concludes his arrest scene by noting that all of the disciples "deserted him and fled" (14:50). Luke, however, begins the Mount of Olives scene by adding the phrase, "the disciples followed him" (22:39). They rightly do what disciples are supposed to do. Jesus only finds the disciples sleeping on one occasion in Luke, and Jesus does not upbraid them for doing so (22:45-46; cf. Mark 14:37, 41). Luke informs his readers that the disciples fall asleep because grief overwhelms them as they fear for Jesus' safety (22:45). Finally, Luke does not draw attention to the failures of the disciples during Jesus' arrest. Instead, Luke shows his readers that the disciples are prepared to fight from the beginning, and he never documents their departure from the scene.

(1) Luke 22:39-46. When Luke describes Jesus' time of prayer, he accentuates Jesus' role as a combatant, the vulnerability of the disciples, and the importance of prayer. Though clearly reliant on Mark's Gospel as a source text, Luke opts to depict the Mount of Olives as a battlefield where Jesus counters Satan's attacks (Arterbury, "Battle on the Mount of Olives," 37–51).

For example, in Luke's Gospel Jesus requests that the Father remove the cup—a reference to Jesus' suffering and death—from him; first and foremost, however, Jesus seeks to be obedient to the Father (22:42). Next, even though 22:43-44 are missing in many early manuscripts, recent scholarship indicates that these verses were more likely expunged from the original version of Luke's Gospel in response to heretical interpretations of them rather than added later by scribes (Clivaz, *L'Ange*, 603–607; Blumell, "Luke 22:43-44," 5–7). At the very least, since Christian writers like Justin Martyr, Irenaeus, Tatian, and Hippolytus drew upon 22:43-44 as early as the mid-second century, the evidence suggests that the earliest readers of Luke's Gospel likely read verses 43-44 in conjunction with this passage (Caird, *Saint Luke*, 243). If so, 22:43-44 function as God's immediate response to the prayer that Jesus voices in 22:42. The Father does not remove the cup, but the Father immediately commissions an angel to strengthen Jesus amid this time of hardship.

Some have interpreted 22:42-44 and Jesus' prayer for the removal of the cup as evidence that Jesus is wavering in his resolve to die as an innocent martyr—something that Jesus resolved to do as far back as 9:51. Frequently, these scholars translate the Greek word *agōnia* in 22:43 as a type of "fearful anxiety" that places Jesus in desperate need of divine comfort. Some scholars disregard 22:43-44 altogether as a later corruption precisely because of this translation. They argue that Jesus is not overwhelmed by his emotions at any other place in Luke's Gospel. As a result, they deem 22:43-44 to be inauthentic (e.g., Ehrman and Plunkett, "The Angel," 401–16). Others consider 22:43-44 to be authentic, but they envision 22:42-44 as Jesus' second temptation (cf. 4:1-13; e.g., Marshall, *Luke*, 828). They suggest that Jesus struggles to remain obedient to the Father at the end of his life just as he did at the beginning.

Luke, however, has already informed his readers in 4:13 that Jesus resisted *all* (Gk. *pas*) of the devil's temptations from the beginning. As a result, perhaps it is better to envision Luke 22:39-43 as the temptation of Jesus' disciples. Luke has already revealed Satan's behind-the-scenes work when Satan takes possession of Judas and colludes with the chief priests and scribes (22:1-6). Furthermore, as his parting words in the upper room, Jesus informs his disciples that Satan demanded to sift all of them like wheat, to shake them loose violently (22:31). He even encouraged them to buy swords and ready themselves for battle (22:36). Even more, whereas Mark portrays Jesus as grieved (Mark 14:34), Luke attributes grief to the disciples not Jesus (22:45). Satan's sifting of the disciples begins while Jesus and his disciples are on the Mount of Olives in 22:39-46. Their time of vulnerability begins as soon as they depart the upper room.

So if Jesus is not full of anxious fearfulness, why does the Lord's angel need to strengthen Jesus? Many have noted that the better translation of the Greek word *agōnia* in 22:44 connotes that Jesus is in a state of "strain" or "combat" rather than a state of "agony" or "anguish." For example, the word *agōnia* was commonly employed in antiquity to speak about wrestlers or athletes who strained in competitive contexts (see e.g., Clivaz, *L'Ange*, 624–26; Brown, *Death of the Messiah*, 1:190). As a result, rather than showing Jesus' fearful anxiety, Luke portrays Jesus as a wrestler or combatant who takes on the unseen "power of darkness" (22:31-32, 53). The Lord strengthens Jesus so that he can battle even more effectively.

This reading of the text fits better with the sequence of events that Luke narrates. For example, Jesus clearly asks that the cup of suffering be removed from him. Next, even though the suffering (the impending crucifixion) is not removed, God nevertheless sends an angel to strengthen Jesus. Jesus does not then become weaker with anxiety after the angel arrives to strengthen him, as if God's assistance is ineffectual (cf. Ehrman and Plunkett, "The Angel," 401–16). Instead, Jesus relies on the strength that God's angel provides to pray even "more earnestly" as he battles the unseen "power of darkness" (22:53). Like a wrestler, the divine assistance now buttresses Jesus as he battles the sifting work of Satan (22:31-32). He prays so earnestly that he sweats like an athlete or a combatant striving to overcome a foe.

Obviously, if *agōnia* is translated to refer to Jesus' straining in a manner akin to an athlete, then Luke has greatly accentuated the importance of prayer in Luke 22:39-46 in much the same way that he has accentuated the importance of prayer throughout his Gospel (see Luke 1:8-25 above). Notice, for example, that only Luke includes two injunctions by Jesus whereby he instructs the disciples to pray. Jesus exhorts them to pray before the time of prayer on the Mount of Olives (22:40) and before the time of the arrest on the Mount of Olives (22:46). Prayer is the proper response in both cases.

Moreover, Jesus explains to them clearly why they need to pray. He asks them to pray so that they "may not come into the time of trial" or "temptation." The Greek word *peirasmos* can connote either an outward trial or an inward temptation (22:40, 46). Furthermore, Jesus' words recall the model prayer that Jesus shared with his disciples in 11:1-4. His last petition was, "And do not bring us into the time of trial" (*peirasmos*) (11:4). In both Luke 11 and 22, Jesus teaches his disciples to pray to God for assistance when facing trials and/or temptations.

In addition, given that Jesus just warned his disciples that Satan was about to "sift" them like wheat (22:31) and encouraged them to ready themselves for battle by buying swords (22:36), Jesus' injunctions to pray appear to fall within the context of a cosmic battle. Prayer is the means by which Jesus exhorts the disciples to face their time of trial and/or temptation. Prayer is depicted as the weapon—or perhaps the armor—that they need more than physical swords (22:38, 50-51). Most important, Jesus has already informed his disciples in 22:31-32 that he has countered/will counter Satan's attempt to destroy Peter's faith as well as the faith of all the disciples. Strikingly, the only explanation that Jesus gives for the survival of Peter's faith is that he has prayed for Peter. In essence, even Jesus relies on prayer when seeking to counter Satan's attacks against the disciples.

Jesus therefore appears to employ prayer as his primary defense on the Mount of Olives. As Satan begins to sift the disciples and their faith like wheat (22:31-32), Jesus does what the disciples are incapable of doing for themselves. He stays awake and prays. Like a boxer who has been strengthened in his corner, Jesus relies on divine strength and charges forth to pray even more earnestly (22:44). He seeks to protect his followers from the unseen assault of Satan himself by means of prayer (22:31-32). Moreover, Jesus teaches his disciples that prayer is the proper response amid both their temptations (e.g., the temptation to fall asleep at a pivotal moment) and their trials (e.g., the arrest of their leader) (Arterbury, "Battle on the Mount of Olives," 45–51).

(2) Luke 22:47-53. Luke then moves seamlessly from the unseen attack of Satan in 22:39-46 to the visible manifestation of Satan's plot to end Jesus' life—a plot that Satan first put into place back in 22:1-6 when Satan took possession of Judas and colluded with the chief priests and scribes. Now, Luke's readers can see that the times of prayer (22:39-46) and arrest (22:47-53) parallel one another. Just as Satan's sifting of the disciples begins when the disciples attempt to pray but instead fall asleep, so now Satan's sifting grows and intensifies during Jesus' arrest. The agents of Satan—Judas (22:47-48) and "the chief priests, the officers of the temple police, and the elders" (22:52)—now lead the mob that arrests Jesus. Furthermore, Luke

identifies those who arrest Jesus as none other than a manifestation of "the power of darkness" (22:53; cf. Eph 6:12). Thus, both the disciples' sleep and the arrest contribute to Satan's bigger strategy, which includes putting Jesus to death (22:1-6) and sifting Jesus' disciples like wheat (22:31).

The disciples, perhaps ramped up in the wake of Jesus' conversation about buying swords (22:35-38), are now awake and ready to fight to defend Jesus (22:49). One disciple even wounds a slave with his sword. Jesus, however, instructs his disciples to "permit this for now" (Matson, "Pacifist Jesus?" 157–76). It is not yet time for the Son of Man (22:48) to reign as king and judge (cf. 21:25-33). It is not yet time for Jesus to conquer God's adversaries as the divine warrior-king (cf. Zech 14:3-4). Rather, it is time for Jesus to die as an innocent martyr in conjunction with the overarching, salvific work of God in the world (9:21-22, 44; 13:31-34; 22:42; 24:19-20, 26). Consequently, he instructs his disciples to "permit this for now" (22:51).

Jesus' Trials and Innocence (22:54–23:25)
Luke 22:54–23:25 chronicles the time between Jesus' arrest and his crucifixion. After the Last Supper and his arrest, Jesus is held at the home of the high priest for the rest of that night. In the process, the high priest's guards treat him harshly. Once the day arrives, the Jewish Sanhedrin, Pontius Pilate, and Herod Antipas examine Jesus. Even though his Roman interrogators ultimately find Jesus innocent of all charges, Pontius Pilate nevertheless condemns Jesus to death in order to please the Jewish religious leaders and the Jewish people. As Luke narrates this material, he once again reinforces the portrait of Jesus as a faithful prophet, and he greatly accentuates the innocence of Jesus, God's Messiah.

(1) Luke 22:54-62. Here Luke builds on the previously established theme of Jesus as a prophet of God who speaks truthfully about the present and the future (cf. 4:24; 7:16, 39; 13:33; 24:19). Previously, while they were still in the upper room, Jesus informed Peter that he would deny Jesus three times before the rooster crows (22:34). Now, in an act of collusion with Judas and by extension Satan (22:1-6), the religious leaders have arrested Jesus and taken him to the home of the high priest (22:54). Peter is brave enough to follow the cabal to the high priest's home and sit among those who seized Jesus at the Mount of Olives. Due to this ominous context, however, Peter folds beneath the pressure. Satan's sifting temporarily works (22:31-32). Three different people identify Peter as one of Jesus' cohorts. Two of them recognize Peter by sight, and the third recognizes Jesus by his Galilean accent. Peter, however, denies that he knows who Jesus is (22:57),

denies that he is one of Jesus' followers (22:58), and denies his own heritage as a Galilean (22:59-60).

When the rooster signals the arrival of the day, Jesus looks at Peter and Peter recalls "the word of the Lord" as Jesus announced it (22:61; cf. 22:34). Jesus' prophetic words prove true once again. Peter has indeed faltered as Jesus predicted. Unlike Judas, however, Peter has not committed apostasy. His weeping and his deep remorse signal that while Satan has indeed sifted him like wheat, Peter's faith in Jesus has not failed (22:31-32). The ending of Luke's Gospel will show that Peter has not been shaken loose (24:12).

(2) Luke 22:63-65. In 22:63-65, it becomes clear that others in the high priest's courtyard do not and perhaps cannot recognize Jesus' identity as God's prophet. Those who guard him mistreat him. They blindfold him and then beat him. Afterward, they ask him to "prophesy" regarding who just hit him. By means of their abusive game, they mock the idea of Jesus speaking and ministering as one of God's prophets. Ironically, though, Jesus' prophecy about Peter's denials is coming true at the precise moment that Jesus' guards are demanding that he prophesy (cf. 22:34, 54-62). At that point, Peter (and Luke's readers) fully understands Jesus' prophetic identity, but the guards who strike him remain completely in the dark. Jesus' words from 13:33 echo forth even here: "Yet today, tomorrow, and the next day I must be on my way, because it is impossible for a prophet to be killed outside of Jerusalem."

(3) Luke 22:66-71. Once the day arrives, Jesus experiences a series of examinations by the Jewish Sanhedrin, Pontius Pilate (the Roman governor of Judea), and Herod Antipas (the son of Herod the Great and tetrarch of Galilee). Throughout this series of interrogations, Luke portrays Jesus as an innocent martyr. Those who examine him repeatedly and consistently judge Jesus to be innocent of all criminal activity against the Roman state (23:4, 14-15, 22, 41, 47).

First, Luke discusses Jesus' interrogation before the Jewish council or assembly—the Sanhedrin. It was composed of religious leaders who together served as a tribunal that made decisions about religious matters involving the Jewish people (22:66). Throughout his Gospel and especially in the Lukan passion narrative, Luke has painted a highly negative portrait of the chief priests and scribes who are interrogating Jesus (9:22; 19:47; 20:1, 19; 22:2, 4, 52; cf. 23:10; 24:20).

Here, they ask Jesus whether he is "the Messiah" (Gk. *christos*, which means the "Anointed One"), and he sidesteps their question (22:67). Jesus has been identified as God's "Anointed One" or Messiah from the beginning of this Gospel. The angel of the Lord announces that Jesus is the Messiah at his birth (2:11). The Holy Spirit reveals the news to Simeon when Jesus is eight days old (2:26). The demons know that Jesus is the Messiah from the outset of his ministry (4:41), and even Peter realizes that Jesus is the Messiah before Jesus and the disciples depart for Jerusalem (9:20). Yet Luke portrays the chief priests and scribes as both hard-hearted and cynical. Had they been listening to the angel of the Lord or the Holy Spirit, they would know for certain that Jesus is the Messiah. Instead, they have elected to listen to Judas, the one possessed by Satan (22:1-6). Consequently, Jesus responds by first commenting on their identity rather than his own. In particular, he draws attention in 22:67-68 to their lack of belief and obstinacy.

Thereafter, Jesus reveals his identity to them in 22:69, though still in a somewhat vague manner. Jesus refers to himself as the Son of Man. While the phrase "the Son of Man" may at times in the biblical literature refer to an ordinary person (e.g., Ps 8:4; 144:3) or a prophetic figure (e.g., Ezek 2:1; 3:1), at numerous points in Luke's Gospel Jesus utilizes the phrase "the Son of Man" to refer to the apocalyptic figure whom God will commission to judge and to rule the earth (e.g., Dan 7:13-14; cf. Luke 5:24; 9:26; 12:8, 40; 17:24; 21:27, 36; Acts 7:56). Furthermore, Jesus prophesies that from now on he, as the Son of Man, "will be seated at the right hand of the power of God" (22:69). In hindsight, Jesus' words clearly describe Jesus' exaltation on the other side of his resurrection and ascension (Acts 2:33; 7:55-56). At this point, however, the chief priests and scribes are uncertain of Jesus' precise meaning when he speaks of the Son of Man. This confusion forces them to ask more questions as they seek to understand his comments.

Finally, Jesus' interrogation amid the Jewish council ends when they ask him whether he is the Son of God (22:70). Akin to what he has done with the title "Messiah," Luke has been informing his readers that Jesus is the Son of God since the beginning of this book. At the annunciation of his conception, Gabriel proclaims that Jesus will be the Son of God (1:31, 35). At Jesus' baptism and at his transfiguration, God proclaims that Jesus is God's beloved Son (3:22; 9:35). On two occasions the demons recognize Jesus as Son of God (4:41; 8:28). Even Jesus identifies himself to his disciples as the Son of God (10:22). Now, however, the skeptical religious elders want to know whether Jesus considers himself to be the Son of God. When Jesus places the words of the religious leaders back on their own lips by saying "*You* say that I am," the chief priests and scribes conclude that Jesus has blasphemed (22:70-71).

(4) Luke 23:1-7. In 23:1-7, the entire (or the whole; Gk. *hapas*) assembly of Jewish elders, including both chief priests and scribes, then takes Jesus to Pontius Pilate, the Roman governor of Judea, and formally accuses him of wrongdoing. Despite the fact that the Jewish assembly interrogated Jesus

exclusively about theological matters in the previous verses (22:66-71), when they bring Jesus before Pilate they do not discuss their theological concerns with Pilate. They know that Pilate will not act based on an intra-Jewish, theological debate. Instead, the religious leaders bring criminal charges against Jesus.

In particular, the Jewish religious leaders make three accusations against Jesus. They claim that Jesus is: (a) "perverting our nation," (b) "forbidding us to pay taxes to the emperor," and (c) saying that God has anointed him to be king (23:2). In essence, the chief priests and scribes depict Jesus as a revolutionary teacher/leader who poses a threat to the Roman Empire (23:5, 14). Notably, similar allegations will be made about Paul and Silas in Acts 17:6-7 and Paul in Acts 24:5. In short, they depict Jesus as a rival to Caesar, an offense that could carry a punishment of death (Wolter, *Gospel According to Luke*, 2:502–503).

In the process, Luke depicts the assembly of chief priests and scribes as exceedingly dishonest (Wolter, *Gospel According to Luke*, 2:503). For instance, the chief priests and scribes asked Jesus directly in 20:22 whether the Jewish people should pay taxes to Caesar, and Jesus said, "give to the emperor the things that are the emperor's" (22:25a). Yet here, the chief priests and scribes fail to speak the truth when they report to Pilate that Jesus forbids the Jews from paying taxes to the emperor (23:2). Similarly, the Sanhedrin asked Jesus in 22:67 whether he is the Messiah or God's Anointed One—a phrase that was initially associated with those whom God "anointed" to be king over Israel (e.g., 1 Sam 9:16; 15:1; 16:3, 12). Jesus, however, elected not to answer their question directly. Instead, Jesus voiced his conviction that the Jewish religious leaders would not believe him either way (22:67). Yet again, the chief priests misreport Jesus' words to Pilate (23:2).

As a result, Pilate begins to question Jesus about the charges that the Jewish religious leaders have leveled against him. As Pilate does so, he starts with the most serious charge. Pilate asks Jesus whether he is "the king of the Jews" (23:3). Notably, as far as we know, only Josephus among ancient Jewish writers uses the phrase "the king of the Jews" (see e.g., Josephus, *Ant.* 6.98; 7.72; and 15.373, 409; Wolter, *Gospel According to Luke*, 2:503). Generally, Jewish writers refer to their kingly figure as "God's Messiah" or "God's Anointed One" (22:67). Pilate, however, has opted for the secular phrase, "the king of the Jews" (Nolland, *Luke*, 3:1118).

Consequently, it is difficult to know for certain how Luke hoped his readers would make sense of Jesus' response. Jesus does not wholeheartedly embrace the title that Pilate articulates, but neither does he outright deny the title. John Nolland contends that Jesus asks Pilate a question when he responds—essentially asking Pilate whether he himself just voiced the opinion that Jesus is indeed the king of the Jews (23:3) (*Luke*, 3:1118). Alternatively, Jesus may simply respond to Pilate in the same manner that he responded to the assembly in 22:70—essentially saying, "*You* say so" (23:3) (Carroll, *Luke*, 456). Regardless, at that point, Pilate immediately declares Jesus innocent of the charge that Jesus is "king of the Jews." Pilate knows of no action that Jesus has taken that proves he is a revolutionary, and the Sanhedrin and Jesus appear to have conflicting reports about Jesus' self-proclaimed identity. As a result, Pilate seeks to dismiss the charges altogether in 23:4.

The entire membership of the Sanhedrin (23:1), however, objects. They persist in their accusations and demand that Pilate deal with Jesus (23:5). They claim that as a revolutionary, Jesus has been stirring up people throughout the entire province of Judea including in the region of Galilee, where Jesus was raised. Once the Jewish religious leaders bring up Jesus' impact on Galilee, Pilate sees a path of escape from this escalating conflict. After confirming that Jesus is indeed a Galilean, Pilate, the Roman governor of Judea, elects to transfer the case to Herod Antipas, the client-ruler and tetrarch of Galilee and Perea (23:7; cf. 3:1, 19; 9:7).

(5) *Luke 23:8-12*. Because Herod Antipas happens to be in Jerusalem (likely due to Passover), Pilate is able to transfer Jesus over to Herod quickly. As a result, when Herod questions Jesus, it functions as the third interrogation of Jesus all within the same day. Moreover, it should be noted that when Pilate transfers Jesus from his custody to Herod's custody, Pilate also cleverly transfers the angry crowd of chief priests and scribes over to Herod as well. They all accompany Jesus and complain to Herod while "vehemently accusing" Jesus of wrongdoing (23:10).

Herod Antipas had heard reports about Jesus' Galilean ministry for some time. At one point, he had hoped to meet Jesus (9:7-9). At another, he wanted to kill Jesus (13:31). Now, however, Herod Antipas sees an opportunity not only to meet Jesus but also "to see him perform some sign" (23:8). Despite Herod's questions, however, Jesus again elects not to defend himself against the accusations leveled against him (23:9). Furthermore, Luke implies that Jesus does not "perform" any deeds of power or signs in Herod's presence. In response, Herod, like the Jewish religious leaders in his midst, mistreats Jesus and mocks him. In addition, since the Jewish assembly accuses Jesus of claiming to be God's anointed king, Herod dresses Jesus up in a kingly robe (23:11; cf. John 19:2-3). Ultimately, though, Herod finds Jesus innocent of any wrongdoing (23:15) and returns him to Pilate (23:11).

(6) *Luke 23:13-25*. Once Jesus is returned to Pilate's custody, Pilate now hopes that the angry crowd of religious leaders has been mollified. The

chief priests and scribes have mistreated Jesus (22:63-65) and watched as a governing official mistreated him (23:11). They have been able to articulate their grievances with vigor to both Pilate (23:2) and Herod Antipas (23:10). Perhaps Pilate reasons that the anger of the religious leaders has been deflated. Perhaps he thinks they can now consider the matter from a more reasonable viewpoint.

As a result, Pilate calls together the religious leaders along with "the people" (23:13)—those whom Jesus has supposedly stirred up (23:5) and perverted with his teachings (23:14). Notably, up to this point the common people (Gk. *laos*) have displayed a pronounced receptivity toward Jesus (e.g., 19:47; 20:1, 6; 21:38) and a lack of appreciation for the views of the chief priests and scribes who wish to harm Jesus (e.g., 20:6, 19; 22:2). Once Pilate has assembled the crowd, he announces that he finds Jesus innocent of all charges (23:14; cf. 23:2, 5). Furthermore, he announces that Herod Antipas likewise examined Jesus and found him innocent (23:15). Consequently, because Jesus has "done nothing to deserve death," Pilate seeks to assuage the crowd's anger by disciplining (or beating) Jesus and releasing him (23:15-16).

Unfortunately, for a second time, Pilate's declaration of Jesus' innocence is met with riotous shouts from the Jewish religious leaders (23:4-5, 14-15). At this point, though, even "the people" appear to join in the uproar (23:18; Carroll, *Luke*, 459). All together the people of Jerusalem demand that Barabbas, a prisoner accused of an insurrection that led to the loss of lives, be released (23:18-19). They want Jesus to take Barabbas's place. When Pilate attempts to reason further with the crowd, they respond by escalating their demands. They now cry, "Crucify, crucify him!" (23:21). They want Pilate to release the guilty murderer (cf. Acts 3:13-14) and murder the innocent prophet (13:33-34).

Finally, Pilate reiterates his original verdict regarding Jesus' innocence for the third time (23:22), but the will of the unruly crowd prevails (23:23). Likely fearing the physical and political impact of a violent riot within the city of Jerusalem, the Roman governor elects to appease the crowd. He chooses to prevent the pot from boiling over, which could weaken his status among his Roman superiors. As a result, Pilate condemns Jesus to death as the residents of Jerusalem demand, and he releases Barabbas (23:25). The insurrectionist whose rebellion caused innocent people to die goes free while the messianic prophet who came to seek and to save the lost will die.

Rhetorically, it is clear that Luke wanted his first readers to hear the verdict of the Roman authorities regarding Jesus loud and clear. Despite a wide array of accusations against Jesus (23:2, 5, 14), Pontius Pilate—the prefect of the Roman province of Judea and a Roman himself—not only finds no reason to execute Jesus (23:15, 22) but also declares Jesus innocent of all charges (23:14, 22). He declares Jesus innocent on three occasions (23:4, 14, 22), perhaps echoing the three accusations that the Jewish assembly originally leveled against Jesus (23:2). Furthermore, Pilate only condemns Jesus to death to placate the crowd in Jerusalem (23:24-25). Even Herod Antipas—an ostensibly Jewish client-ruler for the Roman Empire, tetrarch of Galilee and Perea, and the ruler who executed John the Baptist (9:9) and who previously desired to kill Jesus (13:31)—finds Jesus innocent of all charges (23:15). Even a ruler who observed many Jewish customs and festivals finds Jesus innocent of wrongdoing. In short, even though Jesus will die the death of a Roman dissident, Luke goes to great lengths to show that Jesus' death was not merited on the grounds of Roman law (cf. 23:41, 47). Instead, the Romans put Jesus to death to appease the Jewish religious leaders and crowds (23:25). Luke portrays the Romans as unwitting and weak accomplices in the death of Jesus. The lion's share of the responsibility for Jesus' death, however, rests on the shoulders of the Jewish religious leaders and those in Jerusalem who followed their lead. Luke reinforces this same conclusion in the book of Acts (Acts 3:13; 13:27-28).

Jesus' Crucifixion and Burial (23:26-56a)
Having firmly established the innocence of Jesus during his trials, Luke now continues to build on that theme during Jesus' crucifixion. Alongside Jesus' innocence, Luke adds an emphasis on Jesus' martyrdom. He dies because he is a faithful prophet who trusts and obeys the Father (13:33-34). Moreover, Jesus' death as an innocent martyr provides an opportunity to offer a witness to the truth of his prophetic identity, message, and ministry. Finally, Luke also introduces his readers to a variety of minor characters in this unit whose presence demonstrates that Jesus is not alone. He remains in the company of the Father and many followers who will later function as witnesses (Bovon, *Luke*, 3:294).

(1) Luke 23:26-31. As soon as Pilate hands Jesus over to be crucified, the Roman soldiers begin marching Jesus to "The Skull," the place where Jesus will die (23:26, 33). Perhaps due to the beatings that Jesus has already received (22:63; 23:11), the Roman soldiers require a bystander, Simon of Cyrene, to carry the *patibulum* or "the transverse, horizontal part of the cross" for Jesus (Bovon, *Luke*, 3:300). Luke does not, however, clarify whether Simon was a pilgrim who was visiting Jerusalem during Passover or a resident of Jerusalem who migrated from Cyrene.

Regardless, Luke depicts Simon "as an example of a disciple" for Jesus' followers and his own readers. Recall that in 9:23 and 14:27 Jesus declares that anyone who wishes to be his disciple must be willing to do two things. He or she must be willing to carry his or her cross, and he or she must be willing to follow Jesus. In 23:26, Simon of Cyrene does just that. He carries a cross, and he follows behind Jesus (Bovon, *Luke*, 3:301). From Luke's perspective, Simon illustrates the experiences of a true follower of Jesus. Immediately thereafter, Luke also mentions that "a great number of people followed him, and among them were women" (23:27). Here, Luke indicates that a large group of disciples follows in the wake of both Jesus and Simon of Cyrene. These disciples can see Jesus' suffering as well as Simon's forced labor. They are not under any illusions about the risks that following Jesus entails. Nevertheless, they follow him.

To establish further this point about the need for Jesus' disciples to anticipate suffering, Luke indicates that Jesus turns and speaks to the female disciples who have already begun the mourning process for Jesus (Caird, *Saint Luke*, 249). When Jesus speaks to them, however, he instructs them to turn their grief, focus, and energies to themselves, to the suffering that they will soon experience (23:28-31). Those with young children will suffer doubly. They will mourn both for themselves and their children.

(2) *Luke 23:32-49.* When Luke narrates Jesus' crucifixion, he provides few details about the death itself. In particular, Luke does not accentuate the physical pain or the emotional anguish that Jesus surely endures. Rather, Luke focuses his attention on Jesus' conversations and interactions with those around him. In 23:32-49, for instance, Jesus dialogues with both a criminal beside him and his heavenly Father. In addition, Luke wants his readers to observe the manner in which the soldiers, crowds, and disciples respond to Jesus before, during, and after his crucifixion.

(a) First, in Luke 23:32-33 Luke sets the scene of Jesus' crucifixion. Despite Pontius Pilate declaring Jesus innocent of all crimes against the state, the Romans nevertheless crucify him (23:18-25). Even more, they crucify him as a criminal and between two criminals who have likewise been condemned to death.

(b) Second, Jesus immediately responds to this undeserved and shameful death, as well as their mischaracterization of him as a criminal, by uttering the first of his three statements from the cross in the Gospel of Luke. In 23:34 Jesus says, "Father, forgive them; for they do not know what they are doing." To begin with, it is important to observe that Jesus turns to God in prayer while he is on the cross. This development is fitting given the emphasis that Luke places on prayer within his Gospel; both the first (23:34) and third (23:46) statements that Jesus makes from the cross in Luke are prayers to the Father. In Luke's Gospel, Jesus prays at his baptism (3:21-22);

he prays throughout the night before he selects the twelve apostles (6:12-16); he prays prior to his transfiguration (9:28-36); and he prays prior to his arrest (22:41-44). As a result, it is not surprising to see Jesus pray on two occasions from the cross in Luke's Gospel.

Jesus prays in both Mark 15:34 and Matt 27:46 as well when he addresses God with his question about abandonment (i.e., "My God, my God, why have you forsaken me?"). When Luke captures Jesus' prayer wish in 23:34, however, he shows his readers that Jesus' focus is not on himself or his own suffering. Rather, even amid his martyrdom, Jesus displays concern for those around him. In particular, Jesus exhibits compassion for those who are putting him to death when he asks God to forgive them.

Forgiveness has also been a major theme in Luke's Gospel. For instance, Jesus shows compassionate restraint in response to the mob from the Nazareth synagogue that wishes to kill him in 4:28-30 and the Samaritans who reject him in 9:51-56. In addition, he grants forgiveness to the paralytic (5:20) and the woman who anoints his feet with ointment (7:48). Jesus will explain after his resurrection that "repentance and forgiveness of sins is to be proclaimed in his name" (24:47). The Lukan theme of forgiveness also holds a prominent place in the book of Acts. In particular, in Acts 7:60, when Stephen likewise dies as an innocent martyr (Acts 6:8–8:1), he mimics Jesus' own words when he prays to God and says, "Lord, do not hold this sin against them."

(c) Third, those who unjustly put Jesus to death, both the Jewish religious leaders and the Roman soldiers, do so with great malevolence. The soldiers confiscate his clothes and divide them among themselves (23:34b; cf. Ps 22:18). Furthermore, both the Jewish religious leaders and the soldiers mock him. In particular, when they scoff at him, their comments revolve around Jesus' ability and/or inability "to save."

The Jewish leaders speak first. They say, "He saved others; let him save himself if he is the Messiah of God, his Chosen One!" Ironically, though they do not believe their words, they begin with a declarative statement that Jesus has indeed saved, healed, or rescued (Gk. *sōzō*) others (cf., Foerster, "*sōzō, sōtēria, sōtēr, sōtērios*," *TDNT* 7:965–1024). Here, Luke implicitly invites his readers to recall the times when Jesus has "saved" others in this Gospel. For example, Jesus assures the woman who anoints his feet with ointment that her faith has saved (Gk. *sōzō*) her (7:50). Witnesses relay how Jesus healed (Gk. *sōzō*) the Gerasene demoniac (8:36). Jesus informs the hemorrhaging woman that her faith has made her well (Gk. *sōzō*) (8:48). Jesus assures a messenger that Jairus's deceased daughter will be saved (Gk. *sōzō*) (8:50). Jesus instructs the Samaritan leper to get up and go because his faith has made him well (Gk. *sōzō*) (17:19). Jesus tells the blind man to receive his sight because his faith has saved him (Gk. *sōzō*) (18:42), and after Zacchaeus announces his plans to give half of his possessions to the poor, Jesus declares that he has come to seek and to save (Gk. *sōzō*) the lost (19:10). Yet the Jewish religious leaders do not believe that Jesus has saved anyone, and they do not believe the claims that Jesus is God's Messiah as we saw in 22:67 and 23:2—the one God anointed to serve as king over God's people.

Similarly, the Roman soldiers mock and mistreat him, saying, "If you are the King of the Jews, save yourself." They even place the inscription above his head declaring Jesus' kingship (23:36-38). Like Pilate (23:3), the Roman soldiers do not use the title of "Messiah," which amounts to a religious confession about God's work in the world. Rather, they use the secular title "King of the Jews," which simply connotes royalty and/or dominion over a particular people group. Regardless, they, too, urge Jesus to save (Gk. *sōzō*) himself (23:37).

Finally, one of the two criminals (or "evil-doers") next to Jesus on the cross ridicules Jesus using the same taunt. The presumably Jewish criminal says, "Are you not the Messiah? Save yourself and us!" Ironically, the criminal asks Jesus to save (Gk. *sōzō*) him. Yet in contrast to the woman who anoints Jesus' feet with ointment (7:50), the hemorrhaging woman (8:48), the Samaritan leper (17:19), and the blind beggar (18:42), this criminal has no faith to accompany his request, and in contrast to Zacchaeus, his words and deeds display no evidence of transformation (19:10).

(d) Fourth, Luke dedicates considerable attention to the two criminals who are crucified alongside Jesus in 23:32-33 and 23:39-43. Only Luke describes the conversation between Jesus and the criminals. As he does so, Luke appears to utilize the two "evil-doers" as illustrations of the two types of responses found among the common people who are present—those who are standing by and watching Jesus die (23:35).

The first criminal mocks Jesus and the idea that he is God's Messiah as we have just discussed. The other criminal, however, speaks with great humility and insight. He not only rebukes the first criminal for failing to fear God but also acknowledges his guilt while declaring Jesus to be completely innocent. Like the members of the crowd who hear John the Baptist preach and seek to repent (3:10-14, 21) and like Peter who confesses his sinfulness when he first encounters Jesus (5:1-11), this evil-doer does not hesitate to confess his wrongdoing. On the other hand, when he says Jesus "has done nothing wrong" (23:41), he contributes to the broader Lukan theme of Jesus as an innocent martyr. Like Pilate (23:4, 14, 22) and Herod (23:15) before him, this criminal declares Jesus to be innocent of any crime (23:41; cf. 23:47).

Ultimately, the second criminal exhibits faith and pleads for mercy from Jesus. This development, in and of itself, is shocking given that Luke gives no indication that this criminal has any prior knowledge of Jesus' teaching or ministry. It appears that his only exposure to Jesus comes through listening to Jesus' prayer in 23:34 when he asks the Father to forgive those who are ignorantly killing him. In essence, even on the cross, prayer in Luke's Gospel proves revelatory (Crump, *Jesus the Intercessor*, 88; Garland, *Luke*, 925). The criminal gains insight about Jesus' identity as Jesus voices his prayer.

Next, the second criminal says, "Jesus, remember me when you come into your kingdom" (23:42). As he does so, the criminal hopes for the type of mercy that will be granted to him well after his death, perhaps at the final judgment (Garland, *Luke*, 925; Marshall, *Luke*, 870). Jesus, in turn, issues his second of three last words from the cross in Luke's Gospel. He does not, however, address the criminal's distant future. Instead, Jesus comments on the criminal's immediate circumstances. Jesus says, "Truly, I tell you, today you will be with me in paradise" (23:43). Jesus' response is significant for at least two reasons.

Remarkably, Jesus claims that the criminal will experience immediate rescue, forgiveness, and/or salvation rather than salvation that is far off in the future (Marshall, *Luke*, 870). Throughout his Gospel, Luke has emphasized the immediate, saving impact of Jesus' presence. For example, at the synagogue in Nazareth, Jesus says, "Today, this scripture has been fulfilled in your hearing" (4:21), and to Zacchaeus, Jesus says, "Today salvation has come to this house" (19:9). In essence, Jesus does not tell the criminal on the cross next to him that he will need to wait on the Day of the Lord or the arrival of the Son of Man in order to experience redemption (21:20-24). Rescue and salvation are linked with Jesus' presence and are immediate realities in Luke's Gospel. Furthermore, from Jesus' first words in this Gospel when he proclaims release to the captives and freedom for the oppressed (4:18) to his last words on the cross (23:34, 43), Jesus remains focused on forgiveness and restoration throughout (Brown, *Death of the Messiah*, 2:1002).

In the process, Jesus comforts the criminal by saying that the man will be with him in paradise. (22:43). "Paradise," a term frequently linked with the Garden of Eden in Jewish and Christian literature (e.g., Gen 2:8-10; *Ps. Sol.* 14.3; Rev 22:2) (Bockmuehl, "Locating Paradise," 194–201; Brown, *Death of the Messiah*, 2:1010-11), is now linked with Jesus' presence. Because of Jesus' innocent martyrdom, the place previously associated with Adam's sin has now become associated with Jesus' rescue: "By bringing this wrongdoer with him into paradise, Jesus is undoing the results of Adam's sin which barred access to the tree of life (Gen 3:24)" (Brown, *Death of the Messiah*, 2:1011–12; cf. Garland, *Luke*, 926, 934).

(e) Fifth, in 23:44-49 Luke narrates Jesus' final moments. As he does so, Luke first refers to two miraculous signs that affirm God's presence and connote God's judgment on the Jewish religious leaders and Roman soldiers who orchestrate and carry out Jesus' crucifixion (Brown, *Death of the Messiah*, 2:1033, 1038). Both the three-hour period of darkness at midday and the rending of the curtain in the temple remind Luke's readers of God's unseen presence and God's displeasure with the religious leaders who oversee the temple (cf. 19:45–21:36).

In response to these extraordinary signs, Jesus voices his third and final statement from the cross in Luke's Gospel. With his last breath, Jesus shouts, "Father, into your hands I commend my spirit" (23:46). With his last breath he again prays to the Father (see 23:34 above) and expresses his trust in the Father by quoting Ps 31:5. The rulers and soldiers who carry out Jesus' crucifixion have not shaken Jesus' confidence in the Father. Rather, Jesus trusts the Father to guide salvation history—God's redemptive work in and plan for the world.

Here, it is important to note that Luke never records Jesus crying out to God in anguish or in a sense of abandonment in his Gospel as we see in Mark 15:34 and Matt 27:46. Both Mark and Matthew show Jesus quoting Ps 22:1 from the cross and saying, "My God, my God, why have you forsaken me?" In Ps 22, the psalmist complains to God about God's silence and absence in the midst of attacks from his enemies (Wilson, *Psalms*, 1:412–19). The psalmist does not attribute the enemies' attacks to God, but the enemies' attacks cause the psalmist to ask theological questions about the righteousness of God. Likewise, in Matthew and Mark, when his enemies are actively killing him, Jesus asks why God is inactive. In essence, both Matthew and Mark indicate that the crucifixion leads Jesus to ask God a dark and probing question.

In Luke's Gospel, Jesus quotes from Ps 31:5 rather than Ps 22:1. He knows the divine will, and he knows his death is necessary. Luke, however, does not tell us why Jesus' death is necessary or offer a detailed theology of atonement. Furthermore, Jesus does not link the behavior of his enemies with the action or the inaction of God. Rather, Jesus knows that his death—regardless of who the enemies may be and what the specifics of his demise may be—is necessary (Cosgrove, "Divine DEI," 168–90; cf. Talbert, *Reading Luke*, 265). He remains confident in his Father and his Father's will. The evil actions of the Jewish religious leaders and of the Roman military do not cause Jesus to question God's righteousness in Luke's Gospel.

Thereafter, Luke shows his readers four positive reactions to Jesus in the wake of his death. First, Luke portrays the Roman centurion who stands by Jesus during the crucifixion in a unique manner. Witnessing the miraculous signs and Jesus' responses to his executioners prompts the Roman soldier to turn his attention—and praise—toward God. Just as we saw above with the second criminal (23:41-42), Jesus' prayer again serves a revelatory function. In the wake of Jesus' prayer in 23:46, the Roman centurion begins to see God and Jesus more clearly.

In response, the Roman centurion exclaims in Luke's Gospel, "Certainly this man was innocent" or righteous (Gk. *dikaios*) (23:47). Here Luke's readers should again detect the Lukan motif of Jesus as an innocent martyr. Previously, Pilate declared Jesus "not guilty" of all charges on three occasions (23:4, 14, 22). Herod Antipas found no guilt in Jesus in 23:15, and the second criminal on the cross proclaimed Jesus innocent of all wrongdoing in 23:41. Now, the Roman centurion who puts Jesus to death likewise watches Jesus die and affirms Jesus' innocence or righteousness (cf. Acts 3:14).

Perhaps it should not be surprising to see Luke characterize a centurion so positively. Luke previously described the Roman centurion in 7:1-10 in positive terms as well, and Jesus claims that the Roman soldier's faith in Jesus' ability to heal his servant exceeds the faith of all those Jesus has encountered in Israel (7:9). Likewise, the Roman centurion at the cross in Luke 23 may well foreshadow future events in Luke's writings. In Acts 10, Cornelius, another Roman centurion, will become the first Gentile convert in Luke's writings.

Second, Luke indicates that the crowds—the residents of Jerusalem along with perhaps some pilgrims—beat their breasts (23:48). As a sign of remorse or grief, they pound their chests like the humble tax collector does when he prays to God and confesses his sins in 18:13-14. Third, Luke indicates that all those who know Jesus (i.e., his followers) watch these events from a distance (23:49). Jesus' disciples serve as courageous witnesses who remain with him until the end. Even brave women—female disciples—who have followed Jesus since his Galilean ministry (8:1-3) continue to follow Jesus to the cross and witness his death (cf. 23:55).

(3) Luke 23:50-56a. After chronicling the positive reactions of the centurion (23:47), the crowds (23:38), and the disciples (23:49), Luke also includes and illustrates the positive and compassionate response to Jesus' death by Joseph of Arimathea (23:50-54). Shockingly, Luke informs his readers that Joseph is a member of the Jewish council or assembly of religious leaders who interrogated Jesus (22:66-71), accused him of wrongdoing before Pilate (23:1-5), and demanded his crucifixion (23:18-25). Yet Luke also informs

his readers that Joseph is a good and righteous man (23:50) who disagreed with the plan and the actions of the Sanhedrin (23:51a) and who eagerly awaits the kingdom of God (23:51b). Here, Luke's characterization of Joseph may have reminded his readers of Luke's characterization of faithful Jews at the beginning of this Gospel (Tannehill, *Luke*, 347–48). For example, Luke describes Simeon as "righteous and devout, looking forward to the consolation of Israel" (2:25). Zechariah, Elizabeth, and Anna are all portrayed in a similar fashion (1:5-6; 2:36-38). In short, Luke shows his readers that despite the role of the Jewish religious leaders in the death of Jesus, some Jewish leaders remain faithful to God and empathetic to the plight of Jesus and his followers.

After characterizing Joseph of Arimathea as a faithful Jew, Luke then describes his actions. Upon Jesus' death, Joseph asks the Roman governor for permission to care for Jesus' body (23:52). Joseph honors Jesus by burying him in a proper and honorable manner (23:53). Rather than leaving Jesus' body exposed and subject to scavengers like birds and wild animals, Joseph buries Jesus as "an act of charity and piety (cf. *Tob.* 1:16–18)" (Tannehill, *Luke*, 348). In the process, Joseph also shows that he follows the Law by caring for the body before the Sabbath begins (23:54, 56b). Consequently, both Jesus' birth and his death unfold in accordance with the Law (2:21-27; 23:54-56).

Finally, Luke continues to highlight the female disciples who faithfully follow Jesus—even after his death (23:55). These particular women began following Jesus in Galilee (8:1-3), watched as Jesus died on the cross (23:49), and now witness his burial (23:55). In each context, Luke depicts them as faithful followers or disciples. They are with Jesus from the beginning to the end, even when others have dispersed. They "are uniquely faithful to Jesus" in Luke's Gospel (Johnson, *Luke*, 385). Furthermore, because they watch Joseph place Jesus in the tomb, they will serve as important witnesses to the resurrection. In the meantime, they prepare spices and ointments so they will be able to care for Jesus even after death (23:56a).

The Resurrection of the Messiah (23:56b–24:53)

The final chapter of Luke's Gospel contains two empty tomb accounts (24:1-8, 9-12), two accounts of Jesus' post-resurrection appearances to his disciples (24:13-35, 36-43), Jesus' commissioning of his disciples (24:44-49), and his ascension (24:50-53) (Talbert, *Reading Luke*, 255). In Luke's Gospel, all of these events take place on the same day in or around Jerusalem. In the process, Jesus invites his disciples to envision his life, death, and resurrection within the grand narrative of God's redemptive work as seen in a comprehensive look at the Law, the Prophets, and the Writings (24:27, 44).

The Empty Tomb (23:56b–24:12)

Jesus' female disciples continue to hold an honored role within the narrative of Luke's Gospel. Because they followed Joseph of Arimathea and watched him place Jesus' lifeless body in an unused tomb (23:53-55), they are now able to take spices and ointments to Jesus' tomb at sunrise on Sunday morning in order to anoint his corpse (23:56a; 24:1). Yet when they arrive, Jesus' body is no longer present (24:2-3). He has been raised from the dead. In essence, the faithfulness of these women to Jesus during his life and death now allows them to be the first witnesses to Jesus' resurrection (24:8-10). The message of the resurrection will initially rest squarely on their shoulders.

To aid the women in understanding what has taken place, two angels (24:23) appear and speak on God's behalf (24:4). The women respond appropriately to a manifestation of God, and the angels declare that Jesus is not present. He has been raised (by divine agency) from the dead (24:5). The Father in whom Jesus placed his trust (23:46) has resurrected Jesus from the dead (Acts 2:32). Jesus' well-founded trust in the Father has been rewarded with the miraculous intervention of God into human history.

Furthermore, the angels remind these female disciples that Jesus, God's messianic prophet, predicted this event. The angels ask the women to recall that Jesus as the Son of Man—the one who will one day rule as judge and king (9:26; 12:8, 40; 17:24; 18:8; 21:27, 36; 22:69; Acts 10:42; cf. Dan 7:13-14)—repeatedly taught his disciples that he must first endure suffering and death before experiencing resurrection and exaltation (9:22, 44; 17:24-25; 22:22; cf. 24:46-47). Significantly, in Luke's writings Jesus is formally exalted to the status of Lord and king after his death and resurrection when he ascends to the right hand of the Father where he awaits the day of the Son of Man (Acts 1:9-11; 2:32-36; cf. Luke 21:25-28).

After Mary Magdalene, Joanna, Mary the mother of James, and the other women recall Jesus' words and report the angels' message to the apostles (24:8-10; cf. 8:1-3), the apostles fail to believe their testimony (24:11). Consequently, Peter and some other disciples elect to inspect the tomb themselves (24:12, 24). When Peter also finds the tomb empty, his disbelief turns to amazement (Gk. *thaumazō*). Much like the shepherds' proclamation about Jesus amazed (Gk. *thaumazō*) those present at his birth (2:18), Simeon's prophecy about Jesus amazed (Gk. *thaumazō*) Jesus' mother and father (2:33), Jesus' gracious words initially amazed (Gk. *thaumazō*) those in the Nazareth synagogue (4:22), the disciples' were amazed (Gk. *thaumazō*)

Jesus in Jerusalem

in the wake of Jesus stilling the storm (8:25), and the crowds were amazed (Gk. *thaumazō*) when Jesus exorcised a mute demon (11:14), so also Peter's struggle to believe morphs into amazement (Gk. *thaumazō*) when he sees the empty tomb and the abandoned linen cloths. His journey from unbelief to investigation to amazement and finally to belief (24:34) not only provides a model for others to emulate (cf. 24:41) but likewise establishes Peter as a reliable witness to the resurrection.

In essence, even though Luke highlights the role of the female disciples as the first witnesses to the resurrection, he also demonstrates for his first readers that others witnessed the resurrection as well (24:24). In particular, Peter's trip to the empty tomb (24:12) provides

> a second witness to support the testimony of the women in 24:1-11 (cf. Num 35:30; Deut 17:6f.; 19:15; . . .). Given Jewish assumptions, the witness of the men would have been needed: Josephus (*Ant.* 4.8.15) says, "From women let not evidence be accepted, because of the levity and temerity of their sex" (cf. Mishna, *Rosh Hashana*, 1:8). In order to be persuasive in a Jewish context, the second episode was necessary to buttress the first. (Talbert, *Reading Luke*, 256–57)

On the Road to Emmaus (24:13-35)

After narrating two empty tomb episodes in 24:1-8 and 24:9-12, Luke narrates the first of two episodes in which Jesus appears to his disciples in 24:13-35. In particular, Jesus appears to two of his disciples on the road from Jerusalem to Emmaus. Like the two empty tomb episodes, this event takes place on the same day as Jesus' resurrection.

(1) Luke 24:13-24. When Jesus first appears to the two disciples who are returning to Emmaus from Jerusalem, he does so in an incognito manner (24:13-16). Here, Luke depicts Jesus as a resurrected human being who now relies on divine power to disguise his identity from his own followers. Their inability to recognize Jesus (cf. 24:31) then allows Jesus to ask the pair about their thoughts and reactions in the wake of his crucifixion and to hear their unvarnished responses (24:17, 19). Apparently, Luke believed it was important for his first readers to see how the disciples initially grappled with Jesus' death and their own sadness (24:17). Luke alone includes this story in his Gospel.

Cleopas, one of the two disciples to whom Jesus appears, articulates his impressions along with those of the other disciples in 24:18-24. As we have seen, Luke has repeatedly depicted Jesus as a faithful prophet of God in this Gospel (e.g., 7:11-17). Not surprisingly, Cleopas does the same. He describes Jesus as "a prophet mighty in deed and word before God and all the people" (24:19). Also unsurprising given Jesus' comments about the death of prophets in 13:33-34, Cleopas knows that the chief priests and leaders sought to put Jesus to death due in part to his prophetic critique of the temple and its leadership (24:20; cf. 19:45–21:38).

Yet Cleopas further expresses his sadness when he claims that the disciples had hoped Jesus would "redeem Israel" or set Israel free (24:21; cf. 2:25, 38; 23:51; Acts 1:6). Just as King David ousted the Philistines, firmly established the nation of Israel, and sought to solidify the proper worship of God, so also Jesus' disciples hoped Jesus was the Messiah (or the anointed ruler) who would free the Jewish people from their Roman overlords and inaugurate a new era of faithfulness to God. Jesus' death, however, initially appears to have dashed these hopes and left the disciples with grief or sadness (24:17) (Nolland, *Luke*, 3:1203).

Finally, Cleopas mentions the news of that morning. Some of the female disciples discovered that Jesus' tomb was empty on the morning of the third day, received the message from two angels that Jesus is alive, and reported this news to the other disciples (24:22-23). In addition, some of the disciples, including Peter (24:12), likewise investigated and found the tomb empty (24:24). In essence, Cleopas indicates that he and his fellow disciples are uncertain what to make of the empty tomb and the angels' words. They are uncertain whether these events constitute hopeful signs or more tragic news.

(2) Luke 24:25-27. Jesus' response to this pair of disciples provides them with needed clarity, and Luke also relies on Jesus' words to encapsulate the importance of Jesus' suffering and death for his own readers. First, Jesus says, "Oh, how foolish you are, and how slow of heart to believe all that the prophets have declared!" (24:25). In short, Jesus rebukes the disciples for so quickly losing faith in Jesus as God's Messiah (24:21). Instead, Jesus characterizes his suffering and death as a fulfillment of prophecy. In the whole sweep of God's redemptive work in the world, Jesus characterizes his death as an expected event. Had they listened well to the prophets or even Jesus, the disciples would have anticipated Jesus' suffering and death (e.g., 9:22; 13:32-33).

Next Jesus says, "Was it not necessary that the Messiah should suffer these things and then enter into his glory?" (24:26). By not correcting Cleopas's conclusion that Jesus was "a prophet mighty in deed and word," Jesus implicitly affirms the accuracy of that title (24:19). Jesus goes on, however, to redirect Cleopas's statement about the disciples' past hopes regarding Jesus as "the one to redeem Israel" (24:21). Here, Jesus reiterates the accuracy of the messianic title (24:26). Jesus affirms that the disciples were right to believe that Jesus is "the one to redeem Israel" (24:21). Jesus is indeed both God's prophet and the Messiah.

In essence, the disciples' confusion grows out of their misunderstanding in regard to the role of God's Messiah or Anointed One. Jesus claims that before the Messiah rules as king, it is necessary for the Anointed One to suffer and die as prophet prior to entering into his glory (cf. Acts 2:32-36). In particular, these events are "necessary" (Gk. *dei*) within God's plan of salvation history (24:26). In the ancient world, both pagans and Hellenistic Jews "thought of history as unfolding according to a divine necessity or compulsion that could be expressed in terms of *dei* or *deon esti*. It was in these terms that Luke's language about the *dei* of events would have been understood (cf. 2:49; 4:43; 12:12; 13:14; 15:32; 18:1; 19:5; 22:7, 37)" (Talbert, *Reading Luke*, 265). In short, Jesus affirms that he is the Messiah, but he also affirms that it was "necessary" for the Messiah to suffer and die—just as the prophets foretold.

Second, Jesus relies on the Scriptures (or the OT) to substantiate his interpretation of the events that have unfolded among them. Jesus traces the work and word of God through Moses and the prophets (24:27; cf. 24:44-45). Jesus envisions the Scriptures as an overarching narrative about the redemptive work of God that necessitates the Messiah's suffering and death prior to his exaltation and lordship (Acts 2:32-36). Furthermore, Jesus does not simply appeal to recent events or experiences as evidence of God's will. Rather, Jesus seeks to evaluate recent events in light of the Scriptures. While Jesus' death and resurrection should now help his disciples interpret the Scriptures better, he nevertheless weds his disciples to the Scriptures. He does not ask them to choose between Scripture and recent experiences. Instead, he models for his disciples how Scripture and experience must dovetail together in order for one to understand God's will and work properly. Much later in the book of Acts, Luke will show his readers how the early church continues to understand God's will in light of both the Scriptures and new expressions of the Spirit's work (e.g., Acts 15:13-21).

(3) Luke 24:28-35. After extending meritorious hospitality to the traveler (24:28-29), the two disciples then feed their guest. At that point, Jesus takes the bread, blesses it, breaks it, and gives it to them (24:30). Here, Jesus engages in the same series of actions that we saw when Jesus fed the five thousand (9:16) and shared the Last Supper with his disciples (22:19). In the process, the two disciples from Emmaus experience revelation; their eyes are opened. They can now recognize Jesus before he vanishes (24:31-32).

Up to this point in Luke's Gospel, prayer (e.g., 3:21-22; 6:12-13; 9:29; 22:46-47) and the Scriptures (e.g., 24:27) have served revelatory functions.

In conjunction with prayer and the Scriptures, the Father's will and Jesus' identity have been made known. Now, in addition to prayer (24:30) and the Scriptures (24:27), Jesus' identity and purposes are revealed to this pair of disciples as they break bread in a manner that echoes the Last Supper (22:14-23). In other words, the disciples begin to see and experience Jesus amid the breaking of bread (or the Eucharist). For Luke's readers, in addition to recalling Jesus' death and reminding participants of the "new covenant" that God has forged with his people (22:20), the commemorative meal that Jesus instituted in 22:21 now contributes to the revelation of Jesus' identity and work in a post-resurrection context, along with prayer and the Scriptures (24:35; cf. Acts 2:42).

Finally, with great excitement Cleopas and his fellow disciple return to Jerusalem late on that same day to relay their encounter with Jesus to the eleven apostles (minus Judas) and the other disciples (24:33-35). While the disciples in Jerusalem speak about an unnarrated, post-resurrection appearance of Jesus to Peter (24:34; cf. 1 Cor 15:5), the two disciples from Emmaus relay their own story about Jesus' appearance to them. Just like the women in 24:8-11, all of the disciples gathered in Jerusalem have begun to provide a witness to Jesus' resurrection. They testify to the events that have been fulfilled among them (cf. 1:1). In essence, providing a witness about Jesus' resurrection has become an essential activity for Jesus' disciples in a post-resurrection context.

Appearing to the Disciples (24:36-43)

In addition to his appearances to the two disciples on the road to Emmaus (24:13-32) and to Peter (24:34; cf. 1 Cor 15:5), Jesus now appears to the full cohort of disciples who are gathered in Jerusalem in 24:36-43. As Luke narrates this encounter between the risen Jesus and his disciples, he initially seeks to accomplish one main task. Luke relies on this pericope to verify the corporeal nature of Jesus' resurrection.

When Jesus first greets his disciples, they think they are seeing a ghost (24:37). Rather than Jesus in bodily form, the disciples think they see a vision of Jesus or perhaps his disembodied spirit. While dialoguing with the disciples, however, Jesus instructs them to touch his hands and feet—presumably the same hands and feet that his crucifixion marred (24:39) (Carroll, *Luke*, 491). Furthermore, Jesus asks for food and eats it (24:41-43). In the ancient world, it was believed that one could distinguish spirits from humans based on their response to food. Not even the angels of God ate food (e.g., *Tob.* 12:19; Josephus, *Ant.* 1.9.2; Philo, *Abr.* 110, 118, *QG* 4.9). Only humans were capable of eating. As a result, despite the fact that the resurrected Jesus no longer seems confined by time or space, the message is loud and clear: Jesus' physical body fully participates in the resurrection. Jesus' resurrection defeats physical death and provides a foretaste of the resurrected experience that all his disciples will one day experience (Talbert, *Reading Luke*, 257).

Commissioning the Disciples (24:44-49)

While still appearing to his disciples in Jerusalem (24:36-43), Jesus then teaches and commissions them prior to his ascension (24:44-49). As he instructs them, Jesus asks his disciples to recall the words that he spoke throughout his ministry. In particular, Jesus demonstrates that his life, death, and resurrection fulfill the promises and prophecies of God as the Scriptures chronicle—the Law, the Prophets, and the Writings (24:44).

Luke begins his Gospel with an emphasis on this exact point: God's promises and prophecies reach their fulfillment through God's work in Jesus. For example, in 1:1, Luke explains that he desires to write "an orderly account of the events that have been fulfilled among us." In 4:21 at the synagogue at Nazareth, Jesus says, "Today, this scripture has been fulfilled in your hearing." In Acts 3:18, Peter says, "In this way God fulfilled what he had foretold through all the prophets, that his Messiah would suffer." And, in Acts 13:23, Paul speaks in the synagogue at Antioch of Pisidia and claims that "God has brought to Israel a Savior, Jesus, as he promised." In essence, God's faithfulness to Israel is now on display through Jesus' life, death, and resurrection. God has honored God's promises. Furthermore, Luke essentially informs his readers that they cannot rightly understand Jesus apart from Israel's Scriptures.

Consequently, as we saw in 24:27, Jesus again points his disciples back to the Scriptures for true understanding. Just as Jesus had to open the eyes of the two disciples on the road to Emmaus (24:31), so also Jesus now opens the minds of his disciples so they can understand the overarching work of God to which the Scriptures bear witness (24:45). In particular, Jesus again claims that it was necessary for the Messiah to suffer and die before rising from the dead on the third day (24:46).

This knowledge about Jesus' role as a prophetic Messiah (Johnson, *Luke*, 119–20), which includes his death and resurrection, then has direct implications for Jesus' disciples as they move forward. In essence, Jesus' final lesson gives way to a commission for his disciples. Though Jesus does not provide a fully articulated doctrine of atonement, Jesus nevertheless teaches that because he has fulfilled his role as the Messiah who suffers, dies, and rises to life again, the disciples are now obligated to proclaim repentance and forgiveness of sins in Jesus' name to all nations beginning in Jerusalem. John the

Baptist preached repentance and forgiveness of sin in 3:3, but the disciples are to preach repentance and forgiveness of sin in the name of Jesus, the one who baptizes with "the Holy Spirit and fire" (3:16).

In the process, Jesus primarily commissions them not as leaders but as witnesses of his life, death, and resurrection (24:48). In the book of Acts, Luke demonstrates how their witness indeed begins in Jerusalem but then expands to "all the nations" (Acts 1:8). At first, the disciples seek to testify among all the Jews throughout the world. In Acts 10, however, Luke shows his readers how the disciples soon realize that both the scriptural mandate and Jesus' commission pertain to "all the nations" or all the Gentiles as well (Acts 10:34-35), just as Simeon prophesied in 2:29-32.

Finally, Jesus informs his disciples that God will send the Holy Spirit to empower their witness just as God has promised (Acts 2:1-40). As Luke began his biography of Jesus, he was careful to show the numerous ways that God's Spirit intervened in human affairs. It is through the power of the Holy Spirit that Mary conceives without having sexual relations (1:35, 37). The Holy Spirit fills and empowers John the Baptist (1:15). The Holy Spirit enables Zechariah and Simeon to prophesy (1:67; 2:25-27). At the baptism, God anoints and empowers Jesus with the Holy Spirit (3:21-22), and Jesus endures every temptation of the devil while empowered by the Holy Spirit (4:1). Now, Jesus reminds his disciples that God has promised to send the same Spirit that has empowered him to his disciples. Jesus commissions them to provide a witness, but the Holy Spirit will be the one who makes that witness possible.

Jesus' Ascension (24:50-53)

Luke concludes his biography of Jesus by narrating Jesus' ascension. Notably, Luke will also begin the Acts of the Apostles by narrating this same event with some variations and additions (Acts 1:6-11). In the process, Luke indicates that Jesus crosses the Kidron Valley and arrives at Bethany atop the Mount of Olives on the outskirts of Jerusalem (24:50; cf. 19:29; Acts 1:12). Here he blesses his disciples and separates from them before he is carried up (by divine agency) into heaven (24:51).

The disciples have a twofold response to Jesus' ascension. First, they worship him (24:52). Understanding Jesus' identity as the Son of God and prophetic Messiah, they worship him. They perceive the link between the Father and the Son to be so intimate that their decision to worship Jesus is characterized as an act of faithfulness to the God of Abraham, Isaac, and Jacob rather than a violation of the first commandment (Exod 20:3).

Second, in Luke alone, Jesus instructs the disciples to stay in Jerusalem (24:49; Acts 1:4). As a result, rather than travel to Galilee as we see in Matt 28:16 and Mark 16:7, Jesus' disciples obey his instructions. They return to Jerusalem and continually visit the temple and bless God (24:52-53). Significantly, Luke began his Gospel in the temple (1:8-20). Now Luke ends his Gospel in the temple (24:53). Furthermore, the temple will remain an important aspect of the disciples' worship practices in the Acts of the Apostles until Stephen's martyrdom in Acts 6–8 (e.g., Acts 2:46-47).

Works Cited

Alexander, Loveday. *The Preface to Luke's Gospel: Literary Convention and Social Context in Luke 1.1-4 and Acts 1.1.* Society for the New Testament Studies Monograph Series 78. Cambridge: Cambridge University Press, 1993.

Arterbury, Andrew E. "Abraham's Hospitality among Jewish and Early Christian Writers: A Tradition History of Genesis 18:1-16 and Its Relevance for the Study of the New Testament." *Perspectives in Religious Studies* 30/3 (Fall 2003): 359–76.

———. "The Battle on the Mount of Olives: Reading Luke 22:39-46 in its Literary Context." Pages 37–51 in *Texts and Contexts: Gospels and Pauline Studies.* Edited by Todd D. Still. Waco, TX: Baylor University Press, 2017.

———. "The Downfall of Eutychus: How Ancient Understandings of Sleep Illuminate Acts 20:7-12." Pages 201–21 in *Contemporary Studies in Acts.* Edited by Thomas E. Phillips. Macon, GA: Mercer University Press, 2009.

———. *Entertaining Angels: Early Christian Hospitality in Its Mediterranean Setting.* Sheffield: Sheffield Phoenix, 2005.

———. "Entertaining Angels: Hospitality in Luke and Acts." *Christian Reflection* 25 (2007): 20–26.

———. "'I Have Prayed for You': Divine Enablement in the Gospel of Luke." Pages 155–75 in *Getting "Saved": The Whole Story of Salvation in the New Testament* by Charles H. Talbert and Jason A. Whitlark, with other contributions by A. E. Arterbury et al. Grand Rapids: Eerdmans, 2011.

———. "Zacchaeus: 'A Son of Abraham'?" Pages 18–31 in *Biblical Interpretation in Early Christian Gospels; Volume 3: The Gospel of Luke*. Edited by Thomas R. Hatina. Library of New Testament Studies 376. London: T&T Clark, 2009.

Bauckham, Richard. "For Whom Were Gospels Written?" Pages 9–48 in *The Gospel for All Christians: Rethinking the Gospel Audiences*. Edited by Richard Bauckham. Grand Rapids: Eerdmans, 1998.

———. *Gospel Women: Studies in the Named Women in the Gospels*. Grand Rapids: Eerdmans, 2002.

Betsworth, Sharon. *Children in Early Christian Narratives*. Library of Biblical Studies. New York: Bloomsbury T&T Clark, 2015.

Black, C. Clifton. *Mark*. Abingdon New Testament Commentaries. Nashville: Abingdon, 2011.

Blomberg, Craig L. *Interpreting the Parables*. 2nd ed. Downers Grove, IL: InterVarsity Press, 2012.

Blumell, Lincoln H. "Luke 22:43-44: An Anti-Docetic Interpolation or an Apologetic Omission?" *TC: A Journal of Biblical Textual Criticism* 19 (2014): 1–35.

Boccaccini, Gabriele. *Middle Judaism: Jewish Thought, 300 B.C.E. to 200 C.E.* Minneapolis: Fortress, 1991.

Bock, Darrell. *Luke*. 2 vols. Baker Exegetical Commentaries on the New Testament. Grand Rapids: Baker Academic, 1994–1996.

Bockmuehl, Markus. "Locating Paradise." Pages 192–209 in *Paradise in Antiquity: Jewish and Christian Views*. Edited by Markus Bockmuehl and Guy G. Stroumsa. New York: Cambridge University Press, 2010.

Bovon, François. *Luke*. Translated by Christine M. Thomas, Donald S. Deer, and James Crouch. 3 vols. Hermeneia. Minneapolis: Fortress, 2002–2013.

Brawley, Robert L. *Centering on God: Method and Message in Luke-Acts*. Literary Currents in Biblical Interpretation. Louisville: Westminster John Knox, 1990.

Brobst-Renaud, Amanda. "The Elder Son's Quandary and the Rich Man's Fate: Moral Formation, Characterization, and Rhetoric in Luke 15:11-32 and 16:19-31." PhD diss., Baylor University, 2018.

Brown, Raymond E. *The Birth of the Messiah: A Commentary on the Infancy Narratives in Matthew and Luke.* New York: Doubleday, 1977.

———. *The Death of the Messiah: From Gethsemane to the Grace: A Commentary on the Passion Narratives in the Four Gospels.* 2 vols. New York: Doubleday, 1994.

Brown, Raymond E. *An Introduction to the New Testament.* The Anchor Bible Reference Library. New York: Doubleday, 1997.

Bultmann, Rudolf. *The History of the Synoptic Tradition.* Translated by J. Marsh. New York: Harper & Row, 1963.

Burridge, Richard. *What Are the Gospels? A Comparison with Graeco-Roman Biography.* Society for New Testament Studies Monograph Series 70. Cambridge: Cambridge University Press, 1992.

Cadbury, Henry J. *The Making of Luke-Acts.* 2nd ed. London: SPCK, 1958.

Caird, G. B. *Saint Luke.* Westminster Pelican Commentaries. Philadelphia: Westminster, 1963.

Carroll, John T. *Luke: A Commentary.* New Testament Library. Louisville: Westminster John Knox, 2012.

Catchpole, D. R. "The Triumphal Entry." Pages 319–34 in *Jesus and the Politics of His Day.* Edited by E. Bammel & C.F.D. Moule. Cambridge: Cambridge University Press, 1984.

Clivaz, Claire. *L'ange et la sueur de sang (Lc 22,43–44): Ou comment on pourrait bien encore écrire l'histoire.* Leuven: Peeters, 2010.

Conzelmann, Hans. *The Theology of St. Luke.* Translated by Geoffrey Buswell. Philadelphia: Fortress, 1961.

Cosgrove, Charles H. "The Divine DEI in Luke-Acts: Investigations into the Lukan Understanding of God's Providence." *Novum Testamentum* 26 (1984): 168–90.

Craddock, Fred B. *Luke.* Interpretation. Louisville: Westminster John Knox, 1990.

Croatto, J. Severino. "Jesus, Prophet like Elijah, and Prophet-Teacher like Moses in Luke-Acts." *Journal of Biblical Literature* 124:3 (2005): 451–65.

Crump, David. *Jesus the Intercessor: Prayer and Christology in Luke-Acts.* Tübingen: Mohr Siebeck, 1992.

Culpepper, R. Alan. "The Gospel of Luke: Introduction, Commentary, and Reflections." Pages 1–490 in vol. 9 of *The New Interpreter's Bible*. Edited by Leander E. Keck. 12 vols. Nashville: Abingdon, 1995.

Culy, Martin M., Mikeal C. Parsons, and Joshua J. Stigall. *Luke: A Handbook on the Greek Text*. Waco, TX: Baylor University Press, 2010.

Dahl, Nils Alstrup. "The Story of Abraham in Luke-Acts." Pages 139–58 in *Studies in Luke-Acts*. Edited by Leander E. Keck and J. Louis Martyn. Nashville: Abingdon, 1996.

Danker, Frederick W. *Jesus and the New Age: A Commentary on St. Luke's Gospel*. Rev and exp. ed. Philadelphia: Fortress, 1988.

Dowd, Sharyn. *Reading Mark: A Literary and Theological Commentary on the Second Gospel*. Macon, GA: Smyth & Helwys, 2000.

Ehrman, Bart D. and Mark A. Plunkett, "The Angel and the Agony: The Textual Problem of Luke 22:43-44." *Catholic Biblical Quarterly* 45 (1983): 401–16.

Ellis, E. Earle. *The Gospel of Luke*. New Century Bible Commentary. Grand Rapids: Eerdmans, 1974.

Evans, C. F. *Saint Luke*. 2nd ed. Trinity Press International New Testament Commentaries. London: SCM, 2008.

Evans, Craig A. *Luke*. New International Bible Commentary 3. Peabody, MA: Hendrickson, 1990.

———. "Jesus and Evil Spirits in the Light of Psalm 91." *Baptistic Theologies* 1/2 (2009): 43–58.

Fitzmyer, Joseph A. *The Gospel According to Luke*. Anchor Bible 28–28A. Garden City, NY: Doubleday, 1981–1985.

Furfey, Paul H. "PLOUSIOS and Cognates in the New Testament." *Catholic Biblical Quarterly* 5:3 (1943): 243–63.

Garland, David E. *Luke*. Zondervan Exegetical Commentary on the New Testament. Grand Rapids: Zondervan, 2011.

Garrett, Susan R. *The Demise of the Devil: Magic and the Demonic in Luke's Writings*. Minneapolis: Fortress, 1989.

Green, Joel B. *The Gospel of Luke*. New International Commentary on the New Testament. Grand Rapids: Eerdmans, 1997.

Gregory, Andrew. *The Reception of Luke and Acts in the Period before Irenaeus: Looking for Luke in the Second Century.* Wissenshaftliche Untersuchungen zum Neuen Testament 2/169. Tübingen: Mohr Siebeck, 2003.

Hamilton, Victor P. *The Book of Genesis: Chapters 18–50.* Grand Rapids: Eerdmans, 1995.

Hays, Richard B. *Echoes of Scripture in the Gospels.* Waco, TX: Baylor University Press, 2016.

———. *The Moral Vision of the New Testament: Community, Cross, New Creation; A Contemporary Introduction to New Testament Ethics.* New York: HarperCollins, 1996.

———. "The One Who Redeems Israel: Reading Scripture with Luke." Pages 55–74 in *Reading Backwards: Figural Christology and the Fourfold Gospel Witness.* Waco, TX: Baylor University Press, 2014.

Henning, Meghan. *Educating Early Christians through the Rhetoric of Hell.* Tübingen: Mohr Siebeck, 2014.

Hooker, Morna D. *The Gospel According to Saint Mark.* Black's New Testament Commentaries. London: A. & C. Black, 1991. Repr., Peabody, MA: Hendrickson, 2005.

Johnson, Luke Timothy. *The Gospel of Luke.* Sacra Pagina 3. Collegeville, MN: Liturgical Press, 1991.

Kaminsky, Joel and Anne Stewart. "God of All the World: Universalism and Developing Monotheism in Isaiah 40–66." *Harvard Theological Review* 99:2 (2006): 139–63.

Kittel, Gerhard, and Gerhard Friedrich, eds. *Theological Dictionary of the New Testament.* Translated by Geoffrey W. Bromiley. 10 vols. Grand Rapids: Eerdmans, 1964–1976.

Koester, Helmut. *Ancient Christian Gospels: Their History and Development.* Harrisburg, PA: Trinity Press International, 1990.

Levin, Christoph. "The Poor in the Old Testament: Some Observations." *Religion and Theology* 8/3 (2001): 253–73.

Malina, Bruce J. and Richard L. Rohrbaugh. *Social Scientific Commentary on the Synoptic Gospels.* Minneapolis: Fortress, 1992.

Marshall, I. Howard. *The Gospel of Luke: A Commentary on the Greek Text.* New International Greek Testament Commentary. Grand Rapids: Eerdmans, 1978.

Matson, David Lertis. "Pacifist Jesus? The (Mis)Translation of *eate heōs toutou* in Luke 22:51." *Journal of Biblical Literature* 134/1 (2015): 157–76.

Metzger, Bruce M. "Seventy or Seventy-two Disciples?" *New Testament Studies* 5 (1958–59): 299–306.

Meyers, Carol L., and Eric M. Meyers. *Zechariah 9–14: A New Translation with Introduction and Commentary.* The Anchor Bible 25C. New York: Doubleday, 1993.

Nolland, John. *Luke.* 3 vols. Word Biblical Commentary. Dallas: Word Books, 1989–93.

Parsons, Mikeal C. *Luke.* Paideia Commentaries on the New Testament. Grand Rapids, MI: Baker Academic, 2015.

———. *Luke: Storyteller, Interpreter, Evangelist.* Peabody, MA: Hendrickson, 2007.

Parsons, Mikeal C., and Richard I. Pervo. *Rethinking the Unity of Luke and Acts.* Minneapolis: Fortress, 1993.

Scobie, Charles H. H. "A Canonical Approach to Interpreting Luke: The Journey Motif as a Hermeneutical Key." Pages 327–49 in *Reading Luke: Interpretation, Reflections, Formation.* Edited by Craig Bartholomew, Joel B. Green, and Anthony Thiselton. Grand Rapids: Zondervan, 2005.

Scott, Bernard Brandon. *Hear Then the Parable: A Commentary on the Parables of Jesus.* Minneapolis: Augsburg Fortress, 1989.

Shimoff, Sandra R. "Banquets: The Limits of Hellenization." *Journal for the Study of Judaism* 27 (1996): 440–52.

Stanton, Graham. *The Gospels and Jesus.* 2nd ed. Oxford: Oxford University Press, 2002.

Sterling, Gregory E. *Historiography and Self-Definition: Josephus, Luke-Acts and Apologetic Historiography.* Supplements to Novum Testamentum 64. Leiden: Brill, 1992.

Stern, Frank. *A Rabbi Looks at Jesus' Parables*. Lanham, MD: Rowman & Littlefield, 2006.

Streeter, B. H. *The Four Gospels*. London: Macmillan, 1930.

Talbert, Charles H. *What is a Gospel? The Genre of the Canonical Gospels*. Philadelphia: Fortress, 1977.

———. *Reading Luke: A Literary and Theological Commentary on the Third Gospel*. Rev. ed. Reading the New Testament. Macon, GA: Smyth & Helwys, 2002.

Tannehill, Robert C. *The Narrative Unity of Luke-Acts: A Literary Interpretation*. 2 vols. Foundations and Facets. Minneapolis: Fortress, 1986–90.

———. *Luke*. Abingdon New Testament Commentaries. Nashville: Abingdon, 1996.

Tiede, David L. *Luke*. Augsburg Commentary on the New Testament. Minneapolis: Augsburg, 1988.

Tucker, W. Dennis, Jr. and Jamie A. Grant. *Psalms, Volume 2*. The NIV Application Commentary. Grand Rapids, MI: Zondervan, 2018.

van Unnik, W. C. "Die Motivierung der Feindesliebe in Lukas VI 32–35." *Novum Testamentum* 8 (1966): 284–300.

Verheyden, Jozef, ed. *The Unity of Luke-Acts*. Bibliotheca Ephemeridum theologicarum Lovaniensium 142. Leuven: Peeters, 1998.

Walton, Steve. "Calling the Church Names: Learning about Christian Identity from Acts." *Perspectives in Religious Studies* 41/3 (2014): 223–42.

Werline, Rodney. *Pray Like This: Understanding Prayer in the Bible*. New York: T&T Clark, 2007.

Wilson, Gerald H. *Psalms, Volume 1*. The NIV Application Commentary. Grand Rapids, MI: Zondervan, 2002.

Wolter, Michael. *The Gospel According to Luke*. 2 vols. Translated by Wayne Coppins and Christoph Heilig. Waco, TX: Baylor University Press/ Mohr Siebeck, 2016–2017.

www.ingramcontent.com/pod-product-compliance
Lightning Source LLC
Chambersburg PA
CBHW061938220426
43662CB00012B/1945